GEORGE BERNARD SHAW (1856–1950) is one of the world's greatest literary figures. Born in Dublin, Ireland, he left school at fourteen and in 1876 went to London, where he began his literary career with a series of unsuccessful novels. In 1884 he became a founder of the Fabian Society, the famous British socialist organization. After becoming a reviewer and drama critic, he published a study of the Norwegian dramatist Henrik Ibsen in 1891 and became determined to create plays as he felt Ibsen did: to shake audiences out of their moral complacency and to attack social problems. However, Shaw was an irrepressible wit, and his plays are as entertaining as they are socially provocative. Basically shy, Shaw created a public persona for himself: G.B.S., a bearded eccentric, crusading social critic, antivivisectionist, language reformer, strict vegetarian, and renowned public speaker. The author of fifty-three plays, hundreds of essays, reviews, and letters, and several books, Shaw is best known for *Widowers' Houses* (1892), *Mrs Warren's Profession* (1893), *Arms and the Man* (1894), *Caesar and Cleopatra* (1901), *Man and Superman* (1903), *Major Barbara* (1905), *Pygmalion* (1913), *Heartbreak House* (1919), and *Saint Joan* (1923). He was awarded the Nobel Prize for Literature in 1925.

# HEARTBREAK HOUSE AND MISALLIANCE

BY

## GEORGE BERNARD SHAW

*With an Introduction by*
*Rodelle and Stanley Weintraub*

BANTAM BOOKS
NEW YORK TORONTO LONDON SYDNEY AUCKLAND
A BANTAM CLASSIC

HEARTBREAK HOUSE
AND MISALLIANCE

*A Bantam Classic Book / March 1995*

*PUBLISHING HISTORY*
Misalliance *was published in New York*
*by Brentano's, 1914.* Heartbreak House
*was published in New York by Brentano's, 1919.*

*'The North-West Passage," 1874, by John Everett*
*Millais. Courtesy of the Tate Gallery, London/Art*
*Resource, NY.*

ISBN 0-553-21442-X

*Published simultaneously in the United States and Canada*

Bantam Books are published by Bantam Books, a division of Bantam Doubleday Dell
Publishing Group, Inc. Its trademark, consisting of the words "Bantam Books" and the
portrayal of a rooster, is Registered in U.S. Patent and Trademark Office and in other
countries. Marca Registrada. Bantam Books, 1540 Broadway, New York, New York 10036.

PRINTED IN THE UNITED STATES OF AMERICA

OPM 0 9 8 7 6 5 4 3 2 1

# CONTENTS

# THE
# ENCHANTED
# COUNTRY
# HOUSE: AN
# INTRODUCTION

As in *Howards End* and *The Remains of the Day,* novelists in the twentieth century have employed the country-house setting as symbol for England. So, too, have playwrights, most notably Bernard Shaw, in a series of sardonic comedies culminating with *Heartbreak House,* and Noel Coward, who began his career in high comedy in the 1920s as a disciple of Shaw. The English country house was always much more than a house in the country. It was the retreat to which the comfortable classes removed themselves to escape a crowded city and the barbarians who lived there. Undisturbed, they could enjoy the good life earned by inheritance, marriage, or new money.

Shaw began *Misalliance* on September 8, 1909, in the sunset of the Edwardian years of confidence and affluence. Although he claimed in his preface to have begun *Heartbreak House* before the Great War, he did not actually begin writing it until March 4, 1916, nearly midway through the war that diminished country-house England. For all their extravagance and humor, both plays reveal the enchanted country houses in which they are set as endangered and menacing. John Tarleton's pleasant, sunny place in Surrey even has that typical adjunct, a greenhouse—but in the first minutes of the play its roof is shattered by the crash of an airplane. Captain Shotover's nautically inspired house in Sussex (the ship of state is another obvious metaphor) has become drab and rickety and, by the end of the play, is in danger of being shattered in an air raid.

In the optimistic Shavian play written before the watershed of World War I, and the pessimistic one, written as the war reached its climax, the often absurd goings-on are possibly the stuff of dreams. As *Misalliance* opens, Johnny Tarleton, "an ordinary young business man" to whom the world is not in the least zany, is "reclining, novel in hand, in a swinging chair with a little awning above" in the sunny pavilion of his family's country home in Kent. Under such circumstances it is difficult to remain awake, and perhaps Johnny does not. A wish-fulfillment dream need not be a sleeping dream but only a reverie or daydream; whichever the case may be, Johnny and his father (and mother) discuss the "stark raving nonsense" of the afternoon's happenings in terms of "dreaming." Although they cannot "all be dreaming the same thing," as Johnny tells his father, John Tarleton replies, "Of course not, you duffer; but then I'm dreaming you as well as the lady. . . ." In *Heartbreak House* the lady whose entrance is the inciting force in the play is also the dreamer, dozing over a copy of *Othello,* after which the stark, raving nonsense begins.

In each play the dreamer's dilemmas are confronted. Johnny's father, in whose enterprises the younger Tarleton works and to which he will succeed, thinks he is not "worth tuppence as a man of business," while his mother still treats him as a child. Ellie in *Heartbreak House* may dream of an Othello who will save her from an arranged marriage to an older man of business, with her rescuer a cinematic idol who boasts, like Shakespeare's hero, of impossible accomplishments when his own workaday courage is heroic enough.

Both dreams involve experiences impossible in real life: John's confrontation with the sexually charged aviatrix Lina Szczepanowska, an erotic—if farcical—"Lady of Pain" in *Misalliance,* and Ellie's with the exotic screen-lover type, complete to his Rudolph Valentino garb, in *Heartbreak House.* (Shaw anticipated the romantic film *The Sheik* [1921] in the latter and the booted, sadomasochistic fantasy figure of Jean Genet's *The Balcony* [1956] in the earlier play.)

Both also suggest in the dream device, as well as in their absurdist elements, Shaw's exploitation of Lewis Carroll's *Alice's Adventures in Wonderland* and *Through the Looking-Glass,* the mid-Victorian classics then part of every theatergoer's experience. John Tarleton seems to echo Alice, who says to Tweedledum, "Besides, if *I'm* only a thing in his dream, what are *you,* I should like to know?" In *Misalliance* there is a reference to a looking-glass in which the false is shown to be true and references to rabbits: in "Bunny" (Bentley) Summerhays, "starting a hare," having "started a rabbit," and "Welsh rabbit." The play's events in general suggest that the ordinary world has been turned upside down and backward. Joey Percival echoes Alice when he describes Hypatia Tarleton's "pursuit of me. She runs faster and faster. I run slower and slower. And these woods of yours are full of magic." The overbearing aviatrix may suggest the impertinent and eager-to-punish Red Queen. If Shaw's echoes of Carroll are intentional, they are subtle and inexact.

While both plays include, more lightly than in *Looking-Glass,* mock trials ("Gunner" in one, "Boss" Mangan in the other), the closest parallels are in *Heartbreak House,* which even opens, once Ellie falls asleep, with a mad tea party. Again there is a punishing queen (Lady Utterword), and, even more than in *Misalliance,* nothing is what it seems.

How much Shaw intended likenesses in the two country-house plays is difficult to gauge. With the exception of the onset of the Great War in 1914, he wrote both out of the same store of experience. In *Misalliance* the house is posh, boasting every last improvement, as befits the residence of a nouveau-riche businessman. Prominent are a solarium and greenhouse, and just arrived and unpacked is a new Turkish bath. *Heartbreak House* itself, as befits the aged sea captain who owns it, is run-down and seedy, and resembles in some ways the interior of a ship. While Shaw makes the crash of an airplane into a greenhouse—the first occasion when the new invention is used onstage—the major opening incident of *Misalliance,* in *Heartbreak House* the play ends with an air raid that scatters some of the inhabitants while turning some of the others, jaded by ordinary life, ecstatic with pleasure.

Both plays involve businessmen: one benevolent but slightly less than respectable, the other respectable but dishonest. Both are interrupted by burglars, each a family connection, it turns out, and each more con man than thief. Neither is what he seems to be, yet each evokes a sense of threat and menace to the well-ordered (if false) society into which he intrudes.

The businessmen themselves represent the changes that only a few eventful years have brought. Risen in class like Mangan of *Heartbreak House,* Tarleton radiates optimism; the sour and cynical Mangan, one learns, has little but his status, and lives on expense accounts. Everything turns darker in the wartime play, as fits Shaw's outlook. While both plays involve romantic misalliances and end with some (although others are thwarted), they turn grotesque in *Heartbreak House,* with a "mystic marriage" that at least psychologically is incestuous. The pattern is already established in *Misalliance*, where an elderly father proposes marriage to his future daughter-in-law.

That the change in outlook and the many dimensions of *Heartbreak House* evolve from the ongoing catastrophe of the war is evident from the contrasting array of characters in each play. Written in the late-Edwardian afternoon, *Misalli-*

*ance* is full of the potential of the mobile new society in which new technology and political change are opening possibilities to people who mere decades earlier could only watch from the sidelines. Before the play ends, Tarleton's comfortable home has seen come and go the young and old of several segments of the English class structure, which is breaking down for the better. In *Heartbreak House,* apart from its ingenue figure Ellie Dunn, there are no young people. Planning the play in midwar, after compulsory military service had been instituted, Shaw not only anticipated wartime performance by excluding roles for males of draft age, but foreshadowed the postwar decades in which there would be few remaining men of Ellie's generation. The women, but for Ellie, are in their mid-forties or older—women who had married prior to the war and whose husbands had been just old enough to have been exempted from service and slaughter. In the England of *Heartbreak House,* the heartbreak is becoming real.

Shaw implies in his preface to *Misalliance* that his play merely stages his prose treatise on parents and children, which deals with the poor job contemporary society has done in liberating parent-child relationships and in educating the "experiment" that each child is for a productive role in the world. "The child of the future, then," he wrote, "if there is to be any future but one of decay," would benefit from some work experience before being admitted to a university. "If such persons are to read and talk and criticize to any purpose, they must know the world outside the university at least as well as the shopkeeper in the High Street does." After the 1914–18 war, many would know it better than that, having been translated to the trenches. But Shaw's point throughout seven decades of writing remained much the same—that the worth of existence comes from one's usefulness in bettering it rather than from marginalism or parasitism. "This is the true joy in life," Shaw wrote in the preface to *Man and Superman* (1903), "the being used for a purpose recognized by yourself as a mighty one; the being thoroughly worn out before you are thrown on the scrap heap; the being a force of Nature instead of a feverish selfish little clod of ailments and grievances complaining that the world will not devote itself to making you happy." The lines could be a gloss to both plays.

Of the many dimensions in Shaw's drama, one is almost inevitably Shakespearean. He claimed that *Misalliance* "is on the plan of *The Taming of the Shrew*." Always inverting the obvious, Shaw's version demonstrates the chastening of a series of males, young and old, by a domineering terror of a woman, his aviatrix. He also read his protégé Harley Granville Barker's play *The Madras House,* suggested revisions to Barker, then borrowed elements of it for his own script, in particular the background of the drapery trade (Tarleton makes his manufacturing, rather than retailing, fortune in it) and the atmosphere of sexual power, promiscuity, and need. Constantine Madras even refers to "my friend Tarleton." Shaw's use of the name was very likely his undisguised bow to Barker. Yet by accident of the availability of theaters, *Misalliance* opened in London on February 23, 1910, two weeks before the March ninth premiere of Barker's play.

Shaw both read and saw Gilbert Murray's adaptation of Euripides' classic Greek tragedy *The Bacchae* in 1908. The aviatrix Lina, who falls from the airplane that crashes into Tarleton's greenhouse, may be a version of the avenging god descending from heaven onto a Dionysian grape arbor. It is possible that Shaw was also borrowing from the birth of British aviation, in which he was interested enough to go up in balloons and early airplanes. In 1909 there were a number of attempts to break briefly held duration records for flying with a passenger—as Joey Percival does. London newspapers also gave a lot of coverage to the barnstorming career of the balloonist and parachutist Dolly Shepherd, who jumped in a mannish knickerbocker suit and high boots. In June 1908 she was even involved in a dramatic midair rescue, transferring, at eleven thousand feet, a parachutist from a runaway balloon to her own rigging and trapeze bar. Many in Shaw's audience would have known of the attractive and daring "parachute queen." His own acrobatic heroine clutches Joey Percival, her partner, in midair as he falls. Lord Summerhays, who does not know that the male-clad rescuer is a woman, reports to Percival in awe: "It was extraordinary. When you were thrown out he held on to the top bar with one hand. You came past him in the air, going straight for the glass. He caught you and turned you off into the flower bed, and then lighted beside you like a bird." When Lina is asked if she has been "up much" she answers: "Not in an aeroplane, I've parachuted. . . ." Lina is happiest in a life with risks; domesticity is a bore.

"Gunner" emerges from the Turkish bath brandishing a pistol and declaring that he is Tarleton's illegitimate son by "Lucinda Titmus." Shaw was preoccupied in his plays by foundlings and illegitimate sons, very likely because he worried over his own paternity. Could he really be the son of an unambitious, failed alcoholic nobody? He pondered the possibility of having been sired instead by George John Vandeleur Lee, a charismatic Dublin conductor and music teacher who not only coached Mrs. Shaw (whose name was Lucinda) but shared a house with the family. For print, Shaw put his concerns aside and determined he looked enough like his despised father to have been George Carr Shaw's son. Percival boasts in *Misalliance* of having had, like Shaw, three fathers—a legitimate one, a tame philosopher who lived with the family, and his Italian mother's confessor. Shaw's philosopher was Dr. Walter Gurly, Mrs. Shaw's brother, who stayed often, and the exotic "confessor" was Lee.

Lina throws off her cloak and asks for a Bible, a music stand, and six oranges ("billiard balls will do quite as well"), for life is a juggle. Nothing is normal in the Hindhead house in which the topsy-turvy behavior is even more outrageous than the talk. Hindhead, where Shaw knew Arthur Conan Doyle's house, Undershaw, was located, seems a very appropriately named setting for such goings-on. The *Times*'s critic called Shaw's play a "lunatic asylum," and other contemporaries objected to its "unreality" and to its arbitrariness and illogic. Those aspects of *Misalliance* have become its box office strength in a disorderly world where logic, truth, and sanity are often at odds with reality.

In the preface to *Heartbreak House,* Shaw claimed that when he began the play "not a shot had been fired" in the 1914–18 war, and in the 1919 first edition he even put the dates "1913–16" to the play. Through this fiction he may have been trying to establish a claim to prescience about the war. It is true that nearly a year before the war began in August 1914, his friend Lena Ashwell, the actress who had played Lina Szczepanowska in the first production of *Misalliance,* told him about her father, Charles Ashwell Botelar Pocock, a sea captain who had lived with his family on the *Wellesley,* an old sailing ship that worked out of the River Tyne. Shaw intended to put the eccentric old man, whom he called a "captain of souls," into a play, and the country house is fitted out to remind Captain Shotover of his sea years. Nevertheless, the character owes less to Captain Pocock than to Thomas Carlyle. Shaw admired the cranky, eccentric Victorian philosopher for whom a dominant metaphor for England was the ship that must navigate Cape Horn and keep off the rocks. In *Past and Present* (1843) Carlyle wrote of a character named Undershot, a name that may echo in Shotover's remark that at eighty-eight his last bolt had been shot long before. (Undershot/Shotover also demonstrates Shaw's passion for inversion.)

A letter to actress "Mrs. Pat" Campbell, the Eliza Doolittle of his *Pygmalion,* confirms that Shaw began his shorthand draft of the play on March 4, 1916. Once begun, he wrote her, he had been "creeping through" it with no real sense of how it was going to end. Events would furnish him with an ending, and by mid-1917 he had a complete play—too long for production, but cutting it proved easier than the writing had been. Charged with symbolism and prophecy about what he saw as the moral paralysis of England, it presented a vision of what he called "cultured, leisured Europe" drifting toward catastrophe. There is no sense through the play that a war is actually in progress, but an arms race leading to war is ongoing, and the outbreak of war comes as no surprise.

The country house "in the middle of the north edge of Sussex" was a real place, and the character of Ariadne—Lady Utterword—is linked to it. On May 10, 1940, in the first year of yet another world war, Shaw wrote flatteringly and somewhat erroneously to Virginia Woolf: "There is a play of mine called *Heartbreak House* which I always connect with you because I conceived it in that house somewhere in Sussex where I first met you and, of course, fell in love with you. I suppose every man did." The house was Windham Croft, not far from the London-Brighton railway line, first blamed for the distant sounds that prove in Act III to be the first intimations of war. On a long weekend in mid-June 1916 Charlotte and Bernard Shaw and Virginia and Leonard Woolf were the guests there of Shaw's longtime Fabian friends Beatrice and Sidney Webb, who had rented the house for the summer months. The experience apparently spurred Shaw's shorthand, and the attractive but haughty and high-strung Virginia Woolf seems to have furnished Shaw with the attributes of the handsome, imperious Lady Utterword.

At Windham Croft, Leonard Woolf remembered many years later, Shaw would go out into the garden that is the setting of Act III, and, each morning, add new lines to the play "on a writing pad on his knee." There may even be a nod to Woolf himself in the play. An ex-colonial official, he is suggested in the unseen Sir Hastings Utterword, "governor of all the crown colonies in succession." This was hardly a generous bow to Woolf, given Sir Hastings's arbitrary ruling manner (as described by Ariadne), which recalls Warren Hastings (1732–1818), the ruthless empire builder of Bengal. (At another level, Sir Hastings is a further echo of *Misalliance*, where Lord Summerhays, retired from the governorship of the mythical Indian princely state of Jinghiskahn, has sternly suppressed "the muddle and the folly and the amateurness" of "democratic games.")

Three years after *Heartbreak House* was performed, Virginia Woolf would write her own free-spirited version of the play, *Freshwater,* acted privately in 1935. Ostensibly it took place in the home of her great-aunt, Julia Cameron, on the Isle of Wight, but its reverberations of *Heartbreak House* are recognizable.

A few other characters echo real people. Shaw confessed to Mrs. Campbell that Hesione Hushabye was drawn from her. When she had been a blowsy yet still sultry beauty of forty-eight, Shaw had wanted to run off with her at whatever cost to their careers. Hector Hushabye is largely a portrait of Sir Robert Cunninghame Graham, a soldier of fortune, traveler, and M.P. whom Shaw knew well in the 1880s and 1890s. And Alfred Mangan was drawn from Hudson Kearley, who became Lord Devonport. Founder of a successful chain of food stores, he became food minister in Lloyd George's late-1916 "business government" when submarine warfare was deepening food shortages in Britain. To Shaw the merchant peer was a "political imbecile."

Actual events, too, turn up in the play. Shotover supports, in his old age, the aimless, spendthrift household where the handsome, restless Hector is a kept husband, by inventing tools of war—efficient explosives, an antitank weapon (tanks were not used in warfare until September 15, 1916, after Act I had been completed), and antisubmarine devices. Hostile action is not suggested until late in Act III, when the "sort of splendid drumming in the sky" heard by Mrs. Hushabye turns into an urgent need for air raid precautions. Yet that the attack is intended on a symbolic level is clear in that Shaw never has his characters venture on the identity of the intruders.

The raid was real. Zeppelin raids over the northern outskirts of London, where Shaw lived at Ayot St. Lawrence, were so frequent during 1916 that he joked about protecting himself from the enemy by lettering large, on his roof, and in German, that Shaw the writer lived there: Please fly on farther.

The zeppelin that intrudes over Heartbreak House (never identified as such except in Shaw's own drawing for the Act III set) was the L-31, shot down on October 1, 1916. Flaming, it fell slowly and awesomely—"like a burning newspaper," Shaw wrote to the Webbs. He went off on his motor bicycle the next morning to see the wreckage, bribing a guard with a shilling to get close.

"What is hardly credible, but true," he added, "is that the sound of the Zepp's engines was so fine, and its voyage through the stars so enchanting, that I positively caught myself hoping next night that there would be another raid." Shaw gave the lines to Ellie and Hesione at the close. He and other spectators at the barrier had been so "pleased at having seen the show" that he had to rebuke his own feelings with a closing, "Pretty lot of animals we are!"

The flaming climax is reflected in the many images of fire in the closing dialogue. Appealing for more light, Hector cries out recklessly, "We should be blazing to the skies," although the rules were for blackout. Ellie urges, "Set fire to the house, Marcus." ("Marcus" had been his Othello pose.) Even Ariadne suggests, sardonically, to her timid brother-in-law and admirer, Randall Utterword, that he play "Keep the Home Fires Burning" on his flute—and he does.

• • •

It took some months before Shaw could entirely transform the experience into the curlicues of his Pitman shorthand. In mid-November, when he was visiting his Irish friend Lady Gregory, the play was still titled *The House in the Clouds,* a clue to its intention as fantasy. He did not date "The End" until May 12, 1917, when he still had the staging details to add. By then *Heartbreak House* had matured into a multilayered high comedy rich in its allusiveness while actable on its surface level. The "overheated drawing-room atmosphere" Shaw described early in his preface owed much to Anton Chekhov. Shaw had seen a prewar performance of *The Cherry Orchard* and had remarked to director Frederick Whelen, who sat in the next seat, "I feel as if I want to tear up all my plays and begin all over again." For Shaw the hysteria beneath the surface of lethargy, combined with his own brand of discursive comedy, seemed exactly right to represent the spiritual bankruptcy of the generation responsible for the war. Very likely his subtitle—"a Fantasia in the Russian manner on English themes"—is owed to Chekhov, although Shaw also knew Leo Tolstoy's dark comedy *The Fruits of Enlightenment,* called by a London paper on its English presentation a year after Shaw's own play "the first of the Heartbreak Houses and the most blighting."

The resonances of *Heartbreak House* are many, each furnishing another dimension and almost certainly, in each case, intended. There are echoes of Henrik Ibsen's *The Master Builder* in Shotover just as there are of August Strindberg. Shaw vastly admired the gloomily symbolic plays of Ibsen's Swedish counterpart, once visiting Strindberg in Stockholm and later targeting his own Nobel Prize money, which he would not otherwise accept, for an Anglo-Scandinavian literary foundation to translate plays unavailable in English, beginning with Strindberg. Strindberg's black farce *The Dance of Death* may have contributed something to *Heartbreak House.*

The antecedents of the play reach back into earlier theater, even to Richard Wagner's music dramas, about which Shaw wrote, in 1899, his influential treatise *The Perfect Wagnerite*. Wagner's operas are even mentioned in the text, and his atmosphere broods over the text. Not only music lent its inspiration to the play. In Shaw's last years he penned a puppet play, *Shakes versus Shav* (1949), in which the two playwrights confront each other and gently challenge the greatness of each other's works, Shaw reaffirming his once-shaken optimism in the face of Shakespeare's alleged pessimism. They even debate each other's lines, as Aristophanes in *The Frogs* once toyed with his contemporaries Aeschylus and Euripides. And when Shakespeare asks "Where is thy *Hamlet*? Couldst thou write *King Lear*?" the Shaw figure has a ready answer.

"Aye," he affirms, "with his daughters all complete. Couldst thou have written *Heartbreak House*? Behold my *Lear*." In Shaw's stage directions: "A transparency is suddenly lit up, shewing Captain Shotover seated, as in [John] Millais' picture called *North-West Passage,* with a woman of virginal beauty." He was identifying his debt to a famous Victorian picture (see cover of this edition), which to him suggested Shotover and Ellie (as well as Lear and Cordelia), and to Shakespeare himself. Although his play begins with a hint of *Othello*, *Heartbreak House* on one level is Shaw's *Lear*, and the play closely echoes some of *Lear*'s lines to reinforce an allusiveness paralleled in many of the characters.

The Hushabyes (the surname suggests generational somnolence) add another dimension of allusion to the play. In Paris in the 1930s Jean Giraudoux would write a prophetic play warning of a new war. Called *The Trojan War Shall Not Take Place* (*Tiger at the Gates* in Christopher Fry's adaptation), it was a mordant look at the failure of humanity to prevent war. Shaw's predecessor to *La Guerre de Trois n'aura pas lieu* might with equal irony have been called *The Great*

*War Shall Not Take Place* and included powerful Trojan themes. Shaw's draft identifies Mrs. Hushabye first as Hecuba, then changes her name to the equally Greek Hesione. She is the daughter of the play's old King Priam (Captain Shotover) rather than his wife, as was Hecuba, or his sister, as was Hesione, the beautiful queen of Asia, while Hector (a Trojan hero in Homer) is the captain's swashbuckling and danger-seeking son-in-law whose fantasy sword is sheathed in a walking stick, rather than Priam's own son.

Shaw's smug and complacent counterpart to Troy also includes forty-two-year-old Ariadne (so he calculated on the reverse of a draft page), younger sister to the "fortyish" Hesione. In myth Ariadne is the non-Trojan daughter of King Minos of Crete, who saves Theseus from the minotaur of the dreaded labyrinth, and who parallels Shaw's own character in that she uses an early marriage to escape Heartbreak House, her own labyrinth.

Although the plays were not planned as companions, or as a pair of dramatic bookends, *Misalliance* and *Heartbreak House* are enriched by their contrasts as well as their similarities. They even conclude with almost identical thoughts: Bentley exclaims, "I hope there will be a storm," and Ellie responds to Hesione's longing for a return of the violence, "Oh, I hope so." The world we inhabit, Shaw concludes in both plays, is less logical than we would like—the reason we impose the lies of artificiality upon it. "The correct thing," Lord Summerhays advises Joey Percival in *Misalliance,* "depends for its success on everybody playing the game very strictly. As a single-handed game, it's impossible." Randall Utterword in *Heartbreak House* finds the "games in this house [are] damned annoying," but Hector warns that the only way to avoid being their victim is to learn to play them. Life is a game, or a pose, and Hector observes: "In this house we know all the poses: our game is to find out the man under the pose." Parallels go only so far, after which the playwright must be allowed the pegs upon which he has hung his play. In both *Misalliance* and *Heartbreak House* the pegs are many, yet the plays can be read, or performed, as high comedies without looking between the lines. Still, in the enchanted country house that is England, Shaw probes beneath the pose.

RODELLE WEINTRAUB
STANLEY WEINTRAUB

# A NOTE ON THE SHAW PREFACES

Both prefaces, in their entirety, are very long—perhaps one hundred and fifty pages in all. We have extracted from them here, furnishing passages most relevant to the plays themselves.

Note, too, that Shaw's spelling and punctuation in both preface and play is sometimes idiosyncratic. He often dispensed with apostrophes and quotation marks and spelled words (shew, Tchekov) in his own fashion. And Shaw sometimes indicated emphasis by broad spacing of letters in a word (as on pp. 140 and 144 in this edition).

# Misalliance

(1909)

# PREFACE
## Parents and Children

### TRAILING CLOUDS OF GLORY

Childhood is a stage in the process of that continual remanufacture of the Life Stuff by which the human race is perpetuated. The Life Force either will not or cannot achieve immortality except in very low organisms: indeed it is by no means ascertained that even the amoeba is immortal. Human beings visibly wear out, though they last longer than their friends the dogs. Turtles, parrots, and elephants are believed to be capable of outliving the memory of the oldest human inhabitant. But the fact that new ones are born conclusively proves that they are not immortal. Do away with death and you do away with the need for birth: in fact if you went on breeding, you would finally have to kill old people to make room for young ones.

Now death is not necessarily a failure of energy on the part of the Life Force. People with no imagination try to make things which will last for ever, and even want to live for ever themselves. But the intelligently imaginative man knows very well that it is waste of labor to make a machine that will last ten years, because it will probably be superseded in half that time by an improved machine answering the same purpose. He also knows that if some devil were to convince us that our dream of personal immortality is no dream but a hard fact, such a shriek of despair would go up from the human race as no other conceivable horror could provoke. With all our perverse nonsense as to John Smith living for a thousand million eons and for ever after, we die voluntarily, knowing that it is time for us to be scrapped, to be remanufactured, to come back, as Wordsworth divined, trailing ever brightening clouds of glory. We must all be born again, and yet again and again. We should like to live a little longer just as we should like £50: that is, we should take it if we could get it for nothing; but that sort of idle liking is not will. It is amazing—considering the way we talk—how little a man will do to get £50: all the £50 notes I have ever known of have been more easily earned than a laborious sixpence; but the difficulty of inducing a man to make any serious effort to obtain £50 is nothing to the difficulty of inducing him to make a serious effort to keep alive. The moment he sees death approach, he gets into bed and sends for a doctor. He knows very well at the back of his conscience that he is rather a poor job and had better be remanufactured. He knows that his death will make room for a birth; and he hopes that it will be a birth of something that he aspired to be and fell short of. He knows that it is through death and rebirth that this corruptible shall become incorruptible, and this mortal put on immortality. Practise as you will on his ignorance, his fears, and his imagination with bribes of paradises and threats of hells, there is only one belief that can rob death of its sting and the grave of its victory; and that is the belief that we can lay down the burden of our wretched little makeshift individualities for ever at each lift towards the goal of evolution, which can only be a being that cannot be improved upon. After all, what man is capable of the insane self-conceit of believing that an eternity of himself would be tolerable even to himself? Those who try to believe it postulate that they shall be made perfect first. But if you make me perfect I shall no longer be myself, nor will it be possible for me to conceive my present imperfections (and what I cannot conceive I cannot remember); so that you may just as well give me a new name and face the fact that I am a new person and that the old Bernard Shaw is as dead as mutton. Thus, oddly enough, the conventional belief in the matter comes to this: that if you wish to live for ever you must be wicked enough to be irretrievably damned, since the saved are no longer what they were, and in hell alone do people retain their sinful nature: that is to say, their individuality. And this sort of hell, however convenient as a means of intimidating persons who have practically no honor and no conscience, is not a fact. Death is for many of us the gate of hell; but we are inside on the way out, not outside on the way in. Therefore let us give up telling one another idle stories, and rejoice in death as we rejoice in birth; for without death we cannot be born again; and the man who does not wish to be born again and born better is fit only to represent the City of London in Parliament, or perhaps the university of Oxford.

## THE CHILD IS FATHER TO
## THE MAN

Is he? Then in the name of common sense why do we always treat children on the assumption that the man is father to the child? Oh, these fathers! And we are not content with fathers: we must have godfathers, forgetting that the child is godfather to the man. Has it ever struck you as curious that in a country where the first article of belief is that every child is born with a godfather whom we all call "our father which art in heaven," two very limited individual mortals should be allowed to appear at its baptism and explain that they are its godparents, and that they will look after its salvation until it is no longer a child. I had a godmother who made herself responsible in this way for me. She presented me with a Bible with a gilt clasp and edges, larger than the Bibles similarly presented to my sisters, because my sex entitled me to a heavier article. I must have seen that lady at least four times in the twenty years following. She never alluded to my salvation in any way. People occasionally ask me to act as godfather to their children with a levity which convinces me that they have not the faintest notion that it involves anything more than calling the helpless child George Bernard without regard to the possibility that it may grow up in the liveliest abhorrence of my notions.

A person with a turn for logic might argue that if God is the Father of all men, and if the child is father to the man, it follows that the true representative of God at the christening is the child itself. But such posers are unpopular, because they imply that our little customs, or, as we often call them, our religion, mean something, or must originally have meant something, and that we understand and believe that something.

However, my business is not to make confusion worse confounded, but to clear it up. Only, it is as well to begin by a sample of current thought and practice which shews that on the subject of children we are very deeply confused. On the whole, whatever our theory or no theory may be, our practice is to treat the child as the property of its immediate physical parents, and to allow them to do what they like with it as far as it will let them. It has no rights and no liberties: in short, its condition is that which adults recognize as the most miserable and dangerous politically possible for themselves: namely, the condition of slavery. For its alleviation we trust to the natural affection of the parties, and to public opinion. A father cannot for his own credit let his son go in rags. Also, in a very large section of the population, parents finally become dependent on their children. Thus there are checks on child slavery which do not exist, or are less powerful, in the case of manual and industrial slavery. Sensationally bad cases fall into two classes, which are really the same class: namely, the children whose parents are excessively addicted to the sensual luxury of petting children, and the children whose parents are excessively addicted to the sensual luxury of physically torturing them. There is a Society for the Prevention of Cruelty to Children which has effectually made an end of our belief that mothers are any more to be trusted than stepmothers, or fathers than slave-drivers. And there is a growing body of law designed to prevent parents from using their children ruthlessly to make money for the household. Such legislation has always been furiously resisted by the parents, even when the horrors of factory slavery were at their worst; and the extension of such legislation at present would be impossible if it were not that the parents affected by it cannot control a majority of votes in Parliament. In domestic life a great deal of service is done by children, the girls acting as nursemaids and general servants, and the lads as errand boys. In the country both boys and girls do a substantial share of farm labor. This is why it is necessary to coerce poor parents to send their children to school, though in the relatively small class which keeps plenty of servants it is impossible to induce parents to keep their children at home instead of paying schoolmasters to take them off their hands.

It appears then that the bond of affection between parents and children does not save children from the slavery that denial of rights involves in adult political relations. It sometimes intensifies it, sometimes mitigates it; but on the whole children and parents confront one another as two classes in which all the political power is on one side; and the results are not at all unlike what they would be if there were no immediate consanguinity between them, and one were white and the other black, or one enfranchised and the other disenfranchised, or one ranked as gentle and the other sim-

ple. Not that Nature counts for nothing in the case and political rights for everything. But a denial of political rights,
and the resultant delivery of one class into the mastery of
another, affects their relations so extensively and profoundly
that it is impossible to ascertain what the real natural relations of the two classes are until this political relation is
abolished.

## UNIVERSITY
## SCHOOLBOYISHNESS

Older children might do a good deal before beginning their
collegiate education. What is the matter with our universities
is that the students are school children, whereas it is of the
very essence of university education that they should be
adults. The function of a university is not to teach things
that can now be taught as well or better by University Extension lectures or by private tutors or modern correspon-
dence classes with gramophones. We go to them to be
socialized: to acquire the hall mark of communal training;
to become citizens of the world instead of inmates of the
enlarged rabbit hutches we call homes; to learn manners and
become unchallengeable ladies and gentlemen. The social
pressure which effects these changes should be that of persons who have faced the full responsibilities of adults as
working members of the general community, not that of a
rowdy rabble of half emancipated school children and une-
mancipable pedants. It is true that in a reasonable state of
society this outside experience would do for us very completely what the university does now so corruptly that we
tolerate its bad manners only because they are better than
no manners at all. But the university will always exist in some
form as a community of persons desirous of pushing their

culture to the highest pitch they are capable of, not as solitary students reading in seclusion, but as members of a body of individuals all pursuing culture, talking culture, thinking culture, above all, criticizing culture. If such persons are to read and talk and criticize to any purpose, they must know the world outside the university at least as well as the shop-keeper in the High Street does. And this is just what they do not know at present. You may say of them, paraphrasing Mr Kipling, "What do they know of Plato that only Plato know?" If our universities would exclude everybody who had not earned a living by his or her own exertions for at least a couple of years, their effect would be vastly improved.

## THE NEW LAZINESS

The child of the future, then, if there is to be any future but one of decay, will work more or less for its living from an early age; and in doing so it will not shock anyone, provided there be no longer any reason to associate the conception of children working for their living with infants toiling in a factory for ten hours a day or boys drudging from nine to six under gas lamps in underground city offices. Lads and lasses in their teens will probably be able to produce as much as the most expensive person now costs in his own person (it is retinue that eats up the big income) without working too hard or too long for quite as much happiness as they can enjoy. The question to be balanced then will be, not how soon people should be put to work, but how soon they should be released from any obligation of the kind. A life's work is like a day's work: it can begin early and leave off early or begin late and leave off late, or, as with us, begin too early and never leave off at all, obviously the worst of all possible plans. In any event we must finally reckon work, not as the curse our schools and prisons and capitalist profit factories make it seem today, but as a prime necessity of a tolerable existence. And if we cannot devise fresh wants as fast as we shorten the process of supplying the old ones, there will come a scarcity of work simultaneously with an excess of leisure. Work may have to be shared out among people who want more of it. Our spurious substitute, exercise, will not serve. A new sort of laziness will become the bugbear of society: the laziness that refuses to face the mental toil and adventure of making work by inventing new ideas or extending the domain of knowledge, and insists on a ready-made routine. It may come to forcing people to retire before they are willing to make way for younger ones: that is, to driving all persons of a certain age out of industry, leaving them to find something experimental to occupy them on pain of perpetual holiday. Men will then try to spend twenty thousand a year for the sake of having to earn it. Instead of being what we are now, the cheapest and nastiest of the animals, we shall be the costliest, most fastidious, and best bred. In short, there is no end to the astonishing things that may happen when the curse of Adam becomes first a blessing and then an incurable habit. And in view of that day we must not grudge children their share of it.

## CHILDREN AND GAME: A
## PROPOSAL

Of the many wild absurdities of our existing social order perhaps the most grotesque is the costly and strictly enforced reservation of large tracts of country as deer forests and breeding grounds for pheasants whilst there is so little provision of the kind made for children. I have more than once thought of trying to introduce the shooting of children as a sport, as the children would then be preserved very carefully for ten months in the year, thereby reducing their death rate far more than the fusillades of the sportsmen during the other two would raise it. At present the killing of a fox except by a pack of foxhounds is regarded with horror; but you may and do kill children in a hundred and fifty ways provided you do not shoot them or set a pack of dogs on them. It must be admitted that the foxes have the best of it; and indeed a glance at our pheasants, our deer, and our children will convince the most sceptical that the children have decidedly the worst of it.

This much hope, however, can be extracted from the present state of things. It is so fantastic, so mad, so apparently impossible, that no scheme of reform need ever henceforth be discredited on the ground that it is fantastic or mad or apparently impossible. It is the sensible schemes, unfortunately, that are hopeless in England. Therefore I have great hopes that my own views, though fundamentally sensible, can be made to appear fantastic enough to have a chance.

First, then, I lay it down as a prime condition of sane society, obvious as such to anyone but an idiot, that in any decent community, children should find in every part of their native country, food, clothing, lodging, instruction, and parental kindness for the asking. For the matter of that, so should adults; but the two cases differ in that as these commodities do not grow on the bushes, the adults cannot have them unless they themselves organize and provide the supply, whereas the children must have them as if by magic, with nothing to do but rub the lamp, like Aladdin, and have their needs satisfied.

1914

# MISALLIANCE

J ohnny Tarleton, an ordinary young business man of thirty or less, is taking his weekly Friday to Tuesday in the house of his father, John Tarleton, who has made a great deal of money out of Tarleton's Underwear. The house is in Surrey, on the slope of Hindhead; and Johnny, reclining, novel in hand, in a swinging chair with a little awning above it, is enshrined in a spacious half hemisphere of glass which forms a pavilion commanding the garden, and, beyond it, a barren but lovely landscape of hill profile with fir trees, commons of bracken and gorse, and wonderful cloud pictures.

The glass pavilion springs from a bridgelike arch in the wall of the house, through which one comes into a big hall with tiled flooring, which suggests that the proprietor's notion of domestic luxury is founded on the lounges of week-end hotels. The arch is not quite in the centre of the wall. There is more wall to Johnny's right than to his left; and this space is occupied by a hat rack and umbrella stand in which tennis rackets, white parasols, caps, Panama hats, and other summery articles are bestowed. Just through the arch at this corner stands a new portable Turkish bath, recently unpacked, with its crate beside it, and on the crate the drawn nails and the hammer used in unpacking. Near the crate are open boxes of garden games: bowls and croquet. Nearly in the middle of the glass wall of the pavilion is a door giving on the garden, with a couple of steps to surmount the hot-water pipes which skirt the glass. At intervals round the pavilion are marble pillars with specimens of Viennese pottery on them, very flamboyant in colour and florid in design. Between them are folded garden chairs flung anyhow against the pipes. In the side walls are two doors: one near the hat stand, leading to the interior of the house, the other on the opposite side and at the other end, leading to the vestibule.

There is no solid furniture except a sideboard which stands against the wall between the vestibule door and the pavilion, a small writing table with blotter, rack for telegram forms and stationery, and a wastepaper basket, standing out in the hall near the sideboard, and a lady's worktable, with two chairs at it, towards the other side of the lounge. The writing table has also two chairs at it. On the sideboard there is a tantalus, liqueur bottles, a syphon, a glass jug of lemonade, tumblers, and every convenience for casual drinking. Also a plate of sponge cakes, and a highly ornate punchbowl in the same style as the keramic display in the pavilion. Wicker chairs and little bamboo tables with ash trays and boxes of matches on them are scattered in all directions. In the pavilion, which is flooded with sunshine, is the elaborate patent swing seat and awning in which Johnny reclines with his novel. There are two wicker chairs right and left of him.

Bentley Summerhays, one of those smallish, thinskinned youths, who from 17 to 70 retain unaltered the mental airs of the later and the physical appearance of the earlier age, appears in the garden and comes through the glass door into the pavilion. He is unmistakably a grade above Johnny socially; and though he looks sensitive enough, his assurance and his high voice are a little exasperating.

JOHNNY. Hallo! Wheres your luggage?

BENTLEY. I left it at the station. Ive walked up from Haslemere. [He goes to the hat stand and hangs up his hat].

JOHNNY [shortly] Oh! And whos to fetch it?

BENTLEY. Don't know. Dont care. Providence, probably. If not, your mother will have it fetched.

JOHNNY. Not her business, exactly, is it?

BENTLEY [*returning to the pavilion*] Of course not. Thats why one loves her for doing it. Look here: chuck away your silly week-end novel, and talk to a chap. After a week in that filthy office my brain is simply blue-mouldy. Lets argue about something intellectual. [*He throws himself into the wicker chair on Johnny's right*].

JOHNNY [*straightening up in the swing with a yell of protest*] No. Now seriously, Bunny, Ive come down here to have a pleasant week-end; and I'm not going to stand your confounded arguments. If you want to argue, get out of this and go over to the Congregationalist minister's. He's a nailer at arguing. He likes it.

BENTLEY. You cant argue with a person when his livelihood depends on his not letting you convert him. And would you mind not calling me Bunny? My name is Bentley Summerhays, which you please.

JOHNNY. Whats the matter with Bunny?

BENTLEY. It puts me in a false position. Have you ever considered the fact that I was an afterthought?

JOHNNY. An afterthought? What do you mean by that?

BENTLEY. I—

JOHNNY. No, stop: I dont want to know. It's only a dodge to start an argument.

BENTLEY. Dont be afraid: it wont overtax your brain. My father was 44 when I was born. My mother was 41. There was twelve years between me and the next eldest. I was unexpected. I was probably unintentional. My brothers and sisters are not the least like me. Theyre the regular thing that you always get in the first batch from young parents: quite pleasant, ordinary, do-the-regular-thing sort: all body and no brains, like you.

JOHNNY. Thank you.

BENTLEY. Dont mention it, old chap. Now I'm different. By the time I was born, the old couple knew something. So I came out all brains and no more body than is absolutely necessary. I am really a good deal older than you, though you were born ten years sooner. Everybody feels that when they hear us talk; consequently, though it's quite natural to hear me calling you Johnny, it sounds ridiculous and unbecoming for you to call me Bunny. [*He rises*].

JOHNNY. Does it, by George? You stop me doing it if you can: thats all.

BENTLEY. If you go on doing it after Ive asked you not, youll feel an awful swine (*He strolls away carelessly to the sideboard with his eye on the sponge-cakes*). At least I should; but I suppose youre not so particular.

JOHNNY [*rising vengefully and following Bentley, who is forced to turn and listen*] I'll tell you what it is, my boy: you want a good talking to; and I'm going to give it to you. If you think that because your father's a K.C.B., and you want to marry my sister, you can make yourself as nasty as you please and say what you like, youre mistaken. Let me tell you that except Hypatia, not one person in this house is in favor of her marrying you; and I dont believe shes happy about it herself. The match isnt settled yet: dont forget that. Youre on trial in the office because the Governor isnt giving his daughter money for an idle man to live on her. Youre on trial here because my mother thinks a girl should know what a man is like in the house before she marries him. Thats been going on for two months now; and whats the result? Youve got yourself thoroughly disliked in the office; and youre getting yourself thoroughly disliked here, all through your bad manners and your conceit, and the damned impudence you think clever.

BENTLEY [*deeply wounded and trying hard to control himself*] Thats enough, thank you. You dont suppose, I hope,

that I should have come down if I had known that that was
how you all feel about me. [*He makes for the vestibule door*].

JOHNNY   [*collaring him*] No: you dont run away. I'm going to have this out with you. Sit down: d'y' hear? [*Bentley
attempts to go with dignity. Johnny slings him into a chair at the
writing table, where he sits, bitterly humiliated, but afraid to
speak lest he should burst into tears*]. Thats the advantage of
having more body than brains, you see: it enables me to
teach you manners; and I'm going to do it too. Youre a spoilt
young pup; and you need a jolly good licking. And if youre
not careful youll get it: I'll see to that next time you call me
a swine.

BENTLEY.   I didnt call you a swine. But [*bursting into a
fury of tears*] you are a swine: youre a beast: youre a brute:
youre a cad: youre a liar: youre a bully: I should like to wring
your damned neck for you.

JOHNNY   [*with a derisive laugh*] Try it, my son. [*Bentley
gives an inarticulate sob of rage*]. Fighting isnt in your line.
Youre too small; and youre too childish. I always suspected
that your cleverness wouldnt come to very much when it
was brought up against something solid: some decent chap's
fist, for instance.

BENTLEY.   I hope your beastly fist may come up against
a mad bull or a prizefighter's nose, or something solider than
me. I dont care about your fist; but if everybody here dislikes
me—[*he is checked by a sob*]. Well, I dont care. [*Trying to
recover himself*] I'm sorry I intruded: I didnt know. [*Breaking
down again*] Oh you beast! you pig! Swine, swine, swine,
swine, swine! Now!

JOHNNY.   All right, my lad, all right. Sling your mud as
hard as you please: it wont stick to me. What I want to know
is this. How is it that your father, who I suppose is the
strongest man England has produced in our time—

BENTLEY.   You got that out of your halfpenny paper. A
lot you know about him!

JOHNNY.  I dont set up to be able to do anything but admire him and appreciate him and be proud of him as an Englishman. If it wasnt for my respect for him, I wouldnt have stood your cheek for two days, let alone two months. But what I cant understand is why he didnt lick it out of you when you were a kid. For twenty-five years he kept a place twice as big as England in order: a place full of seditious coffee-colored heathens and pestilential white agitators in the middle of a lot of savage tribes. And yet he couldnt keep you in order. I dont set up to be half the man your father undoubtedly is; but, by George, it's lucky for you you were not my son. I dont hold with my own father's views about corporal punishment being wrong. It's necessary for some people; and I'd have tried it on you until you first learnt to howl and then to behave yourself.

BENTLEY  [contemptuously] Yes: behavior wouldnt come naturally to your son, would it?

JOHNNY  [stung into sudden violence] Now you keep a civil tongue in your head. I'll stand none of your snobbery. I'm just as proud of Tarleton's Underwear as you are of your father's title and his K.C.B., and all the rest of it. My father began in a little hole of a shop in Leeds no bigger than our pantry down the passage there. He—

BENTLEY.  Oh yes: I know. Ive read it. "The Romance of Business, or The Story of Tarleton's Underwear. Please Take One!" I took one the day after I first met Hypatia. I went and bought half a dozen unshrinkable vests for her sake.

JOHNNY.  Well: did they shrink?

BENTLEY.  Oh, dont be a fool.

JOHNNY.  Never mind whether I'm a fool or not. Did they shrink? Thats the point. Were they worth the money?

BENTLEY.  I couldnt wear them: do you think my skin's as thick as your customers' hides? I'd as soon have dressed myself in a nutmeg grater.

JOHNNY. Pity your father didnt give your thin skin a jolly good lacing with a cane!

BENTLEY. Pity you havnt got more than one idea! If you want to know, they did try that on me once, when I was a small kid. A silly governess did it. I yelled fit to bring down the house, and went into convulsions and brain fever and that sort of thing for three weeks. So the old girl got the sack; and serve her right! After that, I was let do what I liked. My father didnt want me to grow up a broken-spirited spaniel, which is your idea of a man, I suppose.

JOHNNY. Jolly good thing for you that my father made you come into the office and shew what you were made of. And it didnt come to much: let me tell you that. When the Governor asked me where I thought we ought to put you, I said "Make him the Office Boy." The Governor said you were too green. And so you were.

BENTLEY. I daresay. So would you be pretty green if you were shoved into my father's set. I picked up your silly business in a fortnight. Youve been at it ten years; and you havnt picked it up yet.

JOHNNY. Dont talk rot, child. You know you simply make me pity you.

BENTLEY. "Romance of Business" indeed! The real romance of Tarleton's business is the story that you understand anything about it. You never could explain any mortal thing about it to me when I asked you. "See what was done the last time": that was the beginning and the end of your wisdom. Youre nothing but a turnspit.

JOHNNY. A what!

BENTLEY. A turnspit. If your father hadnt made a roasting jack for you to turn, youd be earning twenty-four shillings a week behind a counter.

JOHNNY. If you dont take that back and apologize for your bad manners, I'll give you as good a hiding as ever—

BENTLEY. Help! Johnny's beating me! Oh! Murder! [*He throws himself on the ground, uttering piercing yells*].

JOHNNY. Dont be a fool. Stop that noise, will you. I'm not going to touch you. Sh—sh—

*Hypatia rushes in through the inner door, followed by Mrs Tarleton, and throws herself on her knees by Bentley. Mrs Tarleton, whose knees are stiffer, bends over him and tries to lift him. Mrs Tarleton is a shrewed and motherly old lady who has been pretty in her time, and is still very pleasant and likeable and unaffected. Hypatia is a typical English girl of a sort never called typical: that is, she has an opaque white skin, black hair, large dark eyes with black brows and lashes, curved lips, swift glances and movements that flash out of a waiting stillness, boundless energy and audacity held in leash.*

HYPATIA [*pouncing on Bentley with no very gentle hand*] Bentley: whats the matter? Dont cry like that: whats the use? Whats happened?

MRS TARLETON. Are you ill, child? [*They get him up*]. There, there, pet! It's all right: dont cry [*they put him into a chair*]: there! there! there! Johnny will go for the doctor; and he'll give you something nice to make it well.

HYPATIA. What has happened, Johnny?

MRS TARLETON. Was it a wasp?

BENTLEY [*impatiently*] Wasp be dashed!

MRS TARLETON. Oh Bunny! that was a naughty word.

BENTLEY. Yes, I know: I beg your pardon. [*He rises, and extricates himself from them*]. Thats all right. Johnny frightened me. You know how easy it is to hurt me; and I'm too small to defend myself against Johnny.

MRS TARLETON. Johnny: how often have I told you that you must not bully the little ones. I thought youd outgrown all that.

HYPATIA [*angrily*] I do declare, mamma, that Johnny's brutality makes it impossible to live in the house with him.

JOHNNY [*deeply hurt*] It's fourteen years, mother, since

you had that row with me for licking Robert and giving Hypatia a black eye because she bit me. I promised you then that I'd never raise my hand to one of them again; and Ive never broken my word. And now because this young whelp begins to cry out before he's hurt, you treat me as if I were a brute and a savage.

MRS TARLETON.   No dear, not a savage; but you know you musnt call our visitor naughty names.

BENTLEY.   Oh, let him alone—

JOHNNY [*fiercely*] Dont you interfere between my mother and me: d'y' hear?

HYPATIA.   Johnny's lost his temper, mother. We'd better go. Come, Bentley.

MRS TARLETON.   Yes: that will be best. [*To Bentley*] Johnny doesnt mean any harm, dear: he'll be himself presently. Come.

*The two ladies go out through the inner door with Bentley, who turns derisively at the door to cock a snook at Johnny as he goes out.*

*Johnny, left alone, clenches his fists and grinds his teeth, but can find no relief in that way for his rage. After choking and stamping for a moment, he makes for the vestibule door. It opens before he reaches it; and Lord Summerhays comes in. Johnny glares at him, speechless. Lord Summerhays takes in the situation, and quickly takes the punchbowl from the sideboard and offers it to Johnny.*

LORD SUMMERHAYS.   Smash it. Dont hesitate: it's an ugly thing. Smash it: hard. [*Johnny, with a stifled yell, dashes it in pieces, and then sits down and mops his brow*]. Feel better now? [*Johnny nods*]. I know only one person alive who could drive me to the point of having either to break china or commit murder; and that person is my son Bentley. Was it he? [*Johnny nods again, not yet able to speak*]. As the car stopped I heard a yell which is only too familiar to me. It generally means that some infuriated person is trying to thrash Bentley. Nobody has ever succeeded, though almost everybody has tried. [*He seats himself comfortably close to the writing table, and sets to work to collect the fragments of the punchbowl in the wastepaper basket whilst Johnny, with diminishing difficulty, collects himself*]. Bentley is a problem which I confess I have never been able to solve. He was born to be a great success at the age of fifty. Most Englishmen of his class seem to be born to be great successes at the age of twenty-four at most. The domestic problem for me is how to endure Bentley until he is fifty. The problem for the nation is how to get itself governed by men whose growth is arrested when they are little more than college lads. Bentley doesnt really mean to be offensive. You can always make him cry by telling him you dont like him. Only, he cries so loud that the experiment should be made in the open air: in the middle of Salisbury Plain if possible. He has a hard and penetrating intellect and a remarkable power of looking facts in the face; but unfortunately, being very young, he has no idea of how very little of that sort of thing most of us can stand. On the other hand, he is frightfully sensitive and even affectionate; so that he probably gets as much as he gives in the way of hurt feelings. Youll excuse me rambling on like this about my son.

JOHNNY [*who has pulled himself together*] You did it on purpose. I wasnt quite myself: I needed a moment to pull round. Thank you.

LORD SUMMERHAYS. Not at all. Is your father at home?

JOHNNY. No: he's opening one of his free libraries. Thats another nice little penny gone. He's mad on reading. He promised another free library last week. It's ruinous. Itll hit you as well as me when Bunny marries Hypatia. When all Hypatia's money is thrown away on libraries, where will Bunny come in? Cant you stop him?

LORD SUMMERHAYS. I'm afraid not. Hes a perfect whirlwind. Indefatigable at public work. Wonderful man, I think.

JOHNNY. Oh, public work! He does too much of it. It's

really a sort of laziness, getting away from your own serious business to amuse yourself with other people's. Mind: I dont say there isnt another side to it. It has its value as an advertisement. It makes useful acquaintances and leads to valuable business connections. But it takes his mind off the main chance; and he overdoes it.

LORD SUMMERHAYS.   The danger of public business is that it never ends. A man may kill himself at it.

JOHNNY.   Or he can spend more on it than it brings him in: thats how I look at it. What I say is that everybody's business is nobody's business. I hope I'm not a hard man, nor a narrow man, nor unwilling to pay reasonable taxes, and subscribe in reason to deserving charities, and even serve on a jury in my turn; and no man can say I ever refused to help a friend out of a difficulty when he was worth helping. But when you ask me to go beyond that, I tell you frankly I dont see it. I never did see it, even when I was only a boy, and had to pretend to take in all the ideas the Governor fed me up with. I didn't see it; and I dont see it.

LORD SUMMERHAYS.   There is certainly no business reason why you should take more than your share of the world's work.

JOHNNY.   So I say. It's really a great encouragement to me to find you agree with me. For of course if nobody agrees with you, how are you to know that youre not a fool?

LORD SUMMERHAYS.   Quite so.

JOHNNY.   I wish youd talk to him about it. It's no use my saying anything: I'm a child to him still: I have no influence. Besides, you know how to handle men. See how you handled me when I was making a fool of myself about Bunny!

LORD SUMMERHAYS.   Not at all.

JOHNNY.   Oh yes I was: I know I was. Well, if my blessed father had come in he'd have told me to control myself. As if I was losing my temper on purpose!

*Bentley returns, newly washed. He beams when he sees his father, and comes affectionately behind him and pats him on the shoulders.*

BENTLEY.   Hel-lo, commander! have you come? Ive been making a filthy silly ass of myself here. I'm awfully sorry, Johnny, old chap: I beg your pardon. Why dont you kick me when I go on like that?

LORD SUMMERHAYS.   As we came through Godalming I thought I heard some yelling—

BENTLEY.   I should think you did. Johnny was rather rough on me, though. He told me nobody here liked me; and I was silly enough to believe him.

LORD SUMMERHAYS.   And all the women have been kissing you and pitying you ever since to stop your crying, I suppose. Baby!

BENTLEY.   I did cry. But I always feel good after crying: it relieves my wretched nerves. I feel perfectly jolly now.

LORD SUMMERHAYS.   Not at all ashamed of yourself, for instance?

BENTLEY.   If I started being ashamed of myself I shouldnt have time for anything else all my life. I say: I feel very fit and spry. Lets all go down and meet the Grand Cham. [*He goes to the hatstand and takes down his hat*].

LORD SUMMERHAYS.   Does Mr Tarleton like to be called the Grand Cham, do you think, Bentley?

BENTLEY.   Well, he thinks he's too modest for it. He calls himself Plain John. But you cant call him that in his own office: besides, it doesnt suit him: it's not flamboyant enough.

JOHNNY.   Flam what?

BENTLEY.   Flamboyant. Lets go and meet him. He's telephoned from Guildford to say he's on the road. The dear old son is always telephoning or telegraphing: he thinks he's hustling along like anything when hes only sending unnecessary messages.

LORD SUMMERHAYS.   Thank you: I should prefer a quiet afternoon.

BENTLEY.   Right o! I shant press Johnny: he's had enough of me for one week-end [*He goes out through the pavilion into the grounds*].

JOHNNY.   Not a bad idea, that.

LORD SUMMERHAYS.   What?

JOHNNY.   Going to meet the Governor. You know you wouldnt think it; but the Governor likes Bunny rather. And Bunny is cultivating it. I shouldnt be surprised if he thought he could squeeze me out one of these days.

LORD SUMMERHAYS.   You dont say so! Young rascal! I want to consult you about him, if you dont mind. Shall we stroll over to the Gibbet? Bentley is too fast for me as a walking companion; but I should like a short turn.

JOHNNY   [*rising eagerly, highly flattered*] Right you are. Thatll suit me down to the ground. [*He takes a Panama and stick from the hat stand*].

*Mrs Tarleton and Hypatia come back just as the two men are going out. Hypatia salutes Summerhays from a distance with an enigmatic lift of her eyelids in his direction and a demure nod before she sits down at the worktable and busies herself with her needle. Mrs Tarleton, hospitably fussy, goes over to him.*

MRS TARLETON.   Oh, Lord Summerhays, I didn't know you were here. Wont you have some tea?

LORD SUMMERHAYS.   No, thank you: I'm not allowed tea. And I'm ashamed to say Ive knocked over your beautiful punch-bowl. You must let me replace it.

MRS TARLETON.   Oh, it doesnt matter: I'm only too glad to be rid of it. The shopman told me it was in the best taste; but when my poor old nurse Martha got cataract, Bunny said it was a merciful provision of Nature to prevent her seeing our china.

LORD SUMMERHAYS   [*gravely*] That was exceedingly rude of Bentley, Mrs Tarleton. I hope you told him so.

MRS TARLETON.   Oh, bless you! I dont care what he says; so long as he says it to me and not before visitors.

JOHNNY.   We're going out for a stroll, mother.

MRS TARLETON.   All right: dont let us keep you. Never mind about that crock: I'll get the girl to come and take the pieces away. [*Recollecting herself*] There! Ive done it again!

JOHNNY.   Done what?

MRS TARLETON.   Called her the girl. You know, Lord Summerhays, it's a funny thing; but now I'm getting old, I'm dropping back into all the ways John and I had when we had barely a hundred a year. You should have known me when I was forty! I talked like a duchess; and if Johnny or Hypatia let slip a word that was like old times, I was down on them like anything. And now I'm beginning to do it myself at every turn.

LORD SUMMERHAYS.   There comes a time when all that seems to matter so little. Even queens drop the mask when they reach our time of life.

MRS TARLETON.   Let you alone for giving a thing a pretty turn! Youre a humbug, you know, Lord Summerhays. John doesnt know it; and Johnny doesnt know it; but you and I know it, dont we? Now thats something that even you cant answer; so be off with you for your walk without another word.

*Lord Summerhays smiles; bows; and goes out through the vestibule door, followed by Johnny. Mrs Tarleton sits down at the worktable and takes out her darning materials and one of her husband's socks. Hypatia is at the other side of the table, on her mother's right. They chat as they work.*

HYPATIA.   I wonder whether they laugh at us when they are by themselves!

MRS TARLETON.   Who?

HYPATIA.   Bentley and his father and all the toffs in their set.

MRS TARLETON.   Oh, thats only their way. I used to

think that the aristocracy were a nasty sneering lot, and that they were laughing at me and John. Theyre always giggling and pretending not to care much about anything. But you get used to it: theyre the same to one another and to everybody. Besides, what does it matter what they think? It's far worse when theyre civil, because that always means that they want you to lend them money; and you must never do that, Hypatia, because they never pay. How can they? They dont make anything, you see. Of course, if you can make up your mind to regard it as a gift, thats different; but then they generally ask you again; and you may as well say no first as last. You neednt be afraid of the aristocracy, dear: theyre only human creatures like ourselves after all; and youll hold your own with them easy enough.

HYPATIA. Oh, I'm not a bit afraid of them, I assure you.

MRS TARLETON. Well, no, not afraid of them, exactly; but youve got to pick up their ways. You know, dear, I never quite agreed with your father's notion of keeping clear of them, and sending you to a school that was so expensive that they couldnt afford to send their daughters there; so that all the girls belonged to big business families like ourselves. It takes all sorts to make a world; and I wanted you to see a little of all sorts. When you marry Bunny, and go among the women of his father's set, theyll shock you at first.

HYPATIA [incredulously] How?

MRS TARLETON. Well, the things they talk about.

HYPATIA. Oh! scandalmongering?

MRS TARLETON. Oh no: we all do that: that's only human nature. But you know theyve no notion of decency. I shall never forget the first day I spent with a marchioness, two duchesses, and no end of Ladies This and That. Of course it was only a committee: theyd put me on to get a big subscription out of John. I'd never heard such talk in my life. The things they mentioned! And it was the marchioness that started it.

HYPATIA.  What sort of things?

MRS TARLETON.  Drainage!! She tried three systems in her castle; and she was going to do away with them all and try another. I didnt know which way to look when she began talking about it: I thought theyd all have got up and gone out of the room. But not a bit of it, if you please. They were all just as bad as she. They all had systems; and each of them swore by her own system. I sat there with my cheeks burning until one of the duchesses, thinking I looked out of it, I suppose, asked me what system I had. I said I was sure I knew nothing about such things, and hadnt we better change the subject. Then the fat was in the fire, I can tell you. There was a regular terror of a countess with an anaerobic system; and she told me, downright brutally, that I'd better learn something about them before my children died of diphtheria. That was just two months after I'd buried poor little Bobby; and that was the very thing he died of, poor little lamb! I burst out crying: I couldnt help it. It was as good as telling me I'd killed my own child. I had to go away; but before I was out of the door one of the duchesses—quite a young woman—began talking about what sour milk did in her inside and how she expected to live to be over a hundred if she took it regularly. And me listening to her, that had never dared to think that a duchess could have anything so common as an inside! I shouldnt have minded if it had been children's insides: we have to talk about them. But grown-up people! I was glad to get away that time.

HYPATIA.  There was a physiology and hygiene class started at school; but of course none of our girls were let attend it.

MRS TARLETON.  If it had been an aristocratic school plenty would have attended it. Thats what theyre like: theyve nasty minds. With really nice good women a thing is either

decent or indecent; and if it's indecent, we just dont mention
it or pretend to know about it; and theres an end of it. But
all the aristocracy cares about is whether it can get any good
out of the thing. Theyre what Johnny calls cynical-like. And
of course nobody can say a word to them for it. Theyre so
high up that they can do and say what they like.

HYPATIA.   Well, I think they might leave the drains to
their husbands, I shouldnt think much of a man that left
such things to me.

MRS TARLETON.   Oh, dont think that, dear, whatever
you do. I never let on about it to you; but it's me that takes
care of the drainage here. After what that countess said to
me I wasnt going to lose another child nor trust John. And
I dont want my grandchildren to die any more than my
children.

HYPATIA.   Do you think Bentley will ever be as big a man
as his father? I dont mean clever: I mean big and strong.

MRS TARLETON.   Not he. He's overbred, like one of those
expensive little dogs. I like a bit of a mongrel myself, whether
it's a man or a dog: theyre the best for everyday. But we all
have our tastes: whats one woman's meat is another woman's
poison. Bunny's a dear little fellow; but I never could have
fancied him for a husband when I was your age.

HYPATIA.   Yes; but he has some brains. He's not like all
the rest. One cant have everything.

MRS TARLETON.   Oh, youre quite right, dear: quite right.
It's a great thing to have brains: look what it's done for your
father! Thats the reason I never said a word when you jilted
poor Jerry Mackintosh.

HYPATIA   [excusing herself] I really couldnt stick it out
with Jerry, mother. I know you liked him; and nobody can
deny that hes a splendid animal—

MRS TARLETON   [shocked] Hypatia! How can you! The
things that girls say nowadays!

HYPATIA.   Well, what else can you call him? If I'd been

deaf or he'd been dumb, I could have married him. But living with father, Ive got accustomed to cleverness. Jerry would drive me mad: you know very well he's a fool: even Johnny thinks him a fool.

MRS TARLETON [*up in arms at once in defence of her boy*] Now dont begin about my Johnny. You know it annoys me. Johnny's as clever as anybody else in his own way. I dont say he's as clever as you in some ways; but he's a man, at all events, and not a little squit of a thing like your Bunny.

HYPATIA. Oh, I say nothing against your darling: we all know Johnny's perfection.

MRS TARLETON. Dont be cross, dearie. You let Johnny alone; and I'll let Bunny alone. I'm just as bad as you. There!

HYPATIA. Oh, I dont mind your saying that about Bentley. It's true. He is a little squit of a thing. I wish he wasnt. But who else is there? Think of all the other chances Ive had! Not one of them has as much brains in his whole body as Bentley has in his little finger. Besides, theyve no distinction. It's as much as I can do to tell one from the other. They wouldnt even have money if they werent the sons of their fathers, like Johnny. Whats a girl to do? I never met anybody like Bentley before. He may be small; but he's the best of the bunch: you cant deny that.

MRS TARLETON [*with a sigh*] Well, my pet, if you fancy him, theres no more to be said.

*A pause follows this remark: the two women sewing silently.*

HYPATIA. Mother: do you think marriage is as much a question of fancy as it used to be in your time and father's?

MRS TARLETON. Oh, it wasnt much fancy with me, dear: your father just wouldnt take no for an answer; and I was only too glad to be his wife instead of his shop-girl. Still, it's curious; but I had more choice than you in a way, because you see, I was poor; and there are so many more poor men than rich ones that I might have had more of a pick, as you might say, if John hadnt suited me.

HYPATIA. I can imagine all sorts of men I could fall in love with; but I never seem to meet them. The real ones are too small, like Bunny, or too silly, like Jerry. Of course one can get into a state about any man: fall in love with him if you like to call it that. But who would risk marrying a man for love? I shouldnt. I remember three girls at school who agreed that the one man you should never marry was the man you were in love with, because it would make a perfect slave of you. Theres a sort of instinct against it, I think, thats just as strong as the other instinct. One of them, to my certain knowledge, refused a man she was in love with, and married another who was in love with her; and it turned out very well.

MRS TARLETON. Does all that mean that youre not in love with Bunny?

HYPATIA. Oh, how could anybody be in love with Bunny? I like him to kiss me just as I like a baby to kiss me. I'm fond of him; and he never bores me; and I see that he's very clever; but I'm not what you call gone about him, if thats what you mean.

MRS TARLETON. Then why need you marry him?

HYPATIA. What better can I do? I must marry somebody, I suppose. Ive realized that since I was twentythree. I always used to take it as a matter of course that I should be married before I was twenty.

BENTLEY'S VOICE [in the garden] Youve got to keep yourself fresh: to look at these things with an open mind.

JOHN TARLETON'S VOICE. Quite right, quite right: I always say so.

MRS TARLETON. Theres your father, and Bunny with him.

BENTLEY. Keep young. Keep your eye on me. Thats the tip for you.

Bentley and Mr Tarleton (an immense and genial veteran of trade) come into view and enter the pavilion.

JOHN TARLETON.   You think youre young, do you? You think I'm old? [*energetically shaking off his motoring coat and hanging it up with his cap*].

BENTLEY   [*helping him with the coat*] Of course youre old. Look at your face and look at mine. What you call your youth is nothing but your levity. Why do we get on so well together? Because I'm a young cub and youre an old josser. [*He throws a cushion at Hypatia's feet and sits down on it with his back against her knees*].

TARLETON.   Old! Thats all you know about it, my lad. How do, Patsy! [*Hypatia kisses him*]. How is my Chicka-biddy? [*He kisses Mrs Tarleton's hand and poses expansively in the middle of the picture*]. Look at me! Look at these wrinkles, these grey hairs, this repulsive mask that you call old age! What is it? [*Vehemently*] I ask you, what is it?

BENTLEY.   Jolly nice and venerable, old man. Dont be discouraged.

TARLETON.   Nice? Not a bit of it. Venerable? Venerable be blowed! Read your Darwin, my boy. Read your Weismann. [*He goes to the sideboard for a drink of lemonade*].

MRS TARLETON.   For shame, John! Tell him to read his Bible.

TARLETON   [*manipulating the syphon*] Whats the use of telling children to read the Bible when you know they wont. I was kept away from the Bible for forty years by being told to read it when I was young. Then I picked it up one evening in a hotel in Sunderland when I had left all my papers in the train; and I found it wasnt half bad. [*He drinks, and puts down the glass with a smack of enjoyment*]. Better than most halfpenny papers, anyhow, if only you could make people believe it. [*He sits down by the writing-table, near his wife*]. But if you want to understand old age scientifically, read Darwin and Weismann. Of course if you want to understand it romantically, read about Solomon.

MRS TARLETON.   Have you had tea, John?

TARLETON. Yes. Dont interrupt me when I'm improving the boy's mind. Where was I? This repulsive mask—Yes. [*Explosively*] What is death?

MRS TARLETON. John!

HYPATIA. Death is a rather unpleasant subject, Papa.

TARLETON. Not a bit. Not scientifically. Scientifically it's a delightful subject. You think death's natural. Well, it isnt. You read Weismann. There wasnt any death to start with. You go look in any ditch outside and youll find swimming about there as fresh as paint some of the identical little live cells that Adam christened in the Garden of Eden. But if big things like us didnt die, we'd crowd one another off the face of the globe. Nothing survived, sir, except the sort of people that had the sense and good manners to die and make room for the fresh supplies. And so death was introduced by Natural Selection. You get it out of your head, my lad, that I'm going to die because I'm wearing out or decaying. There's no such thing as decay to a vital man. I shall clear out; but I shant decay.

BENTLEY. And what about the wrinkles and the almond tree and the grasshopper that becomes a burden and the desire that fails?

TARLETON. Does it? by George! No, sir: it spiritualizes. As to your grasshopper, I can carry an elephant.

MRS TARLETON. You do say such things, Bunny! What does he mean by the almond tree?

TARLETON. He means my white hairs: the repulsive mask. That, my boy, is another invention of Natural Selection to disgust young women with me, and give the lads a turn.

MRS TARLETON. John: I wont have it. Thats a forbidden subject.

TARLETON. They talk of the wickedness and vanity of women painting their faces and wearing auburn wigs at fifty. But why shouldnt they? Why should a woman allow Nature to put a false mask of age on her when she knows that she's as young as ever? Why should she look in the glass and see a wrinkled lie when a touch of fine art will shew her a glorious truth? The wrinkles are a dodge to repel young men. Suppose she doesnt want to repel young men! Suppose she likes them!

MRS TARLETON. Bunny: take Hypatia out into the grounds for a walk: theres a good boy. John has got one of his naughty fits this evening.

HYPATIA. Oh, never mind me. I'm used to him.

BENTLEY. I'm not. I never heard such conversation: I cant believe my ears. And mind you, this is the man who objected to my marrying his daughter on the ground that a marriage between a member of the great and good middle class with one of the vicious and corrupt aristocracy would be a misalliance. A misalliance, if you please! This is the man Ive adopted as a father!

TARLETON. Eh? Whats that? Adopted me as a father, have you?

BENTLEY. Yes. Thats an idea of mine. I knew a chap named Joey Percival at Oxford (you know I was two months at Balliol before I was sent down for telling the old woman who was head of that silly college what I jolly well thought of him. He would have been glad to have me back, too, at the end of six months; but I wouldnt go: I just let him want; and serve him right!) Well, Joey was a most awfully clever fellow, and so nice! I asked him what made such a difference between him and all the other pups—they were pups, if you like. He told me it was very simple: they had only one father apiece; and he had three.

MRS TARLETON. Dont talk nonsense, child. How could that be?

BENTLEY. Oh, very simple. His father—

TARLETON. Which father?

BENTLEY. The first one: the regulation natural chap. He

kept a tame philosopher in the house: a sort of Coleridge or
Herbert Spencer kind of card, you know. That was the second father. Then his mother was an Italian princess; and she
had an Italian priest always about. He was supposed to take
charge of her conscience; but from what I could make out
she jolly well took charge of his. The whole three of them
took charge of Joey's conscience. He used to hear them arguing like mad about everything. You see, the philosopher
was a freethinker, and always believed the latest thing. The
priest didnt believe anything, because it was sure to get him
into trouble with someone or another. And the natural father
kept an open mind and believed whatever paid him best.
Between the lot of them Joey got cultivated no end. He said
if he could only have had three mothers as well, he'd have
backed himself against Napoleon.

TARLETON [*impressed*] Thats an idea. Thats a most interesting idea: a most important idea.

MRS TARLETON.   You always were one for ideas, John.

TARLETON.   Youre right, Chickabiddy. What do I tell
Johnny when he brags about Tarleton's Underwear? It's not
the underwear. The underwear be hanged! Anybody can
make underwear. Anybody can sell underwear. Tarleton's
Ideas: thats whats done it. Ive often thought of putting that
up over the shop.

BENTLEY.   Take me into partnership when you do, old
man. I'm wasted on the underwear; but I shall come in
strong on the ideas.

TARLETON.   You be a good boy; and perhaps I will.

MRS TARLETON [*scenting a plot against her beloved
Johnny*] Now, John: you promised—

TARLETON.   Yes, yes. All right, Chickabiddy: dont fuss.
Your precious Johnny shant be interfered with. [*Bouncing up,
too energetic to sit still*] But I'm getting sick of that old shop.
Thirty-five years Ive had of it: same blessed old stairs to go
up and down every day: same old lot: same old game: sorry

I ever started it now. I'll chuck it and try something else: something that will give a scope to all my faculties.

HYPATIA.   Theres money in underwear: theres none in wild-cat ideas.

TARLETON.   Theres money in me, madam, no matter what I go into.

MRS TARLETON.   Dont boast, John. Dont tempt Providence.

TARLETON.   Rats! You dont understand Providence. Providence likes to be tempted. Thats the secret of the successful man. Read Browning. Natural theology on an island, eh? Caliban was afraid to tempt Providence: that was why he was never able to get even with Prospero. What did Prospero do? Prospero didnt even tempt Providence: he was Providence. Thats one of Tarleton's ideas; and dont you forget it.

BENTLEY.   You are full of beef today, old man.

TARLETON.   Beef be blowed! Joy of life. Read Ibsen. [*He goes into the pavilion to relieve his restlessness, and stares out with his hands thrust deep in his pockets*].

HYPATIA   [*thoughtful*] Bentley: couldnt you invite your friend Mr Percival down here?

BENTLEY.   Not if I know it. Youd throw me over the moment you set eyes on him.

MRS TARLETON.   Oh, Bunny! For shame!

BENTLEY.   Well, who'd marry me, dyou suppose, if they could get my brains with a full-sized body? No, thank you. I shall take jolly good care to keep Joey out of this until Hypatia is past praying for.

*Johnny and Lord Summerhays return through the pavilion from their stroll.*

TARLETON.   Welcome! welcome! Why have you stayed away so long?

LORD SUMMERHAYS   [*shaking hands*] Yes: I should have come sooner. But I'm still rather lost in England. [*Johnny takes his hat and hangs it up beside his own*]. Thank you. [*Johnny returns to his swing and his novel. Lord Summerhays comes to the writing table*]. The fact is that as Ive nothing to do, I never have time to go anywhere. [*He sits down next Mrs Tarleton*].

TARLETON [*following him and sitting down on his left*] Paradox, paradox. Good. Paradoxes are the only truths. Read Chesterton. But theres lots for you to do here. You have a genius for government. You learnt your job out there in Jinghiskahn. Well, we want to be governed here in England. Govern us.

LORD SUMMERHAYS. Ah yes, my friend; but in Jinghiskahn you have to govern the right way. If you dont, you go under and come home. Here everything has to be done the wrong way, to suit governors who understand nothing but partridge shooting (our English native princes, in fact) and voters who dont know what theyre voting about. I dont understand these democratic games; and I'm afraid I'm too old to learn. What can I do but sit in the window of my club, which consists mostly of retired Indian Civil servants? We look on at the muddle and the folly and amateurishness; and we ask each other where a single fortnight of it would have landed us.

TARLETON. Very true. Still, Democracy's all right, you know. Read Mill. Read Jefferson.

LORD SUMMERHAYS. Yes. Democracy reads well; but it doesnt act well, like some people's plays. No, no, my friend Tarleton: to make Democracy work, you need an aristocratic democracy. To make Aristocracy work, you need a democratic aristocracy. Youve got neither; and theres an end of it.

TARLETON. Still, you know, the superman may come. The superman's an idea. I believe in ideas. Read Whatshisname.

LORD SUMMERHAYS. Reading is a dangerous amusement, Tarleton. I wish I could persuade your free library people of that.

TARLETON.   Why, man, it's the beginning of education.

LORD SUMMERHAYS.   On the contrary, it's the end of it. How can you dare teach a man to read until youve taught him everything else first?

JOHNNY   [*intercepting his father's reply by coming out of the swing and taking the floor*] Leave it at that. Thats good sense. Anybody on for a game of tennis?

BENTLEY.   Oh, lets have some more improving conversation. Wouldnt you rather, Johnny?

JOHNNY.   If you ask me, no.

TARLETON.   Johnny: you dont cultivate your mind. You dont read.

JOHNNY   [*coming between his mother and Lord Summerhays, book in hand*] Yes I do. I bet you what you like that, page for page, I read more than you, though I dont talk about it so much. Only, I dont read the same books. I like a book with a plot in it. You like a book with nothing in it but some idea that the chap that writes it keeps worrying, like a cat chasing its own tail. I can stand a little of it, just as I can stand watching the cat for two minutes, say, when Ive nothing better to do. But a man soon gets fed up with that sort of thing. The fact is, you look on an author as a sort of god. I look on him as a man that I pay to do a certain thing for me. I pay him to amuse me and to take me out of myself and make me forget.

TARLETON.   No. Wrong principle. You want to remember. Read Kipling. "Lest we forget."

JOHNNY.   If Kipling wants to remember, let him remember. If he had to run Tarleton's Underwear, he'd be jolly glad to forget. As he has a much softer job, and wants to keep himself before the public, his cry is, "Dont you forget the sort of things I'm rather clever at writing about." Well, I dont blame him: it's his business: I should do the same in his place. But what he wants and what I want are two different things. I want to forget; and I pay another man to make me forget. If I buy a book or go to the theatre, I want to forget the shop and forget myself from the moment I go in to the moment I come out. Thats what I pay my money for. And if I find that the author's simply getting at me the whole time, I consider that he's obtained my money under false pretences. I'm not a morbid crank: I'm a natural man; and, as such, I dont like being got at. If a man in my employment did it, I should sack him. If a member of my club did it, I should cut him. If he went too far with it, I should bring his conduct before the committee. I might even punch his head, if it came to that. Well, who and what is an author that he should be privileged to take liberties that are not allowed to other men?

MRS TARLETON. You see, John! What have I always told you? Johnny has as much to say for himself as anybody when he likes.

JOHNNY. I'm no fool, mother, whatever some people may fancy. I dont set up to have as many ideas as the Governor; but what ideas I have are consecutive, at all events. I can think as well as talk.

BENTLEY [to Tarleton, chuckling] Had you there, old man, hadnt he? You are rather all over the shop with your ideas, aint you?

JOHNNY [handsomely] I'm not saying anything against you, Governor. But I do say that the time has come for sane, healthy, unpretending men like me to make a stand against this conspiracy of the writing and talking and artistic lot to put us in the back row. It isnt a fact that we're inferior to them: it's a put-up job; and it's they that have put the job up. It's we that run the country for them; and all the thanks we get is to be told we're Philistines and vulgar tradesmen and sordid city men and so forth, and that theyre all angels of light and leading. The time has come to assert ourselves

and put a stop to their stuck-up nonsense. Perhaps if we had
nothing better to do than talking or writing, we could do it
better than they. Anyhow, theyre the failures and refuse of
business (hardly a man of them that didnt begin in an office)
and we're the successes of it. Thank God I havnt failed yet
at anything; and I dont believe I should fail at literature if it
would pay me to turn my hand to it.

BENTLEY. Hear, hear!

MRS TARLETON.    Fancy you writing a book, Johnny! Do
you think he could, Lord Summerhays?

LORD SUMMERHAYS.    Why not? As a matter of fact all the
really prosperous authors I have met since my return to England have been very like him.

TARLETON    [again impressed] Thats an idea. Thats a new
idea. I believe I ought to have made Johnny an author. Ive
never said so before for fear of hurting his feelings, because,
after all, the lad cant help it; but Ive never thought Johnny
worth tuppence as a man of business.

JOHNNY    [sarcastic] Oh! You think youve always kept
that to yourself, do you, Governor? I know your opinion of
me as well as you know it yourself. It takes one man of
business to appreciate another; and you arnt, and you never
have been, a real man of business. I know where Tarleton's
would have been three or four times if it hadnt been for me.
[With a snort and a nod to emphasize the implied warning, he
retreats to the Turkish bath, and lolls against it with an air of
good-humored indifference].

TARLETON.    Well, who denies it? Youre quite right, my
boy. I dont mind confessing to you all that the circumstances
that condemned me to keep a shop are the biggest tragedy
in modern life. I ought to have been a writer. I'm essentially
a man of ideas. When I was a young man I sometimes used
to pray that I might fail, so that I should be justified in giving
up business and doing something: something first-class. But
it was no good: I couldnt fail. I said to myself that if I could

only once go to my Chickabiddy here and shew her a char-
tered accountant's statement proving that I'd made £20 less
than last year, I could ask her to let me chance Johnny's and
Hypatia's future by going into literature. But it was no good.
First it was £250 more than last year. Then it was £700.
Then it was £2000. Then I saw it was no use: Prometheus
was chained to his rock: read Shelley: read Mrs Browning.
Well, well, it was not to be. [*He rises solemnly*]. Lord Summerhays: I ask you to excuse me for a few moments. There
are times when a man needs to meditate in solitude on his
destiny. A chord is touched; and he sees the drama of his
life as a spectator sees a play. Laugh if you feel inclined: no
man sees the comic side of it more than I. In the theatre of
life everyone may be amused except the actor. [*Brightening*]
Theres an idea in this: an idea for a picture. What a pity
young Bentley is not a painter! Tarleton meditating on his
destiny. Not in a toga. Not in the trappings of the tragedian
or the philosopher. In plain coat and trousers: a man like
any other man. And beneath that coat and trousers a human
soul. Tarleton's Underwear! [*He goes out gravely into the vestibule*].

MRS TARLETON   [*fondly*] I suppose it's a wife's partiality,
Lord Summerhays; but I do think John is really great. I'm
sure he was meant to be a king. My father looked down on
John, because he was a rate collector and John kept a shop.
It hurt his pride to have to borrow money so often from
John; and he used to console himself by saying, "After all,
hes only a linendraper." But at last one day he said to me,
"John is a king."

BENTLEY.   How much did he borrow on that occasion?

LORD SUMMERHAYS   [*sharply*] Bentley!

MRS TARLETON.   Oh, dont scold the child: he'd have to
say something like that if it was to be his last word on earth.
Besides, hes quite right: my poor father had asked for his

usual five pounds; and John gave him a hundred in his big
way. Just like a king.

LORD SUMMERHAYS.   Not at all. I had five kings to manage in Jinghiskahn; and I think you do your husband some
injustice, Mrs Tarleton. They pretended to like me because
I kept their brothers from murdering them; but I didnt like
them. And I like Tarleton.

MRS TARLETON.   Everybody does. I really must go and
make the cook do him a Welsh rabbit. He expects one on
special occasions. [*She goes to the inner door*]. Johnny: when
he comes back ask him where we're to put that new Turkish
bath. Turkish baths are his latest. [*She goes out*].

JOHNNY   [*coming forward again*] Now that the Governor
has given himself away, and the old lady's gone, I'll tell you
something, Lord Summerhays. If you study men whove
made an enormous pile in business without being keen on
money, youll find that they all have a slate off. The Governor's a wonderful man; but he's not quite all there, you
know. If you notice, he's different from me; and whatever
my failings may be, I'm a sane man. Erratic: thats what he
is. And the danger is that some day he'll give the whole show
away.

LORD SUMMERHAYS.   Giving the show away is a method
like any other method. Keeping it to yourself is only another
method. I should keep an open mind about it.

JOHNNY.   Has it ever occurred to you that a man with
an open mind must be a bit of a scoundrel? If you ask me,
I like a man who makes up his mind once for all as to whats
right and whats wrong and then sticks to it. At all events
you know where to have him.

LORD SUMMERHAYS.   That may not be his object.

BENTLEY.   He may want to have y o u, old chap.

JOHNNY.   Well, let him. If a member of my club wants
to steal my umbrella, he knows where to find it. If a man
[was] put up for the club who had an open mind on the

subject of property in umbrellas, I should blackball him. An open mind is all very well in clever talky-talky; but in conduct and in business give me solid ground.

LORD SUMMERHAYS. Yes: the quicksands make life difficult. Still, there they are. It's no use pretending theyre rocks.

JOHNNY. I dont know. You can draw a line and make other chaps toe it. Thats what I call morality.

LORD SUMMERHAYS. Very true. But you dont make any progress when youre toeing a line.

HYPATIA [*suddenly, as if she could bear no more of it*] Bentley: do go and play tennis with Johnny. You must take exercise.

LORD SUMMERHAYS. Do, my boy, do. [*To Johnny*] Take him out and make him skip about.

BENTLEY [*rising reluctantly*] I promised you two inches more round my chest this summer. I tried exercises with an indiarubber expander; but I wasnt strong enough: instead of my expanding it, it crumpled me up. Come along, Johnny.

JOHNNY. Do you no end of good, young chap. [*He goes out with Bentley through the pavilion*].

*Hypatia throws aside her work with an enormous sigh of relief.*

LORD SUMMERHAYS. At last!

HYPATIA. At last. Oh, if I might only have a holiday in an asylum for the dumb. How I envy the animals! They cant talk. If Johnny could only put back his ears or wag his tail instead of laying down the law, how much better it would be! We should know when he was cross and when he was pleased; and thats all we know now, with all his talk. It never stops: talk, talk, talk, talk. Thats my life. All the day I listen to mamma talking; at dinner I listen to Papa talking; and when papa stops for breath I listen to Johnny talking.

LORD SUMMERHAYS. You make me feel very guilty. I talk too, I'm afraid.

HYPATIA.  Oh, I dont mind that, because your talk is a
novelty. But it must have been dreadful for your daughters.

LORD SUMMERHAYS.  I suppose so.

HYPATIA.  If parents would only realize how they bore
their children! Three or four times in the last half hour Ive
been on the point of screaming.

LORD SUMMERHAYS.  Were we very dull?

HYPATIA.  Not at all: you were very clever. Thats whats
so hard to bear, because it makes it so difficult to avoid
listening. You see, I'm young; and I do so want something
to happen. My mother tells me that when I'm her age, I shall
be only too glad that nothing's happened; but I'm not her
age; so what good is that to me? Theres my father in the
garden, meditating on his destiny. All very well for him: he's
had a destiny to meditate on; but I havnt had any destiny
yet. Everything's happened to him: nothing's happened to
me. Thats why this unending talk is so maddeningly uninteresting to me.

LORD SUMMERHAYS.  It would be worse if we sat in silence.

HYPATIA.  No it wouldnt. If you all sat in silence, as if
you were waiting for something to happen, then there would
be hope even if nothing did happen. But this eternal cackle,
cackle, cackle about things in general is only fit for old, old,
OLD people. I suppose it means something to them: theyve
had their fling. All I listen for is some sign of it ending in
something; but just when it seems to be coming to a point,
Johnny or Papa just starts another hare; and it all begins over
again; and I realize that it's never going to lead anywhere
and never going to stop. Thats when I want to scream. I
wonder how you can stand it.

LORD SUMMERHAYS.  Well, I'm old and garrulous myself,
you see. Besides, I'm not here of my own free will, exactly.
I came because you ordered me to come.

HYPATIA.  Didnt you want to come?

LORD SUMMERHAYS.   My dear: after thirty years of managing other people's business, men lose the habit of considering what they want or dont want.

HYPATIA.   Oh, dont begin to talk about what men do, and about thirty years experience. If you cant get off that subject, youd better send for Johnny and Papa and begin it all over again.

LORD SUMMERHAYS.   I'm sorry. I beg your pardon.

HYPATIA.   I asked you, didnt you want to come?

LORD SUMMERHAYS.   I did not stop to consider whether I wanted or not, because when I read your letter I knew I had to come.

HYPATIA.   Why?

LORD SUMMERHAYS.   O come, Miss Tarleton! Really! really! Dont force me to call you a blackmailer to your face. You have me in your power; and I do what you tell me very obediently. Dont ask me to pretend I do it of my own free will.

HYPATIA.   I dont know what a blackmailer is. I havnt even that much experience.

LORD SUMMERHAYS.   A blackmailer, my dear young lady, is a person who knows a disgraceful secret in the life of another person, and extorts money from that other person by threatening to make his secret public unless the money is paid.

HYPATIA.   I havnt asked you for money.

LORD SUMMERHAYS.   No; but you asked me to come down here and talk to you; and you mentioned casually that if I didnt youd have nobody to talk about me to but Bentley. That was a threat, was it not?

HYPATIA.   Well, I wanted you to come.

LORD SUMMERHAYS.   In spite of my age and my unfortunate talkativeness?

HYPATIA.   I like talking to you. I can let myself go with you. I can say things to you I cant say to other people.

LORD SUMMERHAYS.   I wonder why?

HYPATIA.   Well, you are the only really clever, grown-up, high-class, experienced man I know who has given himself away to me by making an utter fool of himself with me. You cant wrap yourself up in your toga after that. You cant give yourself airs with me.

LORD SUMMERHAYS.   You mean you can tell Bentley about me if I do.

HYPATIA.   Even if there wasnt any Bentley: even if you didnt care (and I really dont see why you should care so much) still, we never could be on conventional terms with one another again. Besides, Ive got a feeling for you: almost a ghastly sort of love for you.

LORD SUMMERHAYS   [shrinking] I beg you—no, please.

HYPATIA.   Oh, it's nothing at all flattering; and, of course, nothing wrong, as I suppose youd call it.

LORD SUMMERHAYS.   Please believe that I know that. When men of my age—

HYPATIA   [impatiently] Oh, do talk about yourself when you mean yourself, and not about men of your age.

LORD SUMMERHAYS.   I'll put it as bluntly as I can. When, as you say, I made an utter fool of myself, believe me, I made a poetic fool of myself. I was seduced, not by appetites which, thank Heaven, Ive long outlived: not even by the desire of second childhood for a child companion, but by the innocent impulse to place the delicacy and wisdom and spirituality of my age at the affectionate service of your youth for a few years, at the end of which you would be a grown, strong, formed—widow. Alas, my dear, the delicacy of age reckoned, as usual, without the derision and cruelty of youth. You told me that you didnt want to be an old man's nurse, and that you didnt want to have undersized children like Bentley. It served me right: I dont reproach you: I was an old fool. But how you can imagine, after that, that I can suspect you of the smallest feeling for me except the inevitable feeling of early youth for late age, or imagine that I have any feeling for you except one of shrinking humiliation, I cant understand.

HYPATIA. I dont blame you for falling in love with me. I shall be grateful to you all my life for it, because that was the first time that anything really interesting happened to me.

LORD SUMMERHAYS. Do you mean to tell me that nothing of that kind had ever happened before? that no man had ever—

HYPATIA. Oh, lots. Thats part of the routine of life here: the very dullest part of it. The young man who comes a-courting is as familiar an incident in my life as coffee for breakfast. Of course, he's too much of a gentleman to misbehave himself; and I'm too much of a lady to let him; and he's shy and sheepish; and I'm correct and self-possessed; and at last, when I can bear it no longer, I either frighten him off or give him a chance of proposing, just to see how he'll do it, and refuse him because he does it in the same silly way as all the rest. You dont call that an event in one's life, do you? With you it was different. I should as soon have expected the North Pole to fall in love with me as you. You know I'm only a linendraper's daughter when all's said. I was afraid of you: you, a great man! a lord! and older than my father. And then, what a situation it was! Just think of it! I was engaged to your son; and you knew nothing about it. He was afraid to tell you: he brought you down here because he thought if he could throw us together I could get round you because I was such a ripping girl. We arranged it all: he and I. We got Papa and Mamma and Johnny out of the way splendidly; and then Bentley took himself off, and left us— you and me!—to take a walk through the heather and admire the scenery of Hindhead. You never dreamt that it was all a plan: that what made me so nice was the way I was playing up to my destiny as the sweet girl that was to make your boy happy. And then! and then! [*She rises to dance and clap her hands in her glee*].

LORD SUMMERHAYS [*shuddering*] Stop, stop. Can no woman understand a man's delicacy?

HYPATIA [*revelling in the recollection*] And then—ha, ha!—you proposed. You! A father! For your son's girl!

LORD SUMMERHAYS. Stop, I tell you. Dont profane what you dont understand.

HYPATIA. That was something happening at last with a vengeance. It was splendid. It was my first peep behind the scenes. If I'd been seventeen I should have fallen in love with you. Even as it is, I feel quite differently towards you from what I do towards other old men. So [*offering her hand*] you may kiss my hand if that will be any fun for you.

LORD SUMMERHAYS [*rising and recoiling to the table, deeply revolted*] No, no, no. How dare you? [*She laughs mischievously*]. How callous youth is! How coarse! How cynical! How ruthlessly cruel!

HYPATIA. Stuff! It's only that youre tired of a great many things Ive never tried.

LORD SUMMERHAYS. It's not alone that. Ive not forgotten the brutality of my own boyhood. But do try to learn, glorious young beast that you are, that age is squeamish, sentimental, fastidious. If you cant understand my holier feelings, at least you know the bodily infirmities of the old. You know that I darent eat all the rich things you gobble up at every meal; that I cant bear the noise and racket and clatter that affect you no more than they affect a stone. Well, my soul is like that too. Spare it: be gentle with it [*he involuntarily puts out his hands to plead: she takes them with a laugh*]. If you could possibly think of me as half an angel and half an invalid, we should get on much better together.

HYPATIA. We get on very well, I think. Nobody else ever called me a glorious young beast. I like that. Glorious young beast expresses exactly what I like to be.

LORD SUMMERHAYS [*extricating his hands and sitting down*] Where on earth did you get these morbid tastes? You seem to have been well brought up in a normal, healthy, respectable, middle-class family. Yet you go on like the most unwholesome product of the rankest Bohemianism.

HYPATIA. Thats just it. I'm fed up with—

LORD SUMMERHAYS. Horrible expression. Dont.

HYPATIA. Oh, I daresay it's vulgar; but theres no other word for it. I'm fed up with nice things: with respectability, with propriety! When a woman has nothing to do, money and respectability mean that nothing is ever allowed to happen to her. I dont want to be good; and I dont want to be bad: I just dont want to be bothered about either good or bad: I want to be an active verb.

LORD SUMMERHAYS. An active verb? Oh, I see. An active verb signifies to be, to do, or to suffer.

HYPATIA. Just so: how clever of you! I want to be; I want to do; and I'm game to suffer if it costs that. But stick here doing nothing but being good and nice and ladylike I simply wont. Stay down here with us for a week; and I'll shew you what it means: shew it to you going on day after day, year after year, lifetime after lifetime.

LORD SUMMERHAYS. Shew me what?

HYPATIA. Girls withering into ladies. Ladies withering into old maids. Nursing old women. Running errands for old men. Good for nothing else at last. Oh, you cant imagine the fiendish selfishness of the old people and the maudlin sacrifice of the young. It's more unbearable than any poverty: more horrible than any regular-right-down wickedness. Oh, home! home! parents! family! duty! how I loathe them! How I'd like to see them all blown to bits! The poor escape. The wicked escape. Well, I cant be poor: we're rolling in money: it's no use pretending we're not. But I can be wicked; and I'm quite prepared to be.

LORD SUMMERHAYS. You think that easy?

HYPATIA.   Well, isnt it? Being a man, you ought to know.

LORD SUMMERHAYS.   It requires some natural talent, which can no doubt be cultivated. It's not really easy to be anything out of the common.

HYPATIA.   Anyhow, I mean to make a fight for living.

LORD SUMMERHAYS.   Living your own life, I believe the Suffragist phrase is.

HYPATIA.   Living any life. Living, instead of withering without even a gardener to snip you off when youre rotten.

LORD SUMMERHAYS.   Ive lived an active life; but Ive withered all the same.

HYPATIA.   No: youve worn out: thats quite different. And youve some life in you yet or you wouldnt have fallen in love with me. You can never imagine how delighted I was to find that instead of being the correct sort of big panjan-drum you were supposed to be, you were really an old rip like Papa.

LORD SUMMERHAYS.   No, no: not about your father: I really cant bear it. And if you must say these terrible things: these heart-wounding shameful things, at least find some-thing prettier to call me than an old rip.

HYPATIA.   Well, what would you call a man proposing to a girl who might be—

LORD SUMMERHAYS.   His daughter: yes, I know.

HYPATIA.   I was going to say his granddaughter.

LORD SUMMERHAYS.   You always have one more blow to get in.

HYPATIA.   Youre too sensitive. Did you ever make mud pies when you were a kid—beg pardon: a child.

LORD SUMMERHAYS.   I hope not.

HYPATIA.   It's a dirty job; but Johnny and I were vulgar enough to like it. I like young people because theyre not too afraid of dirt to live. Ive grown out of the mud pies; but I like slang; and I like bustling you up by saying things that shock you; and I'd rather put up with swearing and smoking than with dull respectability; and there are lots of things that would just shrivel you up that I think rather jolly. Now!

LORD SUMMERHAYS. Ive not the slightest doubt of it. Dont insist.

HYPATIA. It's not your ideal, is it?

LORD SUMMERHAYS. No.

HYPATIA. Shall I tell you why? Your ideal is an old woman. I daresay she's got a young face; but she's an old woman. Old, old, old. Squeamish. Cant stand up to things. Cant enjoy things: not real things. Always on the shrink.

LORD SUMMERHAYS. On the shrink! Detestable expression.

HYPATIA. Bah! you cant stand even a little thing like that. What good are you? Oh, what good are you?

LORD SUMMERHAYS. Dont ask me. I dont know. I dont know.

*Tarleton returns from the vestibule. Hypatia sits down demurely.*

HYPATIA. Well, Papa: have you meditated on your destiny?

TARLETON [*puzzled*] What? Oh! my destiny. Gad, I forgot all about it: Jock started a rabbit and put it clean out of my head. Besides, why should I give way to morbid introspection? It's a sign of madness. Read Lombroso. [*To Lord Summerhays*] Well, Summerhays, has my little girl been entertaining you?

LORD SUMMERHAYS. Yes. She is a wonderful entertainer.

TARLETON. I think my idea of bringing up a young girl has been rather a success. Dont you listen to this, Patsy: it might make you conceited. She's never been treated like a child. I always said the same thing to her mother. Let her read what she likes. Let her do what she likes. Let her go where she likes. Eh, Patsy?

HYPATIA. Oh yes, if there had only been anything for me to do, any place for me to go, anything I wanted to read.

TARLETON.  There, you see! She's not satisfied. Restless. Wants things to happen. Wants adventures to drop out of the sky.

HYPATIA  [*gathering up her work*]  If youre going to talk about me and my education, I'm off.

TARLETON.  Well, well, off with you. [*To Lord Summerhays*] She's active, like me. She actually wanted me to put her into the shop.

HYPATIA.  Well, they tell me that the girls there have adventures sometimes. [*She goes out through the inner door*].

TARLETON.  She had me there, though she doesnt know it, poor innocent lamb! Public scandal exaggerates enormously, of course; but moralize as you will, superabundant vitality is a physical fact that cant be talked away. [*He sits down between the writing table and the sideboard*]. Difficult question this, of bringing up children. Between ourselves, it has beaten me. I never was so surprised in my life as when I came to know Johnny as a man of business and found out what he was really like. How did you manage with your sons?

LORD SUMMERHAYS.  Well, I really hadnt time to be a father: thats the plain truth of the matter. Their poor dear mother did the usual thing while they were with us. Then of course Eton, Oxford, the usual routine of their class. I saw very little of them, and thought very little about them: how could I? with a whole province on my hands. They and I are—acquaintances. Not, perhaps, quite ordinary acquaintances: theres a sort of—er—I should almost call it a sort of remorse about the way we shake hands (when we do shake hands) which means, I suppose, that we're sorry we dont care more for one another; and I'm afraid we dont meet oftener than we can help. We put each other too much out of countenance. It's really a very difficult relation. To my mind not altogether a natural one.

TARLETON  [*impressed, as usual*] Thats an idea, certainly. I dont think anybody has ever written about that.

LORD SUMMERHAYS.  Bentley is the only one who was really my son in any serious sense. He was completely spoilt. When he was sent to a preparatory school he simply yelled until he was sent home. Eton was out of the question; but we managed to tutor him into Oxford. No use: he was sent down. By that time my work was over; and I saw a good deal of him. But I could do nothing with him—except look on. I should have thought your case was quite different. You keep up the middle-class tradition: the day school and the business training instead of the university. I believe in the day school part of it. At all events, you know your own children.

TARLETON.  Do we? I'm not so sure of it. Fact is, my dear Summerhays, once childhood is over, once the little animal has got past the stage at which it acquires what you might call a sense of decency, it's all up with the relation between parent and child. You cant get over the fearful shyness of it.

LORD SUMMERHAYS.  Shyness?

TARLETON.  Yes, shyness. Read Dickens.

LORD SUMMERHAYS  [*surprised*] Dickens!! Of all authors, Charles Dickens! Are you serious?

TARLETON.  I dont mean his books. Read his letters to his family. Read any man's letters to his children. Theyre not human. Theyre not about himself or themselves. Theyre about hotels, scenery, about the weather, about getting wet and losing the train and what he saw on the road and all that. Not a word about himself. Forced. Shy. Duty letters. All fit to be published: that says everything. I tell you theres a wall ten feet thick and ten miles high between parent and child. I know what I'm talking about. Ive girls in my employment: girls and young men. I had ideas on the subject. I used to go to the parents and tell them not to let their

children go out into the world without instruction in the
dangers and temptations they were going to be thrown into.
What did every one of the mothers say to me? "Oh, sir, how
could I speak of such things to my own daughter?" The men
said I was quite right; but they didnt do it, any more than
I'd been able to do it myself to Johnny. I had to leave books
in his way; and I felt just awful when I did it. Believe me,
Summerhays, the relation between the young and the old
should be an innocent relation. It should be something they
could talk about. Well, the relation between parent and child
may be an affectionate relation. It may be a useful relation.
It may be a necessary relation. But it can never be an innocent relation. Youd die rather than allude to it. Depend on
it, in a thousand years itll be considered bad form to know
who your father and mother are. Embarrassing. Better hand
Bentley over to me. I can look him in the face and talk to
him as man to man. You can have Johnny.

LORD SUMMERHAYS.  Thank you. Ive lived so long in a
country where a man may have fifty sons, who are no more
to him than a regiment of soldiers, that I'm afraid Ive lost
the English feeling about it.

TARLETON  [*restless again*]  You mean Jinghiskahn. Ah
yes. Good thing the empire. Educates us. Opens our minds.
Knocks the Bible out of us. And civilizes the other chaps.

LORD SUMMERHAYS.  Yes: it civilizes them. And it unci-
vilizes us. Their gain. Our loss, Tarleton, believe me, our
loss.

TARLETON.  Well, why not? Averages out the human
race. Makes the nigger half an Englishman. Makes the Englishman half a nigger.

LORD SUMMERHAYS.  Speaking as the unfortunate Englishman in question, I dont like the process. If I had my
life to live over again, I'd stay at home and supercivilize
myself.

TARLETON.  Nonsense! dont be selfish. Think how

youve improved the other chaps. Look at the Spanish empire! Bad job for Spain, but splendid for South America. Look at what the Romans did for Britain! They burst up and had to clear out; but think of all they taught us! They were the making of us: I believe there was a Roman camp on Hindhead: I'll shew it to you tomorrow. Thats the good side of Imperialism: it's unselfish. I despise the Little Englanders: theyre always thinking about England. Smallminded. I'm for the Parliament of man, the federation of the world. Read Tennyson. [*He settles down again*]. Then theres the great food question.

LORD SUMMERHAYS [*apprehensively*] Need we go into that this afternoon?

TARLETON. No; but I wish youd tell the Chickabiddy that the Jinghiskahns eat no end of toasted cheese, and that it's the secret of their amazing health and long life!

LORD SUMMERHAYS. Unfortunately they are neither healthy nor long lived. And they dont eat toasted cheese.

TARLETON. There you are! They would be if they ate it. Anyhow, say what you like, provided the moral is a Welsh rabbit for my supper.

LORD SUMMERHAYS. British morality in a nutshell!

TARLETON [*hugely amused*] Yes. Ha ha! Awful hypocrites, aint we?

*They are interrupted by excited cries from the grounds.*

HYPATIA { Papa! Mamma! Come out as fast as you can. Quick. Quick.

BENTLEY { Hello, governor! Come out. An aeroplane. Look, look.

TARLETON [*starting up*] Aeroplane! Did he say an aeroplane?

LORD SUMMERHAYS. Aeroplane! [*A shadow falls on the pavilion; and some of the glass at the top is shattered and falls on the floor*].

*Tarleton and Lord Summerhays rush out through the pavilion into the garden.*

| | |
|---|---|
| HYPATIA | Take care. Take care of the chimney. |
| BENTLEY | Come this side: it's coming right where youre standing. |
| TARLETON | Hallo! where the devil are you coming? youll have my roof off. |
| LORD SUMMERHAYS | He's lost control. |

MRS. TARLETON. Look, look, Hypatia. There are two people in it.

BENTLEY. Theyve cleared it. Well steered!

| | |
|---|---|
| TARLETON | Yes; but they're coming slam into the greenhouse. |
| LORD SUMMERHAYS | Look out for the glass. |
| MRS TARLETON | Theyll break all the glass. Theyll spoil all the grapes. |
| BENTLEY | Mind where youre coming. He'll save it. No: theyre down. |

*An appalling crash of breaking glass is heard. Everybody shrieks.*

| | |
|---|---|
| MRS TARLETON | Oh, are they killed? John: are they killed? |
| LORD SUMMERHAYS | Are you hurt? Is anything broken? Can you stand? |
| HYPATIA | Oh, you must be hurt. Are you sure? Shall I get you some water? Or some wine? |
| TARLETON | Are you all right? Sure you wont have some brandy just to take off the shock. |

THE AVIATOR. No, thank you. Quite right. Not a scratch. I assure you I'm all right.

BENTLEY. What luck! And what a smash! You are a lucky chap, I can tell you.

*The Aviator and Tarleton come in through the pavilion, followed by Lord Summerhays and Bentley, the Aviator on Tarleton's right. Bentley passes the Aviator and turns to have an admiring look at him. Lord Summerhays overtakes Tarleton less pointedly on the opposite side with the same object.*

THE AVIATOR. I'm really very sorry. I'm afraid Ive knocked your vinery into a cocked hat. (*Effusively*) You dont mind, do you?

TARLETON. Not a bit. Come in and have some tea. Stay to dinner. Stay over the week-end. All my life Ive wanted to fly.

THE AVIATOR [*taking off his goggles*] Youre really more than kind.

BENTLEY. Why, it's Joey Percival.

PERCIVAL. Hallo, Ben! That you?

TARLETON. What! The man with three fathers!

PERCIVAL. Oh! has Ben been talking about me?

TARLETON. Consider yourself as one of the family—if you will do me the honor. And your friend too. Wheres your friend?

PERCIVAL. Oh, by the way! before he comes in: let me explain. I dont know him.

TARLETON. Eh?

PERCIVAL. Havnt even looked at him. I'm trying to make a club record with a passenger. The club supplied the passenger. He just got in; and Ive been too busy handling the aeroplane to look at him. I havnt said a word to him; and I cant answer for him socially; but he's an ideal passenger for a flyer. He saved me from a smash.

LORD SUMMERHAYS. I saw it. It was extraordinary. When you were thrown out he held on to the top bar with one hand. You came past him in the air, going straight for the glass. He caught you and turned you off into the flower bed, and then lighted beside you like a bird.

PERCIVAL. How he kept his head I cant imagine. Frankly, I didnt.

*The Passenger, also begoggled, comes in through the pavilion with Johnny and the two ladies. The Passenger comes between Percival and Tarleton, Mrs. Tarleton between Lord Summerhays and her husband, Hypatia between Percival and Bentley, and Johnny to Bentley's right.*

TARLETON. Just discussing your prowess, my dear sir. Magnificent. Youll stay to dinner. Youll stay the night. Stay over the week. The Chickabiddy will be delighted.

MRS TARLETON. Wont you take off your goggles and have some tea?

*The passenger begins to remove the goggles.*

TARLETON. Do. Have a wash. Johnny: take the gentleman to your room: I'll look after Mr Percival. They must—

*By this time the passenger has got the goggles off, and stands revealed as a remarkably good-looking woman.*

| | | |
|---|---|---|
| MRS TARLETON | Well I never!!! | |
| BENTLEY | [*in a whisper*] Oh, I say! | |
| JOHNNY | By George! | |
| LORD SUMMERHAYS | A lady! | *All together.* |
| HYPATIA | A woman! | |
| TARLETON | [*to Percival*] You never told me— | |
| PERCIVAL | I hadnt the least idea— | |

*An embarrassed pause.*

PERCIVAL. I assure you if I'd had the faintest notion that my passenger was a lady I shouldnt have left you to shift for yourself in that selfish way.

LORD SUMMERHAYS. The lady seems to have shifted for both very effectually, sir.

PERCIVAL. Saved my life. I admit it most gratefully.

TARLETON. I must apologize, madam, for having offered you the civilities appropriate to the opposite sex. And yet, why opposite? We are all human: males and females of the same species. When the dress is the same the distinction vanishes. I'm proud to receive in my house a lady of evident refinement and distinction. Allow me to introduce myself: Tarleton: John Tarleton (*seeing conjecture in the passenger's eye*)—yes, yes: Tarleton's Underwear. My wife, Mrs Tarleton: youll excuse me for having in what I had taken to be a confidence between man and man alluded to her as the Chickabiddy. My daughter Hypatia, who has always wanted some adventure to drop out of the sky, and is now, I hope, satisfied at last. Lord Summerhays: a man known wherever the British flag waves. His son Bentley, engaged to Hypatia. Mr Joseph Percival, the promising son of three highly intellectual fathers.

HYPATIA [*startled*] Bentley's friend? [*Bentley nods*].

TARLETON [*continuing, to the passenger*] May I now ask to be allowed the pleasure of knowing your name?

THE PASSENGER. My name is Lina Szczepanowska [*pronouncing it Sh-Chepanovska*].

PERCIVAL. Sh—I beg your pardon?

LINA. Szczepanowska.

PERCIVAL [*dubiously*] Thank you.

TARLETON [*very politely*] Would you mind saying it again?

LINA. Say fish.

TARLETON. Fish.

LINA. Say church.

TARLETON. Church.

LINA. Say fish church.

TARLETON [*remonstrating*] But it's not good sense.

LINA  [*inexorable*] Say fish church.

TARLETON.  Fish church.

LINA.  Again.

TARLETON.  No, but—[*resigning himself*] fish church.

LINA.  Now say Szczepanowska.

TARLETON.  Szczepanowska. Got it, by Gad. [*A sibilant whispering becomes audible: they are all saying Sh-ch to themselves*]. Szczepanowska! Not an English name, is it?

LINA.  Polish. I'm a Pole.

TARLETON  [*dithyrambically*] Ah yes. What other nation, madame, could have produced your magical personality? Your countrywomen have always appealed to our imagination. Women of Destiny! beautiful! musical! passionate! tragic! You will be at home here: my own temperament is pre-eminently Polish. Wont you sit down?

*The group breaks up. Johnny and Bentley hurry to the pavilion and fetch the two wicker chairs. Johnny gives his to Lina. Hypatia and Percival take the chairs at the worktable. Lord Summerhays gives the chair at the vestibule end of the writing table to Mrs Tarleton; and Bentley replaces it with a wicker chair, which Lord Summerhays takes. Johnny remains standing behind the worktable, Bentley behind his father.*

MRS TARLETON  [*to Lina*] Have some tea now, wont you?

LINA.  I never drink tea.

TARLETON  [*sitting down at the end of the writing table nearest Lina*] Bad thing to aeroplane on, I should imagine. Too jumpy. Been up much?

LINA.  Not in an aeroplane. Ive parachuted; but thats child's play.

MRS TARLETON.  But arnt you very foolish to run such a dreadful risk?

LINA.  You cant live without running risks.

MRS TARLETON.  Oh, what a thing to say! Didnt you know you might have been killed?

LINA. That was why I went up.

HYPATIA. Of course. Cant you understand the fascination of the thing? the novelty! the daring! the sense of something happening!

LINA. Oh no. It's too tame a business for that. I went up for family reasons.

TARLETON. Eh? What? Family reasons?

MRS TARLETON. I hope it wasnt to spite your mother?

PERCIVAL [*quickly*] Or your husband?

LINA. I'm not married. And why should I want to spite my mother?

HYPATIA [*aside to Percival*] That was clever of you, Mr Percival.

PERCIVAL. What?

HYPATIA. To find out.

TARLETON. I'm in a difficulty. I cant understand a lady going up in an aeroplane for family reasons. It's rude to be curious and ask questions; but then it's inhuman to be indifferent, as if you didnt care.

LINA. I'll tell you with pleasure. For the last hundred and fifty years, not a single day has passed without some member of my family risking his life—or her life. It's a point of honor with us to keep up that tradition. Usually several of us do it; but it happens that just at this moment it is being kept up by one of my brothers only. Early this morning I got a telegram from him to say that there had been a fire, and that he could do nothing for the rest of the week. Fortunately I had an invitation from the Aerial League to see this gentleman try to break the passenger record. I appealed to the President of the League to let me save the honor of my family. He arranged it for me.

TARLETON. Oh, I must be dreaming. This is stark raving nonsense.

LINA [*quietly*] You are quite awake, sir.

JOHNNY. We cant all be dreaming the same thing, Governor.

TARLETON. Of course not, you duffer; but then I'm dreaming you as well as the lady.

MRS TARLETON. Dont be silly, John. The lady is only joking, I'm sure. [*To Lina*] I suppose your luggage is in the aeroplane.

PERCIVAL. Luggage was out of the question. If I stay to dinner I'm afraid I cant change unless youll lend me some clothes.

MRS TARLETON. Do you mean neither of you?

PERCIVAL. I'm afraid so.

MRS TARLETON. Oh well, never mind: Hypatia will lend the lady a gown.

LINA. Thank you: I'm quite comfortable as I am. I am not accustomed to gowns: they hamper me and make me feel ridiculous; so if you don't mind I shall not change.

MRS TARLETON. Well, I'm beginning to think I'm doing a bit of dreaming myself.

HYPATIA [*impatiently*] Oh, it's all right, mamma. Johnny: look after Mr Percival. [*To Lina, rising*] Come with me.

*Lina follows her to the inner door. They all rise.*

JOHNNY [*to Percival*] I'll shew you.

PERCIVAL. Thank you.

*Lina goes out with Hypatia, and Percival with Johnny.*

MRS TARLETON. Well, this is a nice thing to happen! And look at the greenhouse! Itll cost thirty pounds to mend it. People have no right to do such things. And you invited them to dinner too! What sort of woman is that to have in our house when you know that all Hindhead will be calling on us to see that aeroplane? Bunny: come with me and help me to get all the people out of the grounds: I declare they came running as if theyd sprung up out of the earth [*she makes for the inner door*].

TARLETON. No: dont you trouble, Chickabiddy: I'll tackle em.

MRS TARLETON. Indeed youll do nothing of the kind: youll stay here quietly with Lord Summerhays. Youd invite them all to dinner. Come, Bunny. [*She goes out, followed by Bentley. Lord Summerhays sits down again*].

TARLETON. Singularly beautiful woman, Summerhays. What do you make of her? She must be a princess. Whats this family of warriors and statesmen that risk their lives every day?

LORD SUMMERHAYS. They are evidently not warriors and statesmen, or they wouldn't do that.

TARLETON. Well, then, what the devil are they?

LORD SUMMERHAYS. I think I know. The last time I saw that lady, she did something I should not have thought possible.

TARLETON. What was that?

LORD SUMMERHAYS. Well, she walked backwards along a taut wire without a balancing pole and turned a somersault in the middle. I remember that her name was Lina, and that the other name was foreign; though I dont recollect it.

TARLETON. Szcz! You couldnt have forgotten that if youd heard it.

LORD SUMMERHAYS. I didnt hear it: I only saw it on a program. But it's clear she's an acrobat. It explains how she saved Percival. And it accounts for her family pride.

TARLETON. An acrobat, eh? Good! good! good! Summerhays: that brings her within reach. Thats better than a princess. I steeled this evergreen heart of mine when I thought she was a princess. Now I shall let it be touched. She is accessible. Good.

LORD SUMMERHAYS. I hope you are not serious. Remember: you have a family. You have a position. You are not in your first youth.

TARLETON. No matter.

> Theres magic in the night
> When the heart is young.

My heart is young. Besides, I'm a married man, not a widower like you. A married man can do anything he likes if his wife dont mind. A widower cant be too careful. Not that I would have you think me an unprincipled man or a bad husband. I'm not. But Ive a superabundance of vitality. Read Pepys' Diary.

LORD SUMMERHAYS.　The woman is your guest, Tarleton.

TARLETON.　Well, is she? A woman I bring into my house is my guest. A woman you bring into my house is my guest. But a woman who drops bang down out of the sky into my greenhouse and smashes every blessed pane of glass in it must take her chance.

LORD SUMMERHAYS.　Still, you know that my name must not be associated with any scandal. Youll be careful, wont you?

TARLETON.　Oh Lord, yes! Yes, yes, yes, yes, yes. I was only joking, of course.

*Mrs Tarleton comes back through the inner door.*

MRS TARLETON.　Well I never! John: I dont think that young woman's right in her head. Do you know what she's just asked for?

TARLETON.　Champagne?

MRS TARLETON.　No. She wants a Bible and six oranges.

TARLETON.　What?

MRS TARLETON.　A Bible and six oranges.

TARLETON.　I understand the oranges: she's doing an orange cure of some sort. But what on earth does she want the Bible for?

MRS TARLETON.　I'm sure I cant imagine. She cant be right in her head.

LORD SUMMERHAYS.　Perhaps she wants to read it.

MRS TARLETON. But why should she? on a weekday at all events. What would you advise me to do, Lord Summerhays?

LORD SUMMERHAYS. Well, is there a Bible in the house?

TARLETON. Stacks of em. Theres the family Bible, and the Doré Bible, and the parallel revised version Bible, and the Doves Press Bible, and Johnny's Bible and Bobby's Bible and Patsy's Bible and the Chickabiddy's Bible and my Bible; and I daresay the servants could raise a few more between them. Let her have the lot.

MRS TARLETON. Dont talk like that before Lord Summerhays, John.

LORD SUMMERHAYS. It doesnt matter, Mrs Tarleton: in Jinghiskahn it was a punishable offense to expose a Bible for sale. The empire has no religion.

*Lina comes in. She has left her cap in Hypatia's room, but has made no other change. She stops just inside the door, holding it open, evidently not intending to stay.*

LINA. Oh, Mrs Tarleton, shall I be making myself very troublesome if I ask for a music-stand in my room as well?

TARLETON. Not at all. You can have the piano if you like. Or the gramophone. Have the gramophone?

LINA. No, thank you: no music.

MRS TARLETON [*going towards her*] Do you think it's good for you to eat so many oranges? Arnt you afraid of getting jaundice?

LINA. Not in the least. But billiard balls will do quite as well.

MRS TARLETON. But you cant eat billiard balls, child!

TARLETON. Get em, Chickabiddy. I understand. [*He imitates a juggler tossing up balls*]. Eh?

LINA [*going to him, past his wife*] Just so.

TARLETON. Billiard balls and cues? Plates, knives, and forks? Two paraffin lamps and a hatstand?

LINA. No: that is popular low-class business. In our

family we touch nothing but classical work. Anybody can do lamp and hatstands. *I* can do silver bullets. That is really hard. [*She passes on to Lord Summerhays, and looks gravely down at him as he sits by the writing table*].

MRS TARLETON.   Well, I'm sure I dont know what youre talking about; and I only hope you know yourselves. However, you shall have what you want, of course. [*She goes out through the inner door*].

LORD SUMMERHAYS.   Will you forgive my curiosity? What is the Bible for?

LINA.   To quiet my soul.

LORD SUMMERHAYS [*with a sigh*] Ah yes, yes. It no longer quiets mine, I am sorry to say.

LINA.   That is because you do not know how to read it. Put it up before you on a stand; and open it at the Psalms. When you can read them and understand them, quite quietly and happily, and keep six balls in the air all the time, you are in perfect condition; and youll never make a mistake that evening. If you find you cant do that, then go and pray until you can. And be very careful that evening.

LORD SUMMERHAYS.   Is that the usual form of test in your profession?

LINA.   Nothing that we Szczepanowskis do is usual, my lord.

LORD SUMMERHAYS.   Are you all so wonderful?

LINA.   It is our profession to be wonderful.

LORD SUMMERHAYS.   Do you never condescend to do as common people do? For instance, do you not pray as common people pray?

LINA.   Common people do not pray, my lord: they only beg.

LORD SUMMERHAYS.   You never ask for anything?

LINA.   No.

LORD SUMMERHAYS.   Then why do you pray?

LINA.   To remind myself that I have a soul.

TARLETON [*walking about*] True. Fine. Good. Beautiful. All this damned materialism: what good is it to anybody? Ive got a soul: dont tell me I havnt. Cut me up and you cant find it. Cut up a steam engine and you cant find the steam. But, by George, it makes the engine go. Say what you will, Summerhays, the divine spark is a fact.

LORD SUMMERHAYS. Have I denied it?

TARLETON. Our whole civilization is a denial of it. Read Walt Whitman.

LORD SUMMERHAYS. I shall go to the billiard room and get the balls for you.

LINA. Thank you.

*Lord Summerhays goes out through the vestibule door.*

TARLETON [*going to her*] Listen to me. [*She turns quickly*]. What you said just now was beautiful. You touch chords. You appeal to the poetry in a man. You inspire him. Come now! Youre a woman of the world: youre independent: you must have driven lots of men crazy. You know the sort of man I am, dont you? See through me at a glance, eh?

LINA. Yes. [*She sits down quietly in the chair Lord Summerhays has just left*].

TARLETON. Good. Well, do you like me? Dont misunderstand me: I'm perfectly aware that youre not going to fall in love at first sight with a ridiculous old shopkeeper. I cant help that ridiculous old shopkeeper. I have to carry him about with me whether I like it or not. I have to pay for his clothes, though I hate the cut of them: especially the waistcoat. I have to look at him in the glass while I'm shaving. I loathe him because he's a living lie. My soul's not like that: it's like yours. I want to make a fool of myself. About you. Will you let me?

LINA [*very calm*] How much will you pay?

TARLETON. Nothing. But I'll throw as many sovereigns as you like into the sea to shew you that I'm in earnest.

LINA. Are those your usual terms?

TARLETON.  No. I never made that bid before.

LINA  [*producing a dainty little book and preparing to write in it*] What did you say your name was?

TARLETON.  John Tarleton. The great John Tarleton of Tarleton's Underwear.

LINA  [*writing*] T-a-r-l-e-t-o-n. Er——? [*She looks up at him inquiringly*].

TARLETON  [*promptly*] Fifty-eight.

LINA.  Thank you. I keep a list of all my offers. I like to know what I'm considered worth.

TARLETON.  Let me look.

LINA  [*offering the book to him*] It's in Polish.

TARLETON.  Thats no good. Is mine the lowest offer?

LINA.  No: the highest.

TARLETON.  What do most of them come to? Diamonds? Motor cars? Furs? Villa at Monte Carlo?

LINA.  Oh yes: all that. And sometimes the devotion of a lifetime.

TARLETON.  Fancy that! A young man offering a woman his old age as a temptation!

LINA.  By the way, you did not say how long.

TARLETON.  Until you get tired of me.

LINA.  Or until you get tired of me?

TARLETON.  I never get tired. I never go on long enough for that. But when it becomes so grand, so inspiring that I feel that everything must be an anti-climax after that, then I run away.

LINA.  Does she let you go without a struggle?

TARLETON.  Yes. Glad to get rid of me. When love takes a man as it takes me—when it makes him great—it frightens a woman.

LINA.  The lady here is your wife, isnt she? Dont you care for her?

TARLETON.  Yes. And mind! she comes first always. I

reserve her dignity even when I sacrifice my own. Youll respect that point of honor, wont you?

LINA.   Only a point of honor?

TARLETON   [impulsively] No, by God! a point of affection as well.

LINA   [smiling, pleased with him] Shake hands, old pal. [She rises and offers him her hand frankly].

TARLETON   [giving his hand rather dolefully] Thanks. That means no, doesnt it?

LINA.   It means something that will last longer than yes. I like you. I admit you to my friendship. What a pity you were not trained when you were young! Youd be young still.

TARLETON.   I suppose, to an athlete like you, I'm pretty awful, eh?

LINA.   Shocking.

TARLETON.   Too much crumb. Wrinkles. Yellow patches that wont come off. Short wind. I know. I'm ashamed of myself. I could do nothing on the high rope.

LINA.   Oh yes: I could put you in a wheelbarrow and run you along, two hundred feet up.

TARLETON   [shuddering] Ugh! Well, I'd do even that for you. Read The Master Builder.

LINA.   Have you learnt everything from books?

TARLETON.   Well, have you learnt everything from the flying trapeze?

LINA.   On the flying trapeze there is often another woman; and her life is in your hands every night and your life in hers.

TARLETON.   Lina: I'm going to make a fool of myself. I'm going to cry. [He crumples into the nearest chair].

LINA.   Pray instead: dont cry. Why should you cry? Youre not the first Ive said no to.

TARLETON.   If you had said yes, should I have been the first then?

LINA. What right have you to ask? Have I asked am *I* the first?

TARLETON. Youre right: a vulgar question. To a man like me, everybody is the first. Life renews itself.

LINA. The youngest child is the sweetest.

TARLETON. Dont probe too deep, Lina. It hurts.

LINA. You must get out of the habit of thinking that these things matter so much. It's linendraperish.

TARLETON. Youre quite right. Ive often said so. All the same, it does matter; for I want to cry. [*He buries his face in his arms on the worktable and sobs*].

LINA [*going to him*] O la la! [*She slaps him vigorously, but not unkindly, on the shoulder*]. Courage, old pal, courage! Have you a gymnasium here?

TARLETON. Theres a trapeze and bars and things in the billiard room.

LINA. Come. You need a few exercises. I'll teach you how to stop crying. [*She takes his arm and leads him off into the vestibule*].

*A young man, cheaply dressed and strange in manner, appears in the garden; steals to the pavilion door; and looks in. Seeing that there is nobody, he enters cautiously until he has come far enough to see into the hatstand corner. He draws a revolver, and examines it, apparently to make sure that it is loaded. Then his attention is caught by the Turkish bath. He looks down the lunette, and opens the panels.*

HYPATIA [*calling in the garden*] Mr Percival! Mr Percival! Where are you?

*The young man makes for the door, but sees Percival coming. He turns and bolts into the Turkish bath, which he closes upon himself just in time to escape being caught by Percival, who runs in through the pavilion, bareheaded. He also, it appears, is in search of a hiding-place; for he stops and turns between the two tables to take a survey of the room; then runs into the corner between the end of the sideboard and the wall. Hypatia, excited, mischievous, her eyes glowing, runs in, precisely on his trail; turns at the same spot; and discovers him just as he makes a dash for the pavilion door. She flies back and intercepts him.*

HYPATIA.   Aha! Arnt you glad Ive caught you?

PERCIVAL   [*illhumoredly turning away from her and coming towards the writing table*] No I'm not. Confound it, what sort of girl are you? What sort of house is this? Must I throw all good manners to the winds?

HYPATIA   [*following him*] Do, do, do, do, do. This is the house of a respectable shopkeeper, enormously rich. This is the respectable shopkeeper's daughter, tired of good manners. [*Slipping her left hand into his right*] Come, handsome young man, and play with the respectable shopkeeper's daughter.

PERCIVAL   [*withdrawing quickly from her touch*] No, no: dont you know you mustnt go on like this with a perfect stranger?

HYPATIA.   Dropped down from the sky. Dont you know that you must always go on like this when you get the chance? You must come to the top of the hill and chase me through the bracken. You may kiss me if you catch me.

PERCIVAL.   I shall do nothing of the sort.

HYPATIA.   Yes, you will: you cant help yourself. Come along. [*She seizes his sleeve*]. Fool, fool: come along. Dont you want to?

PERCIVAL.   No: certainly not. I should never be forgiven if I did it.

HYPATIA.   Youll never forgive yourself if you dont.

PERCIVAL.   Nonsense. Youre engaged to Ben. Ben's my friend. What do you take me for?

HYPATIA.   Ben's old. Ben was born old. Theyre all old here, except you and me and the man-woman or woman-man or whatever you call her that came with you. They never do anything: they only discuss whether what other people do is right. Come and give them something to discuss.

PERCIVAL.  I will do nothing incorrect.

HYPATIA.  Oh, dont be afraid, little boy: youll get nothing but a kiss; and I'll fight like the devil to keep you from getting that. But we must play on the hill and race through the heather.

PERCIVAL.  Why?

HYPATIA.  Because we want to, handsome young man.

PERCIVAL.  But if everybody went on in this way—

HYPATIA.  How happy! oh how happy the world would be!

PERCIVAL.  But the consequences may be serious.

HYPATIA.  Nothing is worth doing unless the consequences may be serious. My father says so; and I'm my father's daughter.

PERCIVAL.  I'm the son of three fathers. I mistrust these wild impulses.

HYPATIA.  Take care. Youre letting the moment slip. I feel the first chill of the wave of prudence. Save me.

PERCIVAL.  Really, Miss Tarleton! [*She strikes him across the face*]. Damn you! [*Recovering himself, horrified at his lapse*] I beg your pardon; but since weve both forgotten ourselves, youll please allow me to leave the house. [*He turns towards the inner door, having left his cap in the bedroom*].

HYPATIA  [*standing in his way*] Are you ashamed of having said "Damn you" to me?

PERCIVAL.  I had no right to say it. I'm very much ashamed of it. I have already begged your pardon.

HYPATIA.  And youre not ashamed of having said "Really, Miss Tarleton!"?

PERCIVAL.  Why should I?

HYPATIA.  O man, man! mean, stupid, cowardly, selfish, masculine male man! You ought to have been a governess. I was expelled from school for saying that the very next person that said "Really, Miss Tarleton!" to me, I would strike across the face. You were the next.

PERCIVAL.  I had no intention of being offensive. Surely there is nothing that can wound any lady in—[*He hesitates, not quite convinced*]. At least—er—I really didnt mean to be disagreeable.

HYPATIA.    Liar.

PERCIVAL.   Of course if youre going to insult me, I am quite helpless. Youre a woman: you can say what you like.

HYPATIA.    And you can only say what you dare. Poor wretch: it isnt much. [*He bites his lip, and sits down, very much annoyed*]. Really, Mr Percival! You sit down in the presence of a lady and leave her standing. [*He rises hastily*]. Ha, ha! Really, Mr Percival! Oh really, really, really, really, really, Mr Percival! How do you like it? Wouldnt you rather I damned you?

PERCIVAL.   Miss Tarleton—

HYPATIA   [*caressingly*] Hypatia, Joey. Patsy, if you like.

PERCIVAL.   Look here: this is no good. You want to do what you like?

HYPATIA.   Dont you!

PERCIVAL.   No. Ive been too well brought up. Ive argued all through this thing; and I tell you I'm not prepared to cast off the social bond. It's like a corset: it's a support to the figure even if it does squeeze and deform it a bit. I want to be free.

HYPATIA.   Well, I'm tempting you to be free.

PERCIVAL.   Not at all. Freedom, my good girl, means being able to count on how other people will behave. If every man who dislikes me is to throw a handful of mud in my face, and every woman who likes me is to behave like Potiphar's wife, then I shall be a slave: the slave of uncertainty: the slave of fear: the worst of all slaveries. How would you like it if every laborer you met in the road were to make love to you? No. Give me the blessed protection of a good stiff conventionality among thoroughly well-brought up ladies and gentlemen.

HYPATIA.  Another talker! Men like conventions because men made them. I didnt make them: I dont like them: I wont keep them. Now, what will you do?

PERCIVAL.  Bolt. [*He runs out through the pavilion*].

HYPATIA.  I'll catch you. [*She dashes off in pursuit*].

*During this conversation the head of the scandalized man in the Turkish bath has repeatedly risen from the lunette, with a strong expression of moral shock. It vanishes abruptly as the two turn towards it in their flight. At the same moment Tarleton comes back through the vestibule door, exhausted by severe and unaccustomed exercise.*

TARLETON  [*looking after the flying figures with amazement*] Hallo, Patsy: whats up? Another aeroplane? [*They are far too preoccupied to hear him; and he is left staring after them as they rush away through the garden. He goes to the pavilion door and looks up; but the heavens are empty. His exhaustion disables him from further inquiry. He dabs his brow with his handkerchief, and walks stiffly to the nearest convenient support, which happens to be the Turkish bath. He props himself upon it with his elbow, and covers his eyes with his hand for a moment. After a few sighing breaths, he feels a little better, and uncovers his eyes. The man's head rises from the lunette a few inches from his nose. He recoils from the bath with a violent start*]. Oh Lord! My brain's gone. [*Calling piteously*] Chickabiddy! [*He staggers down to the writing table*].

THE MAN  [*coming out of the bath, pistol in hand*] Another sound; and youre a dead man.

TARLETON  [*braced*] Am I? Well, youre a live one: thats one comfort. I thought you were a ghost. [*He sits down, quite undisturbed by the pistol*] Who are you; and what the devil were you doing in my new Turkish bath?

THE MAN  [*with tragic intensity*] I am the son of Lucinda Titmus.

TARLETON  [*the name conveying nothing to him*] Indeed? And how is she? Quite well, I hope, eh?

THE MAN. She is dead. Dead, my God! and you are alive.

TARLETON [unimpressed by the tragedy, but sympathetic] Oh! Lost your mother? Thats sad. I'm sorry. But we cant all have the luck to die before our mothers, and be nursed out of the world by the hands that nursed us into it.

THE MAN. Much you care, damn you!

TARTLETON. Oh, don't cut up rough. Face it like a man. You see I didnt know your mother; but Ive no doubt she was an excellent woman.

THE MAN. Not know her! Do you dare to stand there by her open grave and deny that you knew her?

TARLETON [trying to recollect] What did you say her name was?

THE MAN. Lucinda Titmus.

TARLETON. Well, I ought to remember a rum name like that if I ever heard it. But I dont. Have you a photograph or anything?

THE MAN. Forgotten even the name of your victim!

TARLETON. Oh! she was my victim, was she?

THE MAN. She was. And you shall see her face again before you die, dead as she is. I have a photograph.

TARLETON. Good.

THE MAN. Ive two photographs.

TARLETON. Still better. Treasure the mother's pictures. Good boy!

THE MAN. One of them as you knew her. The other as she became when you flung her aside, and she withered into an old woman.

TARLETON. She'd have done that anyhow, my lad. We all grow old. Look at me! [Seeing that the man is embarrassed by his pistol in fumbling for the photographs with his left hand in his breast pocket] Let me hold the gun for you.

THE MAN [retreating to the worktable] Stand back. Do you take me for a fool?

TARLETON.   Well, youre a little upset, naturally. It does you credit.

THE MAN.   Look here, upon this picture and on this. [*He holds out the two photographs like a hand at cards, and points to them with the pistol*].

TARLETON.   Good. Read Shakespear: he has a word for every occasion. [*He takes the photographs, one in each hand, and looks from one to the other, pleased and interested, but without any sign of recognition*] What a pretty girl! Very pretty. I can imagine myself falling in love with her when I was your age. I wasnt a bad-looking young fellow myself in those days. [*Looking at the other*] Curious that we should both have gone the same way.

THE MAN.   You and she the same way! What do you mean?

TARLETON.   Both got stout, I mean.

THE MAN.   Would you have had her deny herself food?

TARLETON.   No: it wouldnt have been any use. It is constitutional. No matter how little you eat you put on flesh if youre made that way. [*He resumes his study of the earlier photograph*].

THE MAN.   Is that all the feeling that rises in you at the sight of the face you once knew so well?

TARLETON   [*too much absorbed in the portrait to heed him*] Funny that I cant remember! Let this be a lesson to you, young man. I could go into court tomorrow and swear I never saw that face before in my life if it wasnt for that brooch [*pointing to the photograph*]. Have you got that brooch, by the way? [*The man again resorts to his breast pocket*]. You seem to carry the whole family property in that pocket.

THE MAN   [*producing a brooch*] Here it is to prove my bona fides.

TARLETON   [*pensively putting the photographs on the table and taking the brooch*] I bought that brooch in Cheapside from a man with a yellow wig and a cast in his left eye. Ive never set eyes on him from that day to this. And yet I remember that man; and I cant remember your mother.

THE MAN. Monster! Without conscience! without even memory! You left her to her shame—

TARLETON [*throwing the brooch on the table and rising pepperily*] Come, come, young man! none of that. Respect the romance of your mother's youth. Dont you start throwing stones at her. I dont recall her features just at this moment; but Ive no doubt she was kind to me and we were happy together. If you have a word to say against her, take yourself out of my house and say it elsewhere.

THE MAN. What sort of a joker are you? Are you trying to put me in the wrong, when you have to answer to me for a crime that would make every honest man spit at you as you passed in the street if I were to make it known?

TARLETON. You read a good deal, dont you?

THE MAN. What if I do? What has that to do with your infamy and my mother's doom?

TARLETON. There, you see! Doom! Thats not good sense; but it's literature. Now it happens that I'm a tremendous reader: always was. When I was your age I read books of that sort by the bushel: the Doom sort, you know. It's odd, isnt it, that you and I should be like one another in that respect? Can you account for it in any way?

THE MAN. No. What are you driving at?

TARLETON. Well, do you know who your father was?

THE MAN. I see what you mean now. You dare set up to be my father! Thank heaven Ive not a drop of your vile blood in my veins.

TARLETON [*sitting down again with a shrug*] Well, if you wont be civil, theres no pleasure in talking to you, is there? What do you want? Money?

THE MAN. How dare you insult me?

TARLETON. Well, what do you want?

THE MAN. Justice.

TARLETON.   Youre quite sure thats all?

THE MAN.   It's enough for me.

TARLETON.   A modest sort of demand, isnt it? Nobody ever had it since the world began, fortunately for themselves; but you must have it, must you? Well, youve come to the wrong shop for it: youll get no justice here: we dont keep it. Human nature is what we stock.

THE MAN.   Human nature! Debauchery! gluttony! self-ishness! robbery of the poor! Is that what you call human nature?

TARLETON.   No: thats what you call it. Come, my lad! Whats the matter with you? You dont look starved; and youve a decent suit of clothes.

THE MAN.   Forty-two shillings.

TARLETON.   They can do you a very decent suit for forty-two shillings. Have you paid for it?

THE MAN.   Do you take me for a thief? And do you suppose I can get credit like you?

TARLETON.   Then you were able to lay your hand on forty-two shillings. Judging from your conversational style, I should think you must spend at least a shilling a week on romantic literature.

THE MAN.   Where would I get a shilling a week to spend on books when I can hardly keep myself decent? I get books at the Free Library.

TARLETON   [*springing to his feet*] What!!!

THE MAN   [*recoiling before his vehemence*] The Free Library. Theres no harm in that.

TARLETON.   Ingrate! I supply you with free books; and the use you make of them is to persuade yourself that it's a fine thing to shoot me. [*He throws himself doggedly back into his chair*]. I'll never give another penny to a Free Library.

THE MAN.   Youll never give another penny to anything. This is the end: for you and me.

TARLETON. Pooh! Come, come, man! talk business. Whats wrong? Are you out of employment?

THE MAN. No. This is my Saturday afternoon. Dont flatter yourself that I'm a loafer or a criminal. I'm a cashier; and I defy you to say that my cash has ever been a farthing wrong. Ive a right to call you to account because my hands are clean.

TARLETON. Well, call away. What have I to account for? Had you a hard time with your mother? Why didn't she ask me for money?

THE MAN. She'd have died first. Besides, who wanted your money? Do you suppose we lived in the gutter? My father maynt have been in as large a way as you; but he was better connected; and his shop was as respectable as yours.

TARLETON. I suppose your mother brought him a little capital.

THE MAN. I dont know. Whats that got to do with you?

TARLETON. Well, you say she and I knew one another and parted. She must have had something off me then, you know. One doesnt get out of these things for nothing. Hang it, young man: do you suppose Ive no heart? Of course she had her due; and she found a husband with it, and set him up in business with it, and brought you up respectably; so what the devil have you to complain of?

THE MAN. Are women to be ruined with impunity?

TARLETON. I havnt ruined any woman that I'm aware of. Ive been the making of you and your mother.

THE MAN. Oh, I'm a fool to listen to you and argue with you. I came here to kill you and then kill myself.

TARLETON. Begin with yourself, if you dont mind. Ive a good deal of business to do still before I die. Havnt you?

THE MAN. No. Thats just it: Ive no business to do. Do you know what my life is? I spend my days from nine to six—nine hours of daylight and fresh air—in a stuffy little den counting another man's money. Ive an intellect: a mind and a brain and a soul; and the use he makes of them is to fix them on his tuppences and his eighteenpences and his two pound seventeen and tenpences and see how much they come to at the end of the day and take care that no one steals them. I enter and enter, and add and add, and take money and give change, and fill cheques and stamp receipts; and not a penny of that money is my own: not one of those transactions has the smallest interest for me or anyone else in the world but him; and even he couldnt stand it if he had to do it all himself. And I'm envied: aye, envied for the variety and liveliness of my job, by the poor devil of a bookkeeper that has to copy all my entries over again. Fifty thousand entries a year that poor wretch makes; and not ten out of the fifty thousand ever has to be referred to again; and when all the figures are counted up and the balance sheet made out, the boss isnt a penny the richer than he'd be if book-keeping had never been invented. Of all the damnable waste of human life that ever was invented, clerking is the very worst.

TARLETON.   Why not join the territorials?

THE MAN.   Because the boss wont let me. He hasnt the sense to see that it would pay him to get some cheap soldiering out of me. How can a man tied to a desk from nine to six be anything—be even a man, let alone a soldier? But I'll teach him and you a lesson. Ive had enough of living a dog's life and despising myself for it. Ive had enough of being talked down to by hogs like you, and wearing my life out for a salary that wouldnt keep you in cigars. Youll never believe that a clerk's a man until one of us makes an example of one of you.

TARLETON.   Despotism tempered by assassination, eh?

THE MAN.   Yes. Thats what they do in Russia. Well, a business office is Russia as far as the clerks are concerned. So dont you take it so coolly. You think I'm not going to do it; but I am.

TARLETON   [rising and facing him] Come, now, as man

to man! It's not my fault that youre poorer than I am; and
it's not your fault that I'm richer than you. And if you could
undo all that passed between me and your mother, you
wouldnt undo it; and neither would she. But youre sick of
your slavery; and you want to be the hero of a romance and
to get into the papers. Eh? A son revenges his mother's
shame. Villain weltering in his gore. Mother: look down from
heaven and receive your unhappy son's last sigh.

THE MAN.   Oh, rot! do you think I read novelettes? And
do you suppose I believe such superstitions as heaven? I go
to church because the boss told me I'd get the sack if I didnt.
Free England! Ha! [*Lina appears at the pavilion door, and
comes swiftly and noiselessly forward on seeing the man with a
pistol in his hand*].

TARLETON.   Youre afraid of getting the sack; but youre
not afraid to shoot yourself.

THE MAN.   Damn you! youre trying to keep me talking
until somebody comes. [*He raises the pistol desperately, but
not very resolutely*].

LINA   [*at his right elbow*] Somebody has come.

THE MAN   [*turning on her*] Stand off. I'll shoot you if you
lay a hand on me. I will, by God.

LINA.   You cant cover me with that pistol. Try.

*He tries, presenting the pistol at her face. She moves round
him in the opposite direction to the hands of a clock with a light
dancing step. He finds it impossible to cover her with the pistol:
she is always too far to his left. Tarleton, behind him, grips his
wrist and drags his arm straight up, so that the pistol points to
the ceiling. As he tries to turn on his assailant, Lina grips his
other wrist.*

LINA.   Please stop. I cant bear to twist anyone's wrist;
but I must if you dont let the pistol go.

THE MAN   [*letting Tarleton take it from him*] All right: I'm
done. Couldnt even do that job decently. Thats a clerk all
over. Very well: send for your damned police and make an

end of it. I'm accustomed to prison from nine to six: I daresay I can stand from six to nine as well.

TARLETON.   Dont swear. Thats a lady. [*He throws the pistol on the writing table*].

THE MAN   [*looking at Lina in amazement*] Beaten by a female! It needed only this. [*He collapses in the chair near the worktable, and hides his face. They cannot help pitying him*].

LINA.   Old pal: dont call the police. Lend him a bicycle and let him get away.

THE MAN.   I cant ride a bicycle. I never could afford one. I'm not even that much good.

TARLETON.   If I gave you a hundred pound note now to go and have a good spree with, I wonder would you know how to set about it. Do you ever take a holiday?

THE MAN.   Take! I got four days last August.

TARLETON.   What did you do?

THE MAN.   I did a cheap trip to Folkestone. I spent sevenpence on dropping pennies into silly automatic machines and peepshows of rowdy girls having a jolly time. I spent a penny on the lift and fourpence on refreshments. That cleaned me out. The rest of the time I was so miserable that I was glad to get back to the office. Now you know.

LINA.   Come to the gymnasium: I'll teach you how to make a man of yourself. [*The man is about to rise irresolutely, from the mere habit of doing what he is told, when Tarleton stops him*].

TARLETON.   Young man: dont. Youve tried to shoot me; but I'm not vindictive. I draw the line at putting a man on the rack. If you want every joint in your body stretched until it's an agony to live—until you have an unnatural feeling that all your muscles are singing and laughing with pain— then go to the gymnasium with that lady. But youll be more comfortable in jail.

LINA   [*greatly amused*] Was that why you went away, old

pal? Was that the telegram you said you had forgotten to send?

*Mrs Tarleton comes in hastily through the inner door.*

MRS TARLETON  [*on the steps*] Is anything the matter, John? Nurse says she heard you calling me a quarter of an hour ago; and that your voice sounded as if you were ill. [*She comes between Tarleton and the man*]. Is anything the matter?

TARLETON.  This is the son of an old friend of mine. Mr—er—Mr Gunner. [*To the man, who rises awkwardly*]. My wife.

MRS TARLETON.  Good evening to you.

GUNNER.  Er—[*He is too nervous to speak, and makes a shambling bow*].

*Bentley looks in at the pavilion door, very peevish, and too preoccupied with his own affairs to pay any attention to those of the company.*

BENTLEY.  I say: has anybody seen Hypatia? She promised to come out with me; and I cant find her anywhere. And wheres Joey?

GUNNER  [*suddenly breaking out aggressively, being incapable of any middle way between submissiveness and violence*] I can tell you where Hypatia is. I can tell you where Joey is. And I say it's a scandal and an infamy. If people only knew what goes on in this so-called respectable house it would be put a stop to. These are the morals of our pious capitalist class! This is your rotten bourgeoisie! This—

MRS TARLETON.  Dont you dare use such language in company. I wont allow it.

TARLETON.  All right, Chickabiddy: it's not bad language: it's only Socialism.

MRS TARLETON.  Well, I wont have any Socialism in my house.

TARLETON  [*to Gunner*] You hear what Mrs Tarleton

says. Well, in this house everybody does what she says or out they go.

GUNNER.  Do you suppose I want to stay? Do you think I would breathe this polluted atmosphere a moment longer than I could help?

BENTLEY  [*running forward between Lina and Gunner*] But what did you mean by what you said about Miss Tarleton and Mr Percival, you beastly rotter, you?

GUNNER  [*to Tarleton*] Oh! is Hypatia your daughter? And Joey is Mister Percival, is he? One of your set, I suppose. One of the smart set! One of the bridge-playing, eighty-horse-power, week-ender set! One of the johnnies I slave for! Well, Joey has more decency than your daughter, anyhow. The women are the worst. I never believed it til I saw it with my own eyes. Well, it wont last for ever. The writing is on the wall. Rome fell. Babylon fell. Hindhead's turn will come.

MRS TARLETON  [*naively looking at the wall for the writing*] Whatever are you talking about, young man?

GUNNER.  I know what I'm talking about. I went into that Turkish bath a boy: I came out a man.

MRS TARLETON.  Good gracious! he's mad. [*To Lina*] Did John make him take a Turkish bath?

LINA.  No. He doesnt need Turkish baths: he needs to put on a little flesh. I dont understand what it's all about. I found him trying to shoot Mr Tarleton.

MRS TARLETON  [*with a scream*] Oh! and John encouraging him, I'll be bound! Bunny: you go for the police. [*To Gunner*] I'll teach you to come into my house and shoot my husband.

GUNNER.  Teach away. I never asked to be let off. I'm ashamed to be free instead of taking my part with the rest. Women—beautiful women of noble birth—are going to prison for their opinions. Girl students in Russia go to the gallows; let themselves be cut in pieces with the knout, or driven through the frozen snows of Siberia, sooner than stand looking on tamely at the world being made a hell for the toiling millions. If you were not all skunks and cowards youd be suffering with them instead of battening here on the plunder of the poor.

MRS TARLETON [*much vexed*] Oh, did you ever hear such silly nonsense? Bunny: go and tell the gardener to send over one of his men to Grayshott for the police.

GUNNER. I'll go with him. I intend to give myself up. I'm going to expose what Ive seen here, no matter what the consequences may be to my miserable self.

TARLETON. Stop. You stay where you are, Ben. Chick-abiddy: youve never had the police in. If you had, youd not be in a hurry to have them in again. Now, young man: cut the cackle; and tell us, as short as you can, what did you see?

GUNNER. I cant tell you in the presence of ladies.

MRS TARLETON. Oh, you are tiresome. As if it mattered to anyone what you saw. Me! A married woman that might be your mother. [*To Lina*] And I'm sure youre not particular, if youll excuse my saying so.

TARLETON. Out with it. What did you see?

GUNNER. I saw your daughter with my own eyes—oh well, never mind what I saw.

BENTLEY [*almost crying with anxiety*] You beastly rotter. I'll get Joey to give you such a hiding—

TARLETON. You cant leave it at that, you know. What did you see my daughter doing?

GUNNER. After all, why shouldnt she do it? The Russian students do it. Women should be as free as men. I'm a fool. I'm so full of your bourgeois morality that I let myself be shocked by the application of my own revolutionary principles. If she likes the man why shouldnt she tell him so?

MRS TARLETON. I do wonder at you, John, letting him talk like this before everybody. [*Turning rather tartly to Lina*]

Would you mind going away to the drawing room just for a few minutes, Miss Chipenoska. This is a private family matter, if you dont mind.

LINA.    I should have gone before, Mrs Tarleton, if there had been anyone to protect Mr Tarleton and the young gentleman. [*She goes out through the inner door*].

GUNNER.    There you are! It's all of a piece here. The men effeminate, the women unsexed—

TARLETON.    Dont begin again, old chap. Keep it for Trafalgar Square.

HYPATIA'S VOICE OUTSIDE.    No, no. [*She breaks off in a stifled half laugh, half scream, and is seen darting across the garden with Percival in hot pursuit. Immediately afterwards she appears again, and runs into the pavilion. Finding it full of people, including a stranger, she stops; but Percival, flushed and reckless, rushes in and seizes her before he, too, realizes that they are not alone. He releases her in confusion*].

*Dead silence. They are all afraid to look at one another except Mrs Tarleton, who stares sternly at Hypatia. Hypatia is the first to recover her presence of mind.*

HYPATIA.    Excuse me rushing in like this. Mr Percival has been chasing me down the hill.

GUNNER.    Who chased him up it? Dont be ashamed. Be fearless. Be truthful.

TARLETON.    Gunner: will you go to Paris for a fortnight? I'll pay your expenses.

HYPATIA.    What do you mean?

GUNNER.    There was a silent witness in the Turkish bath.

TARLETON.    I found him hiding there. Whatever went on here, he saw and heard. Thats what he means.

PERCIVAL    [*sternly approaching Gunner, and speaking with deep but contained indignation*] Am I to understand you as daring to put forward the monstrous and blackguardly lie that this lady behaved improperly in my presence?

GUNNER [*turning white*] You know what I saw and heard.

*Hypatia, with a gleam of triumph in her eyes, slips noiselessly into the swing chair, and watches Percival and Gunner, swinging slightly, but otherwise motionless.*

PERCIVAL. I hope it is not necessary for me to assure you all that there is not one word of truth—not one grain of substance—in this rascally calumny, which no man with a spark of decent feeling would have uttered even if he had been ignorant enough to believe it. Miss Tarleton's conduct, since I have had the honor of knowing her, has been, I need hardly say, in every respect beyond reproach. [*To Gunner*] As for you, sir, youll have the goodness to come out with me immediately. I have some business with you which cant be settled in Mrs Tarleton's presence or in her house.

GUNNER [*painfully frightened*] Why should I go out with you?

PERCIVAL. Because I intend that you shall.

GUNNER. I wont be bullied by you. [*Percival makes a threatening step towards him*]. Police! [*He tries to bolt; but Percival seizes him*]. Leave me go, will you? What right have you to lay hands on me?

TARLETON. Let him run for it, Mr Percival. He's very poor company. We shall be well rid of him. Let him go.

PERCIVAL. Not until he has taken back and made the fullest apology for the abominable lie he has told. He shall do that, or he shall defend himself as best he can against the most thorough thrashing I'm capable of giving him. [*Releasing Gunner, but facing him ominously*] Take your choice. Which is it to be?

GUNNER. Give me a fair chance. Go and stick at a desk from nine to six for a month, and let me have your grub and your sport and your lessons in boxing, and I'll fight you fast enough. You know I'm no good or you darent bully me like this.

PERCIVAL. You should have thought of that before you attacked a lady with a dastardly slander. I'm waiting for your decision. I'm rather in a hurry, please.

GUNNER. I never said anything against the lady.

| MRS TARLETON | } { | Oh, listen to that! |
| BENTLEY | | What a liar! |
| HYPATIA | } { | Oh! |
| TARLETON | | Oh, come! |

PERCIVAL. We'll have it in writing, if you dont mind. [*Pointing to the writing table*] Sit down; and take that pen in your hand. [*Gunner looks irresolutely a little way round; then obeys*]. Now write, "I," whatever your name is—

GUNNER [*after a vain attempt*] I cant. My hand's shaking too much. You see it's no use. I'm doing my best. I cant.

PERCIVAL. Mr Summerhays will write it: you can sign it.

BENTLEY [*insolently to Gunner*] Get up. [*Gunner obeys; and Bentley, shouldering him aside towards Percival, takes his place and prepares to write*].

PERCIVAL. Whats your name?

GUNNER. John Brown.

TARLETON. Oh come! Couldnt you make it Horace Smith? or Algernon Robinson?

GUNNER [*agitatedly*] But my name is John Brown. There are really John Browns. How can I help it if my name's a common one?

BENTLEY. Shew us a letter addressed to you.

GUNNER. How can I? I never get any letters: I'm only a clerk. I can shew you J. B. on my handkerchief. [*He takes out a not very clean one*].

BENTLEY [*with disgust*] Oh, put it up again. Let it go at John Brown.

PERCIVAL. Where do you live?

GUNNER. 4 Chesterfield Parade, Kentish Town, N. W.

PERCIVAL [*dictating*] I, John Brown, of 4 Chesterfield

Parade, Kentish Town, do hereby voluntarily confess that on the 31st May 1909 I—[*To Tarleton*] What did he do exactly?

TARLETON  [*dictating*] —I trespassed on the land of John Tarleton at Hindhead, and effected an unlawful entry into his house, where I secreted myself in a portable Turkish bath—

BENTLEY.  Go slow, old man. Just a moment. "Turkish bath"—yes?

TARLETON  [*continuing*] —with a pistol, with which I threatened to take the life of the said John Tarleton—

MRS TARLETON.  Oh, John! You might have been killed.

TARLETON.  —and was prevented from doing so only by the timely arrival of the celebrated Miss Lina Szczepanowska.

MRS TARLETON.  Is she celebrated? [*Apologetically*] I never dreamt—

BENTLEY.  Look here: I'm awfully sorry; but I cant spell Szczepanowska.

PERCIVAL.  I think it's S, z, c, z—Better say the Polish lady.

BENTLEY  [*writing*] "the Polish lady"?

TARLETON  [*to Percival*] Now it's your turn.

PERCIVAL  [*dictating*] I further confess that I was guilty of uttering an abominable calumny concerning Miss Hypatia Tarleton, for which there was not a shred of foundation.

*Impressive silence whilst Bentley writes.*

BENTLEY.  "foundation"?

PERCIVAL.  I apologize most humbly to the lady and her family for my conduct—[*he waits for Bentley to write*].

BENTLEY.  "conduct"?

PERCIVAL.  —and I promise Mr. Tarleton not to repeat it, and to amend my life—

BENTLEY.  "amend my life"?

PERCIVAL.  —and to do what in me lies to prove worthy of his kindness in giving me another chance—

BENTLEY.   "another chance"?

PERCIVAL.   —and refraining from delivering me up to the punishment I so richly deserve.

BENTLEY.   "richly deserve."

PERCIVAL   [to Hypatia] Does that satisfy you, Miss Tarleton?

HYPATIA.   Yes: that will teach him to tell lies next time.

BENTLEY   [rising to make place for Gunner and handing him the pen] You mean it will teach him to tell the truth next time.

TARLETON.   Ahem! Do you, Patsy?

PERCIVAL.   Be good enough to sign. [Gunner sits down helplessly and dips the pen in the ink]. I hope what you are signing is no mere form of words to you, and that you not only say you are sorry, but that you are sorry.

Lord Summerhays and Johnny come in through the pavilion door.

MRS TARLETON.   Stop. Mr Percival: I think, on Hypatia's account, Lord Summerhays ought to be told about this.

Lord Summerhays, wondering what the matter is, comes forward between Percival and Lina. Johnny stops beside Hypatia.

PERCIVAL.   Certainly.

TARLETON   [uneasily] Take my advice and cut it short. Get rid of him.

MRS TARLETON.   Hypatia ought to have her character cleared.

TARLETON.   You let well alone, Chickabiddy. Most of our characters will bear a little careful dusting; but they wont bear scouring. Patsy is jolly well out of it. What does it matter, anyhow?

PERCIVAL.   Mr. Tarleton: we have already said either too much or not enough. Lord Summerhays: will you be kind enough to witness the declaration this man has just signed?

GUNNER.   I havnt yet. Am I to sign now?

PERCIVAL.   Of course. [Gunner, who is now incapable of

*doing anything on his own initiative, signs*]. Now stand up and read your declaration to this gentleman. [*Gunner makes a vague movement and looks stupidly round. Percival adds peremptorily*] Now, please.

GUNNER [*rising apprehensively and reading without punctuation in a hardly audible voice, like a very sick man*] I John Brown of 4 Chesterfield Parade Kentish Town do hereby voluntarily confess that on the 31st May 1909 I trespassed on the land of John Tarleton at Hindhead and effected an unlawful entry into his house where I secreted myself in a portable Turkish bath with a pistol with which I threatened to take the life of the said John Tarleton and was prevented from doing so only by the timely arrival of the Polish lady. I further confess that I was guilty of uttering an abominable calumny concerning Miss Hypatia Tarleton for which there was not a shred of foundation I apologize most humbly to the lady and her family for my conduct and I promise Mr Tarleton not to repeat it and to amend my life and to do what in me lies to prove worthy of his kindness in giving me another chance and refraining from delivering me up to the punishment I so richly deserve.

*A short and painful silence follows. Then Percival speaks.*

PERCIVAL. Do you consider that sufficient, Lord Summerhays?

LORD SUMMERHAYS. Oh quite, quite.

PERCIVAL [*to Hypatia*] Lord Summerhays would probably like to hear you say that you are satisfied, Miss Tarleton.

HYPATIA [*coming out of the swing, and advancing between Percival and Lord Summerhays*] I must say that you have behaved like a perfect gentleman, Mr Percival.

PERCIVAL [*first bowing to Hypatia, and then turning with cold contempt to Gunner, who is standing helpless*] We need not trouble you any further. [*Gunner turns vaguely towards the pavilion*].

JOHNNY [*with less refined offensiveness, pointing to the pa-*

*vilion]* Thats your way. The gardener will shew you the shortest way into the road. Go the shortest way.

GUNNER  *[oppressed and disconcerted, hardly knows how to get out of the room]* Yes, sir. I—*[He turns again, appealing to Tarleton]* Maynt I have my mother's photographs back again? *[Mrs Tarleton pricks up her ears]*.

TARLETON.  Eh? What? Oh, the photographs! Yes, yes, yes: take them. *[Gunner takes them from the table, and is creeping away, when Mrs Tarleton puts out her hand and stops him]*.

MRS TARLETON.  Whats this, John? What were you doing with his mother's photographs?

TARLETON.  Nothing, nothing. Never mind, Chickabiddy: it's all right.

MRS TARLETON  *[snatching the photographs from Gunner's irresolute fingers, and recognizing them at a glance]* Lucy Titmus! Oh John, John!

TARLETON  *[grimly, to Gunner]* Young man: youre a fool; but youve just put the lid on this job in a masterly manner. I knew you would. I told you all to let well alone. You wouldnt; and now you must take the consequences—or rather *I* must take them.

MRS TARLETON  *[maternally]* Are you Lucy's son?

GUNNER.  Yes!

MRS TARLETON.  And why didnt you come to me? I didnt turn my back on your mother when she came to me in her trouble. Didnt you know that?

GUNNER.  No. She never talked to me about anything.

TARLETON.  How could she talk to her own son? Shy, Summerhays, shy. Parent and child. Shy. *[He sits down at the end of the writing table nearest the sideboard like a man resigned to anything that fate may have in store for him]*.

MRS TARLETON.  Then how did you find out?

GUNNER.  From her papers after she died.

MRS TARLETON  *[shocked]* Is Lucy dead? And I never knew! *[With an effusion of tenderness]* And you here being treated like that, poor orphan, with nobody to take your part! Tear up that foolish paper, child; and sit down and make friends with me.

| | |
|---|---|
| JOHNNY | Hallo, mother: this is all very well, you know— |
| PERCIVAL | But may I point out, Mrs Tarleton, that— |
| BENTLEY | Do you mean that after what he said of— |
| HYPATIA | Oh, look here, mamma: this is really— |

MRS TARLETON. Will you please speak one at a time? *Silence.*

PERCIVAL [*in a very gentlemanly manner*] Will you allow me to remind you, Mrs Tarleton, that this man has uttered a most serious and disgraceful falsehood concerning Miss Tarleton and myself?

MRS TARLETON. I dont believe a word of it. If the poor lad was there in the Turkish bath, who has a better right to say what was going on here than he has? You ought to be ashamed of yourself, Patsy; and so ought you too, Mr Percival, for encouraging her. [*Hypatia retreats to the pavilion, and exchanges grimaces with Johnny, shamelessly enjoying Percival's sudden reverse. They know their mother*].

PERCIVAL [*gasping*] Mrs. Tarleton: I give you my word of honor—

MRS TARLETON. Oh, go along with you and your word of honor. Do you think I'm a fool? I wonder you can look the lad in the face after bullying him and making him sign those wicked lies; and all the time you carrying on with my daughter before youd been half an hour in my house. Fie, for shame!

PERCIVAL. Lord Summerhays: I appeal to you. Have I done the correct thing or not?

LORD SUMMERHAYS. Youve done your best, Mr Percival.

But the correct thing depends for its success on everybody playing the game very strictly. As a single-handed game, it's impossible.

BENTLEY. [*suddenly breaking out lamentably*] Joey: have you taken Hypatia away from me?

LORD SUMMERHAYS. [*severely*] Bentley! Bentley! Control yourself, sir.

TARLETON. Come, Mr Percival! the shutters are up on the gentlemanly business. Try the truth.

PERCIVAL. I am in a wretched position. If I tell the truth nobody will believe me.

TARLETON. Oh yes they will. The truth makes everybody believe it.

PERCIVAL. It also makes everybody pretend not to believe it. Mrs Tarleton: youre not playing the game.

MRS TARLETON. I dont think youve behaved at all nicely, Mr Percival.

BENTLEY. I wouldn't have played you such a dirty trick, Joey. [*Struggling with a sob*] You beast.

LORD SUMMERHAYS. Bentley: you must control yourself. Let me say at the same time, Mr Percival, that my son seems to have been mistaken in regarding you either as his friend or as a gentleman.

PERCIVAL. Miss Tarleton: I'm suffering this for your sake. I ask you just to say that I am not to blame. Just that and nothing more.

HYPATIA [*gloating mischievously over his distress*] You chased me through the heather and kissed me. You shouldnt have done that if you were not in earnest.

PERCIVAL. Oh, this is really the limit. [*Turning desperately to Gunner*] Sir: I appeal to you. As a gentleman! as a man of honor! as a man bound to stand by another man! You were in that Turkish bath. You saw how it began. Could any man have behaved more correctly than I did? Is there a shadow of foundation for the accusations brought against me?

GUNNER [*sorely perplexed*]  Well, what do you want me to say?

JOHNNY.  He has said what he had to say already, hasnt he? Read that paper.

GUNNER.  When I tell the truth, you make me go back on it. And now you want me to go back on myself! What is a man to do?

PERCIVAL [*patiently*]  Please try to get your mind clear, Mr Brown. I pointed out to you that you could not, as a gentleman, disparage a lady's character. You agree with me, I hope.

GUNNER.  Yes: that sounds all right.

PERCIVAL.  But youre also bound to tell the truth. Surely youll not deny that.

GUNNER.  Who's denying it? I say nothing against it.

PERCIVAL.  Of course not. Well, I ask you to tell the truth simply and unaffectedly. Did you witness any improper conduct on my part when you were in the bath?

GUNNER.  No, sir.

JOHNNY ⎫         Then what do you mean by saying
        ⎬              that—
HYPATIA ⎪         Do you mean to say that I—
BENTLEY ⎭         Oh, you are a rotter. Youre
                      afraid—

TARLETON [*rising*]  Stop. [*Silence*]. Leave it at that. Enough said. You keep quiet, Johnny. Mr Percival: youre whitewashed. So are you, Patsy. Honors are easy. Lets drop the subject. The next thing to do is to open a subscription to start this young man on a ranch in some far country thats accustomed to be in a disturbed state. He—

MRS TARLETON.  Now stop joking the poor lad, John: I wont have it. He's been worried to death between you all. [*To Gunner*] Have you had your tea?

GUNNER.  Tea? No: it's too early. I'm all right; only I had

no dinner: I didn't think I'd want it. I didnt think I'd be alive.

MRS TARLETON.   Oh, what a thing to say! You mustnt talk like that.

JOHNNY.   He's out of his mind. He thinks it's past dinnertime.

MRS TARLETON.   Oh, youve no sense, Johnny. He calls his lunch his dinner, and has his tea at half-past six. Havnt you, dear?

GUNNER   [timidly] Hasnt everybody?

JOHNNY   [laughing] Well, by George, thats not bad.

MRS TARLETON.   Now dont be rude, Johnny: you know I dont like it. [To Gunner] A cup of tea will pick you up.

GUNNER.   I'd rather not. I'm all right.

TARLETON   [going to the sideboard] Here! try a mouthful of sloe gin.

GUNNER.   No, thanks. I'm a teetotaler. I cant touch alcohol in any form.

TARLETON.   Nonsense! This isnt alcohol. Sloe gin. Vegetarian, you know.

GUNNER   [hesitating] Is it a fruit beverage?

TARLETON.   Of course it is. Fruit beverage. Here you are. [He gives him a glass of sloe gin].

GUNNER   [going to the sideboard] Thanks. [He begins to drink it confidently; but the first mouthful startles and almost chokes him]. It's rather hot.

TARLETON.   Do you good. Dont be afraid of it.

MRS TARLETON   [going to him] Sip it, dear. Dont be in a hurry.

Gunner sips slowly, each sip making his eyes water.

JOHNNY   [coming forward into the place left vacant by Gunner's visit to the sideboard] Well, now that the gentleman has been attended to, I should like to know where we are. It may be a vulgar business habit; but I confess I like to know where I am.

TARLETON.  I dont. Wherever you are, youre there any-how. I tell you again, leave it at that.

BENTLEY.  I want to know too. Hypatia's engaged to me.

HYPATIA.  Bentley: if you insult me again: if you say an-other word, I'll leave the house and not enter it until you leave it.

JOHNNY.  Put that in your pipe and smoke it, my boy.

BENTLEY  [*inarticulate with fury and suppressed tears*] Oh! Beasts! Brutes!

MRS TARLETON.  Now dont hurt his feelings, poor little lamb!

LORD SUMMERHAYS  [*very sternly*] Bentley: you are not behaving well. You had better leave us until you have re-covered yourself.

*Bentley goes out in disgrace, but gets no further than half way to the pavilion door, when, with a wild sob, he throws himself on the floor and begins to yell.*

| | |
|---|---|
| MRS TARLETON | [*running to him*] Oh, poor child, poor child! Dont cry, duckie: he didnt mean it: dont cry. |
| LORD SUMMERHAYS | Stop that infernal noise, sir: do you hear? Stop it instantly. |
| JOHNNY | Thats the game he tried on me. There you are! Now, mother! Now, Patsy! You see for your-selves. |
| HYPATIA | [*covering her ears*] Oh you little wretch! Stop him, Mr Percival. Kick him. |
| TARLETON | Steady on, steady on. Easy, Bunny, easy. |

LINA    [*appearing at the door*] Leave him to me, Mrs Tarleton. [*Clear and authoritative*] Stand clear, please.

*She quickly lifts the upper half of Bentley from the ground; dives under him; rises with his body hanging across her shoulders; and runs out with him.*

BENTLEY    [*in scared, sobered, humble tones as he is borne off*] What are you doing? Let me down. Please, Miss Szczepanowska—[*they pass out of hearing*].

*An awestruck silence falls on the company as they speculate on Bentley's fate.*

JOHNNY.    I wonder what she's going to do with him.

HYPATIA.    Spank him, I hope. Spank him hard.

LORD SUMMERHAYS.    I hope so. I hope so. Tarleton: I'm beyond measure humiliated and annoyed by my son's behavior in your house. I had better take him home.

TARLETON.    Not at all: not at all. Now, Chickabiddy: as Miss Lina has taken away Ben, suppose you take away Mr Brown for a while.

GUNNER    [*with unexpected aggressiveness*] My name isnt Brown. [*They stare at him: he meets their stare defiantly, pugnacious with sloe gin; drains the last drop from his glass; throws it on the sideboard; and advances to the writing table*]. My name's Baker: Julius Baker. Mister Baker. If any man doubts it, I'm ready for him.

MRS TARLETON.    John: you shouldnt have given him that sloe gin. It's gone to his head.

GUNNER.    Dont you think it. Fruit beverages dont go to the head; and what matter if they did? I say nothing to you, maam: I regard you with respect and affection. [*Lachrymosely*] You were very good to my mother: my poor mother! [*Relapsing into his daring mood*] But I say my name's Baker; and I'm not to be treated as a child or made a slave of by any man. Baker is my name. Did you think I was going to give you my real name? Not likely! Not me!

TARLETON. So you thought of John Brown. That was clever of you.

GUNNER. Clever! yes: we're not all such fools as you think: we clerks. It was the bookkeeper put me up to that. It's the only name that nobody gives as a false name, he said. Clever, eh? I should think so.

MRS TARLETON. Come now, Julius—

GUNNER [reassuring her gravely] Dont you be alarmed, maam. I know what is due to you as a lady and to myself as a gentleman. I regard you with respect and affection. If you had been my mother, as you ought to have been, I should have had more chance. But you shall have no cause to be ashamed of me. The strength of a chain is no greater than its weakest link; but the greatness of a poet is the greatness of his greatest moment. Shakespear used to get drunk. Frederick the Great ran away from a battle. But it was what they could rise to, not what they could sink to, that made them great. They werent good always; but they were good on their day. Well, on my day—on my day, mind you—I'm good for something too. I know that Ive made a silly exhibition of myself here. I know I didnt rise to the occasion. I know that if youd been my mother, youd have been ashamed of me. I lost my presence of mind: I was a contemptible coward. But [slapping himself on the chest] I'm not the man I was then. This is my day. Ive seen the tenth possessor of a foolish face carried out kicking and screaming by a woman. [To Percival] You crowed pretty big over me. You hypnotized me. But when you were put through the fire yourself, you were found wanting. I tell you straight I dont give a damn for you.

MRS TARLETON. No: thats naughty. You shouldnt say that before me.

GUNNER. I would cut my tongue out sooner than say anything vulgar in your presence; for I regard you with respect and affection. I was not swearing. I was affirming my manhood.

MRS TARLETON. What an idea! What puts all these things into your head?

GUNNER. Oh, dont think, because I'm only a clerk, that I'm not one of the intellectuals. I'm a reading man, a thinking man. I read in a book—a high class six shilling book—this precept: Affirm your manhood. It appealed to me. Ive always remembered it. I believe in it. I feel I must do it to recover your respect after my cowardly behavior. Therefore I affirm it in your presence. I tell that man who insulted me that I dont give a damn for him. And neither I do.

TARLETON. I say, Summerhays: did you have chaps of this sort in Jinghiskahn?

LORD SUMMERHAYS. Oh yes: they exist everywhere: they are a most serious modern problem.

GUNNER. Yes. Youre right. [Conceitedly] I'm a problem. And I tell you that when we clerks realize that we're problems! well, look out: thats all.

LORD SUMMERHAYS [suavely, to Gunner] You read a great deal, you say?

GUNNER. Ive read more than any man in this room, if the truth were known, I expect. Thats whats going to smash up your Capitalism. The problems are beginning to read. Ha! We're free to do that here in England. What would you do with me in Jinghiskahn if you had me there?

LORD SUMMERHAYS. Well, since you ask me so directly, I'll tell you. I should take advantage of the fact that you have neither sense enough nor strength enough to know how to behave yourself in a difficulty of any sort. I should warn an intelligent and ambitious policeman that you are a troublesome person. The intelligent and ambitious policeman would take an early opportunity of upsetting your temper by ordering you to move on, and treading on your heels until you were provoked into obstructing an officer in the discharge of his duty. Any trifle of that sort would be sufficient to make a man like you lose your self-possession and put yourself in the wrong. You would then be charged and imprisoned until things quieted down.

GUNNER.    And you call that justice!

LORD SUMMERHAYS.    No. Justice was not my business. I had to govern a province; and I took the necessary steps to maintain order in it. Men are not governed by justice, but by law or persuasion. When they refuse to be governed by law or persuasion, they have to be governed by force or fraud, or both. I used both when law and persuasion failed me. Every ruler of men since the world began has done so, even when he has hated both fraud and force as heartily as I do. It is as well that you should know this, my young friend; so that you may recognize in time that anarchism is a game at which the police can beat you. What have you to say to that?

GUNNER.    What have I to say to it! Well, I call it scandalous: thats what I have to say to it.

LORD SUMMERHAYS.    Precisely: thats all anybody has to say to it, except the British public, which pretends not to believe it. And now let me ask you a sympathetic personal question. Havnt you a headache?

GUNNER.    Well, since you ask me, I have. Ive overexcited myself.

MRS TARLETON.    Poor lad! No wonder, after all youve gone through! You want to eat a little and to lie down. You come with me. I want you to tell me about your poor dear mother and about yourself. Come along with me. [*She leads the way to the inner door*].

GUNNER [*following her obediently*] Thank you kindly, madam. [*She goes out. Before passing out after her, he partly closes the door and lingers for a moment to whisper*] Mind: I'm not knuckling down to any man here. I knuckle down to Mrs Tarleton because she's a woman in a thousand. I affirm my manhood all the same. Understand: I dont give a damn for the lot of you. [*He hurries out, rather afraid of the conse-*

*quences of this defiance, which has provoked Johnny to an impatient movement towards him*].

HYPATIA.  Thank goodness he's gone! Oh, what a bore! WHAT a bore!!! Talk! talk! talk!

TARLETON.  Patsy: it's no good. We're going to talk. And we're going to talk about you.

JOHNNY.  It's no use shirking it, Pat. We'd better know where we are.

LORD SUMMERHAYS.  Come, Miss Tarleton. Wont you sit down? I'm very tired of standing. [*Hypatia comes from the pavilion and takes a chair at the worktable. Lord Summerhays takes the opposite chair, on her right. Percival takes the chair Johnny placed for Lina on her arrival. Tarleton sits down at the end of the writing table. Johnny remains standing. Lord Summerhays continues, with a sigh of relief at being seated*] We shall now get the change of subject we are all pining for.

JOHNNY  [*puzzled*] Whats that?

LORD SUMMERHAYS.  The great question. The question that men and women will spend hours over without complaining. The question that occupies all the novel readers and all the playgoers. The question they never get tired of.

JOHNNY.  But what question?

LORD SUMMERHAYS.  The question which particular young man some young woman will mate with.

PERCIVAL.  As if it mattered!

HYPATIA  [*sharply*] Whats that you said?

PERCIVAL.  I said: As if it mattered.

HYPATIA.  I call that ungentlemanly.

PERCIVAL.  Do you care about that? you who are so magnificently unladylike!

JOHNNY.  Look here, Mr Percival: youre not supposed to insult my sister.

HYPATIA.  Oh, shut up, Johnny. I can take care of myself. Dont you interfere.

JOHNNY.  Oh, very well. If you choose to give yourself

away like that—to allow a man to call you unladylike and then to be unladylike, Ive nothing more to say.

HYPATIA. I think Mr Percival is most ungentlemanly; but I wont be protected. I'll not have my affairs interfered with by men on pretence of protecting me. I'm not your baby. If I interfered between you and a woman, you would soon tell me to mind my own business.

TARLETON. Children: dont squabble. Read Dr Watts. Behave yourselves.

JOHNNY. Ive nothing more to say; and as I dont seem to be wanted here, I shall take myself off. [*He goes out with affected calm through the pavilion*].

TARLETON. Summerhays: a family is an awful thing, an impossible thing. Cat and dog. Patsy: I'm ashamed of you.

HYPATIA. I'll make it up with Johnny afterwards; but I really cant have him here sticking his clumsy hoof into my affairs.

LORD SUMMERHAYS. The question is, Mr Percival, are you really a gentleman, or are you not?

PERCIVAL. Was Napoleon really a gentleman or was he not? He made the lady get out of the way of the porter and said, "Respect the burden, madam." That was behaving like a very fine gentleman; but he kicked Volney for saying that what France wanted was the Bourbons back again. That was behaving rather like a navvy. Now I, like Napoleon, am not all one piece. On occasion, as you have all seen, I can behave like a gentleman. On occasion, I can behave with a brutal simplicity which Miss Tarleton herself could hardly surpass.

TARLETON. Gentleman or no gentleman, Patsy: what are your intentions?

HYPATIA. My intentions! Surely it's the gentleman who should be asked his intentions.

TARLETON. Come now, Patsy! none of that nonsense. Has Mr Percival said anything to you that I ought to know or that Bentley ought to know? Have you said anything to Mr Percival?

HYPATIA.    Mr Percival chased me through the heather and kissed me.

LORD SUMMERHAYS.    As a gentleman, Mr Percival, what do you say to that?

PERCIVAL.    As a gentleman, I do not kiss and tell. As a mere man: a mere cad, if you like, I say that I did so at Miss Tarleton's own suggestion.

HYPATIA.    Beast!

PERCIVAL.    I dont deny that I enjoyed it. But I did not initiate it. And I began by running away.

TARLETON.    So Patsy can run faster than you, can she?

PERCIVAL.    Yes, when she is in pursuit of me. She runs faster and faster. I run slower and slower. And these woods of yours are full of magic. There was a confounded fern owl. Did you ever hear the churr of a fern owl? Did you ever hear it create a sudden silence by ceasing? Did you ever hear it call its mate by striking its wings together twice and whistling that single note that no nightingale can imitate? That is what happened in the woods when I was running away. So I turned; and the pursuer became the pursued.

HYPATIA.    I had to fight like a wild cat.

LORD SUMMERHAYS.    Please dont tell us this. It's not fit for old people to hear.

TARLETON.    Come: how did it end?

HYPATIA.    It's not ended yet.

TARLETON.    How is it going to end?

HYPATIA.    Ask him.

TARLETON.    How is it going to end, Mr Percival?

PERCIVAL.    I cant afford to marry, Mr Tarleton. Ive only a thousand a year until my father dies. Two people cant possibly live on that.

TARLETON.    Oh, cant they? When I married, I should have been jolly glad to have felt sure of the quarter of it.

PERCIVAL. No doubt; but I am not a cheap person, Mr Tarleton. I was brought up in a household which cost at least seven or eight times that; and I am in constant money difficulties because I simply dont know how to live on the thousand a year scale. As to ask a woman to share my degrading poverty, it's out of the question. Besides, I'm rather young to marry. I'm only 28.

HYPATIA. Papa: buy the brute for me.

LORD SUMMERHAYS [*shrinking*] My dear Miss Tarleton: dont be so naughty. I know how delightful it is to shock an old man; but there is a point at which it becomes barbarous. Dont. Please dont.

HYPATIA. Shall I tell Papa about you?

LORD SUMMERHAYS. Tarleton: I had better tell you that I once asked your daughter to become my widow.

TARLETON [*to Hypatia*] Why didnt you accept him, you young idiot?

LORD SUMMERHAYS. I was too old.

TARLETON. All this has been going on under my nose, I suppose. You run after young men; and old men run after you. And I'm the last person in the world to hear of it.

HYPATIA. How could I tell you?

LORD SUMMERHAYS. Parents and children, Tarleton.

TARLETON. Oh, the gulf that lies between them! the impassable, eternal gulf! And so I'm to buy the brute for you, eh?

HYPATIA. If you please, Papa.

TARLETON. Whats the price, Mr Percival?

PERCIVAL. We might do with another fifteen hundred if my father would contribute. But I should like more.

TARLETON. It's purely a question of money with you, is it?

PERCIVAL [*after a moment's consideration*] Practically yes: it turns on that.

TARLETON. I thought you might have some sort of preference for Patsy, you know.

PERCIVAL. Well, but does that matter, do you think? Patsy fascinates me, no doubt. I apparently fascinate Patsy. But, believe me, all that is not worth considering. One of my three fathers (the priest) has married hundreds of couples: couples selected by one another, couples selected by the parents, couples forced to marry one another by circumstances of one kind or another; and he assures me that if marriages were made by putting all the men's names into one sack and the women's names into another, and having them taken out by a blindfolded child like lottery numbers, there would be just as high a percentage of happy marriages as we have here in England. He said Cupid was nothing but the blindfolded child: pretty idea that, I think! I shall have as good a chance with Patsy as with anyone else. Mind: I'm not bigoted about it. I'm not a doctrinaire: not the slave of a theory. You and Lord Summerhays are experienced married men. If you can tell me of any trustworthy method of selecting a wife, I shall be happy to make use of it. I await your suggestions. [*He looks with polite attention to Lord Summerhays, who, having nothing to say, avoids his eye. He looks to Tarleton, who purses his lips glumly and rattles his money in his pockets without a word*]. Apparently neither of you has anything to suggest. Then Patsy will do as well as another, provided the money is forthcoming.

HYPATIA. Oh, you beauty! you beauty!

TARLETON. When I married Patsy's mother, I was in love with her.

PERCIVAL. For the first time?

TARLETON. Yes: for the first time.

PERCIVAL. For the last time?

LORD SUMMERHAYS [*revolted*] Sir: you are in the presence of his daughter.

HYPATIA.  Oh, dont mind me. I dont care. I'm accustomed to Papa's adventures.

TARLETON  [*blushing painfully*] Patsy, my child: that was not—not delicate.

HYPATIA.  Well, Papa, youve never shewn any delicacy in talking to me about my conduct; and I really dont see why I shouldnt talk to you about yours. It's such nonsense! Do you think young people dont know?

LORD SUMMERHAYS.  I'm sure they dont feel. Tarleton: this is too horrible, too brutal. If neither of these young people have any—any—any—

PERCIVAL.  Shall we say paternal sentimentality? I'm extremely sorry to shock you; but you must remember that Ive been educated to discuss human affairs with three fathers simultaneously. I'm an adult person. Patsy is an adult person. You do not inspire me with veneration. Apparently you do not inspire Patsy with veneration. That may surprise you. It may pain you. I'm sorry. It cant be helped. What about the money?

TARLETON.  You dont inspire me with generosity, young man.

HYPATIA  [*laughing with genuine amusement*] He had you there, Joey.

TARLETON.  I havnt been a bad father to you, Patsy.

HYPATIA.  I dont say you have, dear. If only I could persuade you Ive grown up, we should get along perfectly.

TARLETON.  Do you remember Bill Burt?

HYPATIA.  Why?

TARLETON  [*to the others*] Bill Burt was a laborer here. I was going to sack him for kicking his father. He said his father had kicked him until he was big enough to kick back. Patsy begged him off. I asked that man what it felt like the first time he kicked his father, and found that it was just like kicking any other man. He laughed and said that it was the old man that knew what it felt like. Think of that, Summerhays! think of that!

HYPATIA.  I havnt kicked you, Papa.

TARLETON.  Youve kicked me harder thán Bill Burt ever kicked.

LORD SUMMERHAYS.  It's no use, Tarleton. Spare yourself. Do you seriously expect these young people, at their age, to sympathize with what this gentleman calls your paternal sentimentality?

TARLETON  [*wistfully*] Is it nothing to you but paternal sentimentality, Patsy?

HYPATIA.  Well, I greatly prefer your superabundant vitality, papa.

TARLETON  [*violently*] Hold your tongue, you young devil. The young are all alike: hard, coarse, shallow, cruel, selfish, dirty-minded. You can clear out of my house as soon as you can coax him to take you; and the sooner the better. [*To Percival*] I think you said your price was fifteen hundred a year. Take it. And I wish you joy of your bargain.

PERCIVAL.  If you wish to know who I am—

TARLETON.  I dont care a tinker's curse who you are or what you are. Youre willing to take that girl off my hands for fifteen hundred a year: thats all that concerns me. Tell her who you are if you like: it's her affair, not mine.

HYPATIA.  Dont answer him, Joey: it wont last. Lord Summerhays, I'm sorry about Bentley; but Joey's the only man for me.

LORD SUMMERHAYS.  It may—

HYPATIA.  Please dont say it may break your poor boy's heart. It's much more likely to break yours.

LORD SUMMERHAYS.  Oh!

TARLETON  [*springing to his feet*] Leave the room. Do you hear: leave the room.

PERCIVAL.  Arnt we getting a little cross? Dont be angry, Mr Tarleton. Read Marcus Aurelius.

TARLETON. Dont you dare make fun of me. Take your aeroplane out of my vinery and yourself out of my house.

PERCIVAL [*rising, to Hypatia*] I'm afraid I shall have to dine at the Beacon, Patsy.

HYPATIA [*rising*] Do. I dine with you.

TARLETON. Did you hear me tell you to leave the room?

HYPATIA. I did. [*To Percival*] You see what living with one's parents means, Joey. It means living in a house where you can be ordered to leave the room. Ive got to obey: it's his house, not mine.

TARLETON. Who pays for it? Go and support yourself as I did if you want to be independent.

HYPATIA. I wanted to and you wouldnt let me. How can I support myself when I'm a prisoner?

TARLETON. Hold your tongue.

HYPATIA. Keep your temper.

PERCIVAL [*coming between them*] Lord Summerhays: youll join me, I'm sure, in pointing out to both father and daughter that they have now reached that very common stage in family life at which anything but a blow would be an anticlimax. Do you seriously want to beat Patsy, Mr Tarleton?

TARLETON. Yes. I want to thrash the life out of her. If she doesnt get out of my reach, I'll do it. [*He sits down and grasps the writing table to restrain himself*].

HYPATIA [*coolly going to him and leaning with her breast on his writhing shoulders*] Oh, if you want to beat me just to relieve your feelings—just really and truly for the fun of it and the satisfaction of it, beat away. I dont grudge you that.

TARLETON [*almost in hysterics*] I used to think that this sort of thing went on in other families but that it never could happen in ours. And now—[*He is broken with emotion, and continues lamentably*] I cant say the right thing. I cant do the right thing. I dont know what is the right thing. I'm beaten; and she knows it. Summerhays: tell me what to do.

LORD SUMMERHAYS. When my council in Jinghiskahn reached the point of coming to blows, I used to adjourn the sitting. Let us postpone the discussion. Wait until Monday: we shall have Sunday to quiet down in. Believe me, I'm not making fun of you; but I think theres something in this young gentleman's advice. Read something.

TARLETON.    I'll read King Lear.

HYPATIA.    Dont. I'm very sorry, dear.

TARLETON.    Youre not. Youre laughing at me. Serve me right! Parents and children! No man should know his own child. No child should know its own father. Let the family be rooted out of civilization! Let the human race be brought up in institutions!

HYPATIA.    Oh yes. How jolly! You and I might be friends then; and Joey could stay to dinner.

TARLETON.    Let him stay to dinner. Let him stay to breakfast. Let him spend his life here. Dont you say I drove him out. Dont you say I drove you out.

PERCIVAL.    I really have no right to inflict myself on you. Dropping in as I did—

TARLETON.    Out of the sky. Ha! Dropping in. The new sport of aviation. You just see a nice house; drop in; scoop up the man's daughter; and off with you again.

*Bentley comes back, with his shoulders hanging as if he too had been exercised to the last pitch of fatigue. He is very sad. They stare at him as he gropes to Percival's chair.*

BENTLEY.    I'm sorry for making a fool of myself. I beg your pardon. Hypatia: I'm awfully sorry; but Ive made up my mind that I'll never marry. [*He sits down in deep depression*].

HYPATIA    [*running to him*] How nice of you, Bentley! Of course you guessed I wanted to marry Joey. What did the Polish lady do to you?

BENTLEY    [*turning his head away*] I'd rather not speak of her, if you dont mind.

HYPATIA.    You've fallen in love with her. [*She laughs*].

BENTLEY.  It's beastly of you to laugh.

LORD SUMMERHAYS.  You are not the first to fall today under the lash of that young lady's terrible derision, Bentley.

*Lina, her cap on, and her goggles in her hand, comes impetuously through the inner door.*

LINA⸱ [*on the steps*] Mr Percival: can we get that aeroplane started again? [*She comes down and runs to the pavilion door*]. I must get out of this into the air: right up into the blue.

PERCIVAL.  Impossible. The frame's twisted. The petrol has given out: thats what brought us down. And how can we get a clear run to start with among these woods?

LINA  [*swooping back through the middle of the pavilion*] We can straighten the frame. We can buy petrol at the Beacon. With a few laborers we can get her out on to the Portsmouth Road and start her along that.

TARLETON  [*rising*] But why do you want to leave us, Miss Szcz?

LINA.  Old pal: this is a stuffy house. You seem to think of nothing but making love. All the conversation here is about love-making. All the pictures are about love-making. The eyes of all of you are sheep's eyes. You are steeped in it, soaked in it: the very texts on the walls of your bedrooms are the ones about love. It is disgusting. It is not healthy. Your women are kept idle and dressed up for no other purpose than to be made love to. I have not been here an hour; and already everybody makes love to me as if because I am a woman it were my profession to be made love to. First you, old pal. I forgave you because you were nice about your wife.

HYPATIA.  Oh! oh! oh! Oh, Papa!

LINA.  Then you, Lord Summerhays, come to me; and all you have to say is to ask me not to mention that you made love to me in Vienna two years ago. I forgave you because I thought you were an ambassador; and all ambassadors make love and are very nice and useful to people who travel. Then this young gentleman. He is engaged to this young lady; but no matter for that: he makes love to me because I carry him off in my arms when he cries. All these I bore in silence. But now comes your Johnny and tells me I'm a ripping fine woman, and asks me to marry him. I, Lina Szczepanowska, MARRY him !!!!! I do not mind this boy: he is a child: he loves me: I should have to give him money and take care of him: that would be foolish, but honorable. I do not mind you, old pal: you are what you call an old—ouf! but you do not offer to buy me: you say until we are tired—until you are so happy that you dare not ask for more. That is foolish too, at your age; but it is an adventure: it is not dishonorable. I do not mind Lord Summerhays: it was in Vienna: they had been toasting him at a great banquet: he was not sober. That is bad for the health; but it is not dishonorable. But your Johnny! Oh, your Johnny! with his marriage. He will do the straight thing by me. He will give me a home, a position. He tells me I must know that my present position is not one for a nice woman. This to me, Lina Szczepanowska! I am an honest woman: I earn my living. I am a free woman: I live in my own house. I am a woman of the world: I have thousands of friends: every night crowds of people applaud me, delight in me, buy my picture, pay hard-earned money to see me. I am strong: I am skilful: I am brave: I am independent: I am unbought: I am all that a woman ought to be; and in my family there has not been a single drunkard for four generations. And this Englishman! this linendraper! he dares to ask me to come and live with him in this rrrrrrabbit hutch, and take my bread from his hand, and ask him for pocket money, and wear soft clothes, and be his woman! his wife! Sooner than that, I would stoop to the lowest depths of my profession. I would stuff lions with food and pretend to tame them. I would deceive honest people's eyes with conjuring tricks instead of real feats of strength and skill. I would be a clown and set bad examples of conduct to little children. I would sink yet lower and be an actress or an opera singer, imperilling my soul by the wicked lie of pretending to be somebody else. All this I would do sooner than take my bread from the hand of a man and make him the master of my body and soul. And so you may tell your Johnny to buy an Englishwoman: he shall not buy Lina Szczepanowska; and I will not stay in the house where such dishonor is offered me. Adieu. [*She turns precipitately to go, but is faced in the pavilion doorway by Johnny, who comes in slowly, his hands in his pockets, meditating deeply*].

JOHNNY [*confidentially to Lina*] You wont mention our little conversation, Miss Shepanoska. It'll do no good; and I'd rather you didnt.

TARLETON. Weve just heard about it, Johnny.

JOHNNY [*shortly, but without ill-temper*] Oh: is that so?

HYPATIA. The cat's out of the bag, Johnny, about everybody. They were all beforehand with you: Papa, Lord Summerhays, Bentley and all. Dont you let them laugh at you.

JOHNNY [*a grin slowly overspreading his countenance*] Well, theres no use my pretending to be surprised at you, Governor, is there? I hope you got it as hot as I did. Mind, Miss Shepanoska: it wasnt lost on me. I'm a thinking man. I kept my temper. Youll admit that.

LINA [*frankly*] Oh yes. I do not quarrel. You are what is called a chump; but you are not a bad sort of chump.

JOHNNY. Thank you. Well, if a chump may have an opinion, I should put it at this. You make, I suppose, ten pounds a night off your own bat, Miss Lina?

LINA [*scornfully*] Ten pounds a night! I have made ten pounds a minute.

JOHNNY [*with increased respect*] Have you indeed? I didn't know: youll excuse my mistake, I hope. But the principle is the same. Now I trust you wont be offended at what I'm going to say; but Ive thought about this and watched it in daily experience; and you may take it from me that the moment a woman becomes pecuniarily independent, she gets hold of the wrong end of the stick in moral questions.

LINA.  Indeed! And what do you conclude from that, Mister Johnny?

JOHNNY.  Well, obviously, that independence for women is wrong and shouldnt be allowed. For their own good, you know. And for the good of morality in general. You agree with me, Lord Summerhays, dont you?

LORD SUMMERHAYS.  It's a very moral moral, if I may so express myself.

*Mrs Tarleton comes in softly through the inner door.*

MRS TARLETON.  Dont make too much noise. The lad's asleep.

TARLETON.  Chickabiddy: we have some news for you.

JOHNNY [*apprehensively*] Now theres no need, you know, Governor, to worry mother with everything that passes.

MRS TARLETON  [*coming to Tarleton*] Whats been going on? Dont you hold anything back from me, John. What have you been doing?

TARLETON.  Patsy isnt going to marry Bentley.

MRS TARLETON.  Of course not. Is that your great news? I never believed she'd marry him.

TARLETON.  Theres something else. Mr Percival here—

MRS TARLETON  [*to Percival*] Are you going to marry Patsy?

PERCIVAL  [*diplomatically*] Patsy is going to marry me, with your permission.

MRS TARLETON.  Oh, she has my permission: she ought to have been married long ago.

HYPATIA.  Mother!

TARLETON.  Miss Lina here, though she has been so short a time with us, has inspired a good deal of attachment in—I may say in almost all of us. Therefore I hope she'll stay to dinner, and not insist on flying away in that aeroplane.

PERCIVAL. You must stay, Miss Szczepanowska. I cant go up again this evening.

LINA. Ive seen you work it. Do you think I require any help? And Bentley shall come with me as a passenger.

BENTLEY [terrified] Go up in an aeroplane! I darent.

LINA. You must learn to dare.

BENTLEY [pale but heroic] All right. I'll come.

LORD SUMMERHAYS    No, no, Bentley, im-
                   possible. I shall not
MRS TARLETON.      allow it.
                   Do you want to kill the
                   child? He shant go.

BENTLEY. I will. I'll lie down and yell until you let me go. I'm not a coward. I wont be a coward.

LORD SUMMERHAYS. Miss Szczepanowska; my son is very dear to me. I implore you to wait until tomorrow morning.

LINA. There may be a storm tomorrow. And I'll go: storm or no storm. I must risk my life tomorrow.

BENTLEY. I hope there will be a storm.

LINA [grasping his arm] You are trembling.

BENTLEY. Yes: it's terror, sheer terror. I can hardly see. I can hardly stand. But I'll go with you.

LINA [slapping him on the back and knocking a ghastly white smile into his face] You shall. I like you, my boy. We go tomorrow, together.

BENTLEY. Yes: together: tomorrow.

TARLETON. Well, sufficient unto the day is the evil thereof. Read the old book.

MRS TARLETON. Is there anything else?

TARLETON. Well, I—er [he addresses Lina, and stops]. I—er [he addresses Lord Summerhays, and stops]. I—er [he gives it up]. Well, I suppose—er—I suppose theres nothing more to be said.

HYPATIA [fervently] Thank goodness!

# Heartbreak House

## A Fantasia in the Russian Manner on English Themes
### (1919)

# PREFACE
## Heartbreak House and Horseback Hall

### WHERE HEARTBREAK HOUSE STANDS

Heartbreak House is not merely the name of the play which follows this preface. It is cultured, leisured Europe before the war. When the play was begun not a shot had been fired; and only the professional diplomatists and the very few amateurs whose hobby is foreign policy even knew that the guns were loaded. A Russian playwright, Tchekov, had produced four fascinating dramatic studies of Heartbreak House, of which three, The Cherry Orchard, Uncle Vanya, and The Seagull, had been performed in England. Tolstoy, in his Fruits of Enlightenment, had shewn us through it in his most ferociously contemptuous manner. Tolstoy did not waste any sympathy on it: it was to him the house in which Europe was stifling its soul; and he knew that our utter enervation and futilization in that overheated drawing-room atmosphere was delivering the world over to the control of ignorant and soulless cunning and energy, with the frightful consequences which have now overtaken it. Tolstoy was no pessimist: he was not disposed to leave the house standing if he could bring it down about the ears of its pretty and amiable voluptuaries; and he wielded the pickaxe with a will. He treated the case of the inmates as one of opium poisoning, to be dealt with by seizing the patients roughly and exercising them violently until they were broad awake. Tchekov, more of a fatalist, had no faith in these charming people extricating themselves. They would, he thought, be sold up and sent adrift by the bailiffs; therefore he had no scruple in exploiting and even flattering their charm.

## THE INHABITANTS

Tchekov's plays, being less lucrative than swings and round-abouts, got no further in England, where theatres are only ordinary commercial affairs, than a couple of performances by the Stage Society. We stared and said, "How Russian!" They did not strike me in that way. Just as Ibsen's intensely Norwegian plays exactly fitted every middle and professional class suburb in Europe, these intensely Russian plays fitted all the country houses in Europe in which the pleasures of music, art, literature, and the theatre had supplanted hunt-ing, shooting, fishing, flirting, eating, and drinking. The same nice people, the same utter futility. The nice people could read; some of them could write; and they were the only repositories of culture who had social opportunities of contact with our politicians, administrators, and newspaper proprietors, or any chance of sharing or influencing their activities. But they shrank from that contact. They hated pol-itics. They did not wish to realize Utopia for the common people: they wished to realize their favorite fictions and poems in their own lives; and, when they could, they lived without scruple on incomes which they did nothing to earn. The women in their girlhood made themselves look like va-riety theatre stars, and settled down later into the types of beauty imagined by the previous generation of painters. They took the only part of our society in which there was leisure for high culture, and made it an economic, political, and, as far as practicable, a moral vacuum; and as Nature, abhorring the vacuum, immediately filled it up with sex and with all sorts of refined pleasures, it was a very delightful place at its best for moments of relaxation. In other moments it was disastrous. For prime ministers and their like, it was a veritable Capua.

### HORSEBACK HALL

But where were our front benchers to nest if not here? The alternative to Heartbreak House was Horseback Hall, consisting of a prison for horses with an annex for the ladies and gentlemen who rode them, hunted them, talked about them, bought them and sold them, and gave nine-tenths of their lives to them, dividing the other tenth between charity, churchgoing (as a substitute for religion), and conservative electioneering (as a substitute for politics). It is true that the two establishments got mixed at the edges. Exiles from the library, the music room, and the picture gallery would be found languishing among the stables, miserably discontented; and hardy horsewomen who slept at the first chord of Schumann were born, horribly misplaced, into the garden of Klingsor; but sometimes one came upon horsebreakers and heartbreakers who could make the best of both worlds. As a rule, however, the two were apart and knew little of one another; so the prime minister folk had to choose between barbarism and Capua. And of the two atmospheres it is hard to say which was the more fatal to statesmanship.

## REVOLUTION ON THE SHELF

Heartbreak House was quite familiar with revolutionary ideas on paper. It aimed at being advanced and free-thinking, and hardly ever went to church or kept the Sabbath except by a little extra fun at week-ends. When you spent a Friday to Tuesday in it you found on the shelf in your bed-room not only the books of poets and novelists, but of rev-olutionary biologists and even economists. Without at least a few plays by myself and Mr Granville Barker, and a few stories by Mr H. G. Wells, Mr Arnold Bennett, and Mr John Galsworthy, the house would have been out of the move-ment. You would find Blake among the poets, and beside him Bergson, Butler, Scott Haldane, the poems of Meredith and Thomas Hardy, and, generally speaking, all the literary implements for forming the mind of the perfect modern So-cialist and Creative Evolutionist. It was a curious experience to spend Sunday in dipping into these books, and on Mon-day morning to read in the daily paper that the country had just been brought to the verge of anarchy because a new Home Secretary or chief of police, without an idea in his head that his great-grandmother might not have had to apol-ogize for, had refused to "recognize" some powerful Trade Union, just as a gondola might refuse to recognize a 20,000-ton liner.

In short, power and culture were in separate compart-ments. The barbarians were not only literally in the saddle, but on the front bench in the House of Commons, with nobody to correct their incredible ignorance of modern thought and political science but upstarts from the count-inghouse, who had spent their lives furnishing their pockets instead of their minds. Both, however, were practised in dealing with money and with men, as far as acquiring the one and exploiting the other went; and although this is as undesirable an expertness as that of the medieval robber baron, it qualifies men to keep an estate or a business going in its old routine without necessarily understanding it, just as Bond Street tradesmen and domestic servants keep fashionable society going without any instruction in sociology.

## THE CHERRY ORCHARD

The Heartbreak people neither could nor would do anything of the sort. With their heads as full of the Anticipations of Mr H. G. Wells as the heads of our actual rulers were empty even of the anticipations of Erasmus or Sir Thomas More, they refused the drudgery of politics, and would have made a very poor job of it if they had changed their minds. Not that they would have been allowed to meddle anyhow, as only through the accident of being a hereditary peer can anyone in these days of Votes for Everybody get into parliament if handicapped by a serious modern cultural equipment; but if they had, their habit of living in a vacuum would have left them helpless and ineffective in public affairs. Even in private life they were often helpless wasters of their inheritance, like the people in Tchekov's Cherry Orchard. Even those who lived within their incomes were really kept going by their solicitors and agents, being unable to manage an estate or run a business without continual prompting from those who have to learn how to do such things or starve.

From what is called Democracy no corrective to this state of things could be hoped. It is said that every people has the Government it deserves. It is more to the point that every Government has the electorate it deserves; for the orators of the front bench can edify or debauch an ignorant electorate at will. Thus our democracy moves in a vicious circle of reciprocal worthiness and unworthiness.

## THE PRACTICAL BUSINESS MEN

From the beginning the useless people set up a shriek for "practical business men." By this they meant men who had become rich by placing their personal interests before those of the country, and measuring the success of every activity by the pecuniary profit it brought to them and to those on whom they depended for their supplies of capital. The pitiable failure of some conspicuous samples from the first batch we tried of these poor devils helped to give the whole public side of the war an air of monstrous and hopeless farce. They proved not only that they were useless for public work, but that in a well-ordered nation they would never have been allowed to control private enterprise.

## HOW THE FOOLS SHOUTED
## THE WISE MEN DOWN

Thus, like a fertile country flooded with mud, England shewed no sign of her greatness in the days when she was putting forth all her strength to save herself from the worst consequences of her littleness. Most of the men of action, occupied to the last hour of their time with urgent practical work, had to leave to idler people, or to professional rhetoricians, the presentation of the war to the reason and imagination of the country and the world in speeches, poems, manifestoes, picture posters, and newspaper articles. I have had the privilege of hearing some of our ablest commanders talking about their work; and I have shared the common lot of reading the accounts of that work given to the world by the newspapers. No two experiences could be more different. But in the end the talkers obtained a dangerous ascendancy over the rank and file of the men of action; for though the great men of action are always inveterate talkers and often very clever writers, and therefore cannot have their minds formed for them by others, the average man of action, like the average fighter with the bayonet, can give no account of himself in words even to himself, and is apt to pick up and accept what he reads about himself and other people in the papers, except when the writer is rash enough to commit himself on technical points. It was not uncommon during the war to hear a soldier, or a civilian engaged on war work, describing events within his own experience that reduced to utter absurdity the ravings and maunderings of his daily paper, and yet echo the opinions of that paper like a parrot. Thus, to escape from the prevailing confusion and folly, it was not enough to seek the company of the ordinary man of action: one had to get into contact with the master spirits. This was a privilege which only a handful of people could enjoy. For the unprivileged citizen there was no escape. To him the whole country seemed mad, futile, silly, incompetent, with no hope of victory except the hope that the enemy might be just as mad. Only by very resolute reflection and reasoning could he reassure himself that if there was nothing more solid beneath these appalling appearances the war could not possibly have gone on for a single day without a total breakdown of its organization.

## THE EPHEMERAL THRONES AND
## THE ETERNAL THEATRE

To the theatre it will not matter. Whatever Bastilles fall, the theatre will stand. Apostolic Hapsburg has collapsed; All Highest Hohenzollern languishes in Holland, threatened with trial on a capital charge of fighting for his country against England; Imperial Romanoff, said to have perished miserably by a more summary method of murder, is perhaps alive or perhaps dead: nobody cares more than if he had been a peasant; the lord of Hellas is level with his lackeys in republican Switzerland; Prime Ministers and Commanders-in-Chief have passed from a brief glory as Solons and Caesars into failure and obscurity as closely on one another's heels as the descendants of Banquo; but Euripides and Aristophanes, Shakespear and Molière, Goethe and Ibsen remain fixed in their everlasting seats.

## HOW WAR MUZZLES THE
## DRAMATIC POET

As for myself, why, it may be asked, did I not write two plays about the war instead of two pamphlets on it? The answer is significant. You cannot make war on war and on your neighbor at the same time. War cannot bear the terrible castigation of comedy, the ruthless light of laughter that glares on the stage. When men are heroically dying for their country, it is not the time to shew their lovers and wives and fathers and mothers how they are being sacrificed to the blunders of boobies, the cupidity of capitalists, the ambition of conquerors, the electioneering of demagogues, the Pharisaism of patriots, the lusts and lies and rancors and blood-thirsts that love war because it opens their prison doors, and sets them in the thrones of power and popularity. For unless these things are mercilessly exposed they will hide under the mantle of the ideals on the stage just as they do in real life.

And though there may be better things to reveal, it may not, and indeed cannot, be militarily expedient to reveal them whilst the issue is still in the balance. Truth telling is not compatible with the defense of the realm. We are just now reading the revelations of our generals and admirals, unmuzzled at last by the armistice. During the war, General A, in his moving despatches from the field, told how General B had covered himself with deathless glory in such and such a battle. He now tells us that General B came within an ace of losing us the war by disobeying his orders on that occasion, and fighting instead of running away as he ought to have done. An excellent subject for comedy now that the war is over, no doubt; but if General A had let this out at the time, what would have been the effect on General B's soldiers? And had the stage made known what the Prime Minister and the Secretary of State for War who overruled General A thought of him, and what he thought of them, as now revealed in raging controversy, what would have been the effect on the nation? That is why comedy, though sorely tempted, had to be loyally silent; for the art of the dramatic poet knows no patriotism; recognizes no obligation but truth to natural history; cares not whether Germany or England perish; is ready to cry with Brynhild, "Lass' uns verderben, lachend zu grunde geh'n" sooner than deceive or be deceived; and thus becomes in time of war a greater military danger than poison, steel, or trinitrotoluene. That is why I had to withhold Heartbreak House from the footlights during the war; for the Germans might on any night have turned the last act from play into earnest, and even then might not have waited for their cues.

*June* 1919.

# HEARTBREAK HOUSE

## Act I

The hilly country in the middle of the north edge of Sussex, looking very pleasant on a fine evening at the end of September, is seen through the windows of a room which has been built so as to resemble the after part of an old-fashioned high-pooped ship with a stern gallery; for the windows are ship built with heavy timbering, and run right across the room as continuously as the stability of the wall allows. A row of lockers under the windows provides an unupholstered window-seat interrupted by twin glass doors, respectively halfway between the stern post and the sides. Another door strains the illusion a little by being apparently in the ship's port side, and yet leading, not to the open sea, but to the entrance hall of the house. Between this door and the stern gallery are bookshelves. There are electric light switches beside the door leading to the hall and the glass doors in the stern gallery. Against the starboard wall is a carpenter's bench. The vice has a board in its jaws; and the floor is littered with shavings, overflowing from a waste-paper basket. A couple of planes and a centrebit are on the bench. In the same wall, between the bench and the windows, is a narrow doorway with a half door, above which a glimpse of the room beyond shews that it is a shelved pantry with bottles and kitchen crockery.

On the starboard side, but close to the middle, is a plain oak drawing-table with drawing-board, T-square, straightedges, set squares, mathematical instruments, saucers of water color, a tumbler of discolored water, Indian ink, pencils, and brushes on it. The drawing-board is set so that the draughtsman's chair has the window on its left hand. On the floor at the end of the table, on his right, is a ship's fire bucket. On the port side of the room, near the bookshelves, is a sofa with its back to the windows. It is a sturdy mahogany article, oddly upholstered in sailcloth, including the bolster, with a couple of blankets hanging over the back. Between the sofa and the drawing-table is a big wicker chair, with broad arms and a low sloping back, with its back to the light. A small but stout table of teak, with a round top and gate legs, stands against the port wall between the door and the bookcase. It is the only article in the room that suggests (not at all convincingly) a woman's hand in the furnishing. The uncarpeted floor of narrow boards is caulked and holystoned like a deck.

The garden to which the glass doors lead dips to the south before the landscape rises again to the hills. Emerging from the hollow is the cupola of an observatory. Between the observatory and the house is a flagstaff on a little esplanade, with a hammock on the east side and a long garden seat on the west.

A young lady, gloved and hatted, with a dust coat on, is sitting in the window-seat with her body twisted to enable her to look out at the view. One hand props her chin: the other hangs down with a volume of the Temple Shakespear in it, and her finger stuck in the page she has been reading.

A clock strikes six.

The young lady turns and looks at her watch. She rises with an air of one who waits and is almost at the end of her patience. She is a pretty girl, slender, fair, and intelligent looking, nicely but not expensively dressed, evidently not a smart idler.

With a sigh of weary resignation she comes to the draughtsman's chair; sits down; and begins to read Shakespear. Presently the book sinks to her lap; her eyes close; and she dozes into a slumber.

*An elderly womanservant comes in from the hall with three unopened bottles of rum on a tray. She passes through and disappears in the pantry without noticing the young lady. She places the bottles on the shelf and fills her tray with empty bottles. As she returns with these, the young lady lets her book drop, awakening herself, and startling the womanservant so that she all but lets the tray fall.*

THE WOMANSERVANT. God bless us! [*The young lady picks up the book and places it on the table*]. Sorry to wake you, miss, I'm sure; but you are a stranger to me. What might you be waiting here for now?

THE YOUNG LADY. Waiting for somebody to shew some signs of knowing that I have been invited here.

THE WOMANSERVANT. Oh, youre invited, are you? And has nobody come? Dear! dear!

THE YOUNG LADY. A wild-looking old gentleman came and looked in at the window; and I heard him calling out "Nurse: there is a young attractive female waiting in the poop. Go and see what she wants." Are you the nurse?

THE WOMANSERVANT. Yes, miss: I'm Nurse Guinness. That was old Captain Shotover, Mrs Hushabye's father. I heard him roaring; but I thought it was for something else. I suppose it was Mrs Hushabye that invited you, ducky?

THE YOUNG LADY. I understood her to do so. But really I think I'd better go.

NURSE GUINNESS. Oh, dont think of such a thing, miss. If Mrs Hushabye has forgotten all about it, it will be a pleasant surprise for her to see you, wont it?

THE YOUNG LADY. It has been a very unpleasant surprise to me to find that nobody expects me.

NURSE GUINNESS. Youll get used to it, miss: this house is full of surprises for them that dont know our ways.

CAPTAIN SHOTOVER [*looking in from the hall suddenly: an ancient but still hardy man with an immense white beard, in a reefer jacket with a whistle hanging from his neck*] Nurse: there is a hold-all and a handbag on the front steps for everybody to fall over. Also a tennis racquet. Who the devil left them there?

THE YOUNG LADY. They are mine, I'm afraid.

THE CAPTAIN [*advancing to the drawing-table*] Nurse: who is this misguided and unfortunate young lady?

NURSE GUINNESS. She says Miss Hessy invited her, sir.

THE CAPTAIN. And had she no friend, no parents, to warn her against my daughter's invitations? This is a pretty sort of house, by heavens! A young and attractive lady is invited here. Her luggage is left on the steps for hours; and she herself is deposited in the poop and abandoned, tired and starving. This is our hospitality. These are our manners. No room ready. No hot water. No welcoming hostess. Our visitor is to sleep in the toolshed, and to wash in the duck-pond.

NURSE GUINNESS. Now it's all right, Captain: I'll get the lady some tea; and her room shall be ready before she has finished it. [*To the young lady*] Take off your hat, ducky; and make yourself at home. [*She goes to the door leading to the hall*].

THE CAPTAIN [*as she passes him*] Ducky! Do you suppose, woman, that because this young lady has been insulted and neglected, you have the right to address her as you address my wretched children, whom you have brought up in ignorance of the commonest decencies of social intercourse?

NURSE GUINNESS. Never mind him, doty. [*Quite unconcerned, she goes out into the hall on her way to the kitchen*].

THE CAPTAIN. Madam: will you favor me with your name? [*He sits down in the big wicker chair*].

THE YOUNG LADY. My name is Ellie Dunn.

THE CAPTAIN. Dunn! I had a boatswain whose name was Dunn. He was originally a pirate in China. He set up as a ship's chandler with stores which I have every reason to believe he stole from me. No doubt he became rich. Are you his daughter?

ELLIE [*indignant*] No: certainly not. I am proud to be able to say that though my father has not been a successful man, nobody has ever had one word to say against him. I think my father is the best man I have ever known.

THE CAPTAIN. He must be greatly changed. Has he attained the seventh degree of concentration?

ELLIE. I dont understand.

THE CAPTAIN. But how could he, with a daughter? I, madam, have two daughters. One of them is Hesione Hushabye, who invited you here. I keep this house: she upsets it. I desire to attain the seventh degree of concentration: she invites visitors and leaves me to entertain them. [*Nurse Guinness returns with the tea-tray, which she places on the teak table*]. I have a second daughter who is, thank God, in a remote part of the Empire with her numskull of a husband. As a child she thought the figure-head of my ship, the Dauntless, the most beautiful thing on earth. He resembled it. He had the same expression: wooden yet enterprising. She married him, and will never set foot in this house again.

NURSE GUINNESS [*carrying the table, with the tea-things on it, to Ellie's side*] Indeed you never were more mistaken. She is in England this very moment. You have been told three times this week that she is coming home for a year for her health. And very glad you should be to see your own daughter again after all these years.

THE CAPTAIN. I am not glad. The natural term of the affection of the human animal for its offspring is six years. My daughter Ariadne was born when I was forty-six. I am now eighty-eight. If she comes, I am not at home. If she wants anything, let her take it. If she asks for me, let her be informed that I am extremely old, and have totally forgotten her.

NURSE GUINNESS. Thats no talk to offer to a young lady.

Here, ducky, have some tea; and dont listen to him. [*She pours out a cup of tea*].

THE CAPTAIN [*rising wrathfully*] Now before high heaven they have given this innocent child Indian tea: the stuff they tan their own leather insides with. [*He seizes the cup and the tea-pot and empties both into the leathern bucket*].

ELLIE [*almost in tears*] Oh, please! I am so tired. I should have been glad of anything.

NURSE GUINNESS. Oh, what a thing to do! The poor lamb is ready to drop.

THE CAPTAIN. You shall have some of my tea. Do not touch that fly-blown cake: nobody eats it here except the dogs. [*He disappears into the pantry*].

NURSE GUINNESS. Theres a man for you! They say he sold himself to the devil in Zanzibar before he was a captain; and the older he grows the more I believe them.

A WOMAN'S VOICE [*in the hall*] Is anyone at home? Hesione! Nurse! Papa! Do come, somebody; and take in my luggage.

*Thumping heard, as of an umbrella, on the wainscot.*

NURSE GUINNESS. My gracious! It's Miss Addy, Lady Utterword, Mrs Hushabye's sister: the one I told the Captain about. [*Calling*] Coming, Miss, coming.

*She carries the table back to its place by the door, and is hurrying out when she is intercepted by Lady Utterword, who bursts in much flustered. Lady Utterword, a blonde, is very handsome, very well dressed, and so precipitate in speech and action that the first impression (erroneous) is one of comic silliness.*

LADY UTTERWORD. Oh, is that you, Nurse? How are you? You dont look a day older. Is nobody at home? Where is Hesione? Doesnt she expect me? Where are the servants? Whose luggage is that on the steps? Where's Papa? Is everybody asleep? [*Seeing Ellie*] Oh! I beg your pardon. I suppose you are one of my nieces. [*Approaching her with outstretched arms*] Come and kiss your aunt, darling.

ELLIE.  I'm only a visitor. It is my luggage on the steps.

NURSE GUINNESS.  I'll go get you some fresh tea, ducky. [*She takes up the tray*].

ELLIE.  But the old gentleman said he would make some himself.

NURSE GUINNESS.  Bless you! he's forgotten what he went for already. His mind wanders from one thing to another.

LADY UTTERWORD.  Papa, I suppose?

NURSE GUINNESS.  Yes, Miss.

LADY UTTERWORD  [*vehemently*]  Dont be silly, Nurse. Dont call me Miss.

NURSE GUINNESS  [*placidly*]  No, lovey. [*She goes out with the tea-tray*].

LADY UTTERWORD  [*sitting down with a flounce on the sofa*]  I know what you must feel. Oh, this house, this house! I come back to it after twenty-three years; and it is just the same: the luggage lying on the steps, the servants spoilt and impossible, nobody at home to receive anybody, no regular meals, nobody ever hungry because they are always gnawing bread and butter or munching apples, and, what is worse, the same disorder in ideas, in talk, in feeling. When I was a child I was used to it: I had never known anything better, though I was unhappy, and longed all the time—oh, how I longed!—to be respectable, to be a lady, to live as others did, not to have to think of everything for myself. I married at nineteen to escape from it. My husband is Sir Hastings Utterword, who has been governor of all the crown colonies in succession. I have always been the mistress of Government House. I have been so happy: I had forgotten that people could live like this. I wanted to see my father, my sister, my nephews and nieces (one ought to, you know), and I was looking forward to it. And now the state of the house! the way I'm received! the casual impudence of that woman Guinness, our old nurse! really Hesione might at least have been here: some preparation might have been made for me. You must excuse my going on in this way; but I am really very much hurt and annoyed and disillusioned: and if I had realized it was to be like this, I wouldnt have come. I have a great mind to go away without another word. [*She is on the point of weeping*].

ELLIE [*also very miserable*] Nobody has been here to receive me either. I thought I ought to go away too. But how can I, Lady Utterword? My luggage is on the steps; and the station fly has gone.

*The Captain emerges from the pantry with a tray of Chinese lacquer and a very fine tea-set on it. He rests it provisionally on the end of the table; snatches away the drawing-board, which he stands on the floor against the table legs; and puts the tray in the space thus cleared. Ellie pours out a cup greedily.*

THE CAPTAIN. Your tea, young lady. What! another lady! I must fetch another cup. [*He makes for the pantry*].

LADY UTTERWORD [*rising from the sofa, suffused with emotion*] Papa! Dont you know me? I'm your daughter.

THE CAPTAIN. Nonsense! my daughter's upstairs asleep. [*He vanishes through the half door*].

*Lady Utterword retires to the window to conceal her tears.*

ELLIE [*going to her with the cup*] Dont be so distressed. Have this cup of tea. He is very old and very strange: he has been just like that to me. I know how dreadful it must be: my own father is all the world to me. Oh, I'm sure he didnt mean it.

*The Captain returns with another cup.*

THE CAPTAIN. Now we are complete. [*He places it on the tray*].

LADY UTTERWORD [*hysterically*] Papa: you cant have forgotten me. I am Ariadne. I'm little Paddy Patkins. Wont you kiss me? [*She goes to him and throws her arms round his neck*].

THE CAPTAIN [*woodenly enduring her embrace*] How can

you be Ariadne? You are a middle-aged woman: well-preserved, madam, but no longer young.

LADY UTTERWORD.   But think of all the years and years I have been away, Papa. I have had to grow old, like other people.

THE CAPTAIN   [*disengaging himself*] You should grow out of kissing strange men: they may be striving to attain the seventh degree of concentration.

LADY UTTERWORD.   But I'm your daughter. You havnt seen me for years.

THE CAPTAIN.   So much the worse! When our relatives are at home, we have to think of all their good points or it would be impossible to endure them. But when they are away, we console ourselves for their absence by dwelling on their vices. That is how I have come to think my absent daughter Ariadne a perfect fiend; so do not try to ingratiate yourself here by impersonating her. [*He walks firmly away to the other side of the room*].

LADY UTTERWORD.   Ingratiating myself indeed! [*With dignity*] Very well, Papa. [*She sits down at the drawing-table and pours out tea for herself*].

THE CAPTAIN.   I am neglecting my social duties. You remember Dunn? Billy Dunn?

LADY UTTERWORD.   Do you mean that villainous sailor who robbed you?

THE CAPTAIN   [*introducing Ellie*] His daughter. [*He sits down on the sofa*].

ELLIE   [*protesting*] No—
*Nurse Guinness returns with fresh tea.*

THE CAPTAIN.   Take that hogwash away. Do you hear?

NURSE.   Youve actually remembered about the tea! [*To Ellie*] O, miss, he didnt forget you after all! You have made an impression.

THE CAPTAIN   [*gloomily*] Youth! beauty! novelty! They

are badly wanted in this house. I am excessively old. Hesione
is only moderately young. Her children are not youthful.

LADY UTTERWORD.   How can children be expected to be
youthful in this house? Almost before we could speak we
were filled with notions that might have been all very well
for pagan philosophers of fifty, but were certainly quite unfit
for respectable people of any age.

NURSE.   You were always for respectability, Miss Addy.

LADY UTTERWORD.   Nurse: will you please remember
that I am Lady Utterword, and not Miss Addy, nor lovey,
nor darling, nor doty? Do you hear?

NURSE.   Yes, ducky: all right. I'll tell them all they must
call you my lady. [*She takes her tray out with undisturbed
placidity*].

LADY UTTERWORD.   What comfort? what sense is there
in having servants with no manners?

ELLIE   [*rising and coming to the table to put down her empty
cup*] Lady Utterword: do you think Mrs Hushabye really expects me?

LADY UTTERWORD.   Oh, dont ask me. You can see for
yourself that Ive just arrived; her only sister, after twenty-
three years absence! and it seems that *I* am not expected.

THE CAPTAIN.   What does it matter whether the young
lady is expected or not? She is welcome. There are beds:
there is food. I'll find a room for her myself. [*He makes for
the door*].

ELLIE   [*following him to stop him*] Oh please—[*He goes
out*]. Lady Utterword: I dont know what to do. Your father
persists in believing that my father is some sailor who robbed
him.

LADY UTTERWORD.   You had better pretend not to notice
it. My father is a very clever man; but he always forgot things;
and now that he is old, of course he is worse. And I must
warn you that it is sometimes very hard to feel quite sure
that he really forgets.

*Mrs Hushabye bursts into the room tempestuously, and embraces Ellie. She is a couple of years older than Lady Utterword, and even better looking. She has magnificent black hair, eyes like the fishpools of Heshbon, and a nobly modelled neck, short at the back and low between her shoulders in front. Unlike her sister she is uncorseted and dressed anyhow in a rich robe of black pile that shews off her white skin and statuesque contour.*

MRS HUSHABYE. Ellie, my darling, my pettikins [*kissing her*]: how long have you been here? I've been at home all the time: I was putting flowers and things in your room; and when I just sat down for a moment to try how comfortable the armchair was I went off to sleep. Papa woke me and told me you were here. Fancy your finding no one, and being neglected and abandoned. [*Kissing her again*] My poor love! [*She deposits Ellie on the sofa. Meanwhile Ariadne has left the table and come over to claim her share of attention*]. Oh! youve brought someone with you. Introduce me.

LADY UTTERWORD. Hesione: is it possible that you dont know me?

MRS HUSHABYE [*conventionally*] Of course I remember your face quite well. Where have we met?

LADY UTTERWORD. Didnt Papa tell you I was here? Oh! this is really too much. [*She throws herself sulkily into the big chair*].

MRS HUSHABYE. Papa!

LADY UTTERWORD. Yes: Papa. O u r Papa, you unfeeling wretch. [*Rising angrily*] I'll go straight to a hotel.

MRS HUSHABYE [*seizing her by the shoulders*] My goodness gracious goodness, you dont mean to say that youre Addy!

LADY UTTERWORD. I certainly am Addy; and I dont think I can be so changed that you would not have recognized me if you had any real affection for me. And Papa didnt think me even worth mentioning!

MRS HUSHABYE. What a lark! Sit down. [*She pushes her*

*back into the chair instead of kissing her, and posts herself behind it*]. You d o look a swell. Youre much handsomer than you used to be. Youve made the acquaintance of Ellie, of course. She is going to marry a perfect hog of a millionaire for the sake of her father, who is as poor as a church mouse; and you must help me to stop her.

ELLIE. Oh p l e a s e, Hesione.

MRS HUSHABYE. My pettikins, the man's coming here today with your father to begin persecuting you; and everybody will see the state of the case in ten minutes; so whats the use of making a secret of it?

ELLIE. He is not a hog, Hesione. You dont know how wonderfully good he was to my father, and how deeply grateful I am to him.

MRS HUSHABYE [*to Lady Utterword*] Her father is a very remarkable man, Addy. His name is Mazzini Dunn. Mazzini was a celebrity of some kind who knew Ellie's grandparents. They were both poets, like the Brownings; and when her father came into the world Mazzini said "Another soldier born for freedom!" So they christened him Mazzini; and he has been fighting for freedom in his quiet way ever since. Thats why he is so poor.

ELLIE. I am proud of his poverty.

MRS HUSHABYE. Of course you are, pettikins. Why not leave him in it, and marry someone you love?

LADY UTTERWORD [*rising suddenly and explosively*] Hesione: are you going to kiss me or are you not?

MRS HUSHABYE. What do you want to be kissed for?

LADY UTTERWORD. I d o n t want to be kissed; but I do want you to behave properly and decently. We are sisters. We have been separated for twenty-three years. You o u g h t to kiss me.

MRS HUSHABYE. Tomorrow morning, dear, before you make up. I hate the smell of powder.

LADY UTTERWORD. Oh! you unfeeling—[*She is interrupted by the return of the captain*].

THE CAPTAIN [*to Ellie*] Your room is ready. [*Ellie rises*]. The sheets were damp; but I have changed them. [*He makes for the garden door on the port side*].

LADY UTTERWORD. Oh! What about m y sheets?

THE CAPTAIN [*halting at the door*] Take my advice: air them; or take them off and sleep in blankets. You shall sleep in Ariadne's old room.

LADY UTTERWORD. Indeed I shall do nothing of the sort. That little hole! I am entitled to the best spare room.

THE CAPTAIN [*continuing unmoved*] She married a numskull. She told me she would marry anyone to get away from home.

LADY UTTERWORD. You are pretending not to know me on purpose. I will leave the house.

*Mazzini Dunn enters from the hall. He is a little elderly man with bulging credulous eyes and earnest manners. He is dressed in a blue serge jacket suit with an unbuttoned mackintosh over it, and carries a soft black hat of clerical cut.*

ELLIE. At last! Captain Shotover: here is my father.

THE CAPTAIN. This! Nonsense! not a bit like him. [*He goes away through the garden, shutting the door sharply behind him*].

LADY UTTERWORD. I will not be ignored and pretended to be somebody else. I will have it out with Papa now, this instant. [*To Mazzini*] Excuse me. [*She follows the Captain out, making a hasty bow to Mazzini, who returns it*].

MRS HUSHABYE [*hospitably, shaking hands*] How good of you to come, Mr Dunn! You dont mind Papa, do you? He is as mad as a hatter, you know, but quite harmless, and extremely clever. You will have some delightful talks with him.

MAZZINI. I hope so. [*To Ellie*] So here you are, Ellie, dear. [*He draws her arm affectionately through his*]. I must thank you, Mrs Hushabye, for your kindness to my daughter. I'm afraid she would have had no holiday if you had not invited her.

MRS HUSHABYE.   Not at all. Very nice of her to come and attract young people to the house for us.

MAZZINI   [smiling] I'm afraid Ellie is not interested in young men, Mrs Hushabye. Her taste is on the graver, solider side.

MRS HUSHABYE   [with a sudden rather hard brightness in her manner] Wont you take off your overcoat, Mr Dunn? You will find a cupboard for coats and hats and things in the corner of the hall.

MAZZINI   [hastily releasing Ellie] Yes—thank you—I had better—[He goes out].

MRS HUSHABYE   [emphatically] The old brute!

ELLIE.   Who?

MRS. HUSHABYE.   Who! Him. He. It. [Pointing after Mazzini]. "Graver, solider tastes," indeed!

ELLIE   [aghast] You dont mean that you were speaking like that of my father!

MRS HUSHABYE.   I was. You know I was.

ELLIE   [with dignity] I will leave your house at once. [She turns to the door].

MRS HUSHABYE.   If you attempt it, I'll tell your father why.

ELLIE   [turning again] Oh! How can you treat a visitor like this, Mrs Hushabye?

MRS HUSHABYE.   I thought you were going to call me Hesione.

ELLIE.   Certainly not now?

MRS HUSHABYE.   Very well: I'll tell your father.

ELLIE   [distressed] Oh!

MRS HUSHABYE.   If you turn a hair—if you take his part against me and against your own heart for a moment, I'll give that born soldier of freedom a piece of my mind that will stand him on his selfish old head for a week.

ELLIE. Hesione! My father selfish! How little you know—

*She is interrupted by Mazzini, who returns, excited and perspiring.*

MAZZINI. Ellie: Mangan has come: I thought youd like to know. Excuse me, Mrs Hushabye: the strange old gentleman—

MRS HUSHABYE. Papa. Quite so.

MAZZINI. Oh, I beg your pardon: of course: I was a little confused by his manner. He is making Mangan help him with something in the garden; and he wants me to—

*A powerful whistle is heard.*

THE CAPTAIN'S VOICE. Bosun ahoy! [*The whistle is repeated*].

MAZZINI [*flustered*] Oh dear! I believe he is whistling for me. [*He hurries out*].

MRS HUSHABYE. Now my father is a wonderful man if you like.

ELLIE. Hesione: listen to me. You dont understand. My father and Mr Mangan were boys together. Mr Ma—

MRS HUSHABYE. I dont care what they were: we must sit down if you are going to begin as far back as that. [*She snatches at Ellie's waist, and makes her sit down on the sofa beside her*]. Now, pettikins: tell me all about Mr Mangan. They call him Boss Mangan, dont they? He is a Napoleon of industry and disgustingly rich, isnt he? Why isnt your father rich?

ELLIE. My poor father should never have been in business. His parents were poets; and they gave him the noblest ideas; but they could not afford to give him a profession.

MRS HUSHABYE. Fancy your grandparents, with their eyes in fine frenzy rolling! And so your poor father had to go into business. Hasnt he succeeded in it?

ELLIE. He always used to say he could succeed if he only had some capital. He fought his way along, to keep a roof over our heads and bring us up well; but it was always a struggle: always the same difficulty of not having capital enough. I dont know how to describe it to you.

MRS HUSHABYE. Poor Ellie! I know. Pulling the devil by the tail.

ELLIE [*hurt*] Oh no. Not like that. It was at least dignified.

MRS HUSHABYE. That made it all the harder, didnt it? *I* shouldn't have pulled the devil by the tail with dignity. I should have pulled hard—[*between her teeth*] h a r d. Well? Go on.

ELLIE. At last it seemed that all our troubles were at an end. Mr Mangan did an extraordinarily noble thing out of pure friendship for my father and respect for his character. He asked him how much capital he wanted, and gave it to him. I dont mean that he lent it to him, or that he invested it in his business. He just simply made him a present of it. Wasnt that splendid of him?

MRS HUSHABYE. On condition that you married him?

ELLIE. Oh no, no, no. This was when I was a child. He had never even seen me: he never came to our house. It was absolutely disinterested. Pure generosity.

MRS HUSHABYE. Oh! I beg the gentleman's pardon. Well, what became of the money?

ELLIE. We all got new clothes and moved into another house. And I went to another school for two years.

MRS HUSHABYE. Only two years?

ELLIE. That was all; for at the end of two years my father was utterly ruined.

MRS HUSHABYE. How?

ELLIE. I dont know. I never could understand. But it was dreadful. When we were poor my father had never been in debt. But when he launched out into business on a large scale, he had to incur liabilities. When the business went into liquidation he owed more money than Mr Mangan had given him.

MRS HUSHABYE. Bit off more than he could chew, I suppose.

ELLIE. I think you are a little unfeeling about it.

MRS HUSHABYE. My pettikins: you mustnt mind my way of talking. I was quite as sensitive and particular as you once; but I have picked up so much slang from the children that I am really hardly presentable. I suppose your father had no head for business, and made a mess of it.

ELLIE. Oh, that just shews how entirely you are mistaken about him. The business turned out a great success. It now pays forty-four per cent after deducting the excess profits tax.

MRS HUSHABYE. Then why arnt you rolling in money?

ELLIE. I dont know. It seems very unfair to me. You see, my father was made bankrupt. It nearly broke his heart, because he had persuaded several of his friends to put money into the business. He was sure it would succeed; and events proved that he was quite right. But they all lost their money. It was dreadful. I dont know what we should have done but for Mr Mangan.

MRS HUSHABYE. What! Did the Boss come to the rescue again, after all his money being thrown away?

ELLIE. He did indeed, and never uttered a reproach to my father. He bought what was left of the business—the buildings and the machinery and things—from the official trustee for enough money to enable my father to pay six and eightpence in the pound and get his discharge. Everyone pitied Papa so much, and saw so plainly that he was an honorable man, that they let him off at six-and-eight pence instead of ten shillings. Then Mr Mangan started a company to take up the business, and made my father a manager in it to save us from starvation; for I wasnt earning anything then.

MRS HUSHABYE. Quite a romance. And when did the Boss develop the tender passion?

ELLIE. Oh, that was years after, quite lately. He took the chair one night at a sort of people's concert. I was singing there. As an amateur, you know: half a guinea for expenses and three songs with three encores. He was so pleased with my singing that he asked might he walk home with me. I never saw anyone so taken aback as he was when I took him home and introduced him to my father: his own manager. It was then that my father told me how nobly he had behaved. Of course it was considered a great chance for me, as he is so rich. And—and—we drifted into a sort of understanding—I suppose I should call it an engagement— [*She is distressed and cannot go on*].

MRS HUSHABYE [*rising and marching about*] You may have drifted into it; but you will bounce out of it, my pettikins, if I am to have anything to do with it.

ELLIE [*hopelessly*] No: it's no use. I am bound in honor and gratitude. I will go through with it.

MRS HUSHABYE [*behind the sofa, scolding down at her*] You know, of course, that it's not honorable or grateful to marry a man you dont love. Do you love this Mangan man?

ELLIE. Yes. At least—

MRS HUSHABYE. I dont want to know about "the least": I want to know the worst. Girls of your age fall in love with all sorts of impossible people, especially old people.

ELLIE. I like Mr Mangan very much; and I shall always be—

MRS HUSHABYE [*impatiently completing the sentence and prancing away intolerantly to starboard*] —grateful to him for his kindness to dear father. I know. Anybody else?

ELLIE.   What do you mean?

MRS HUSHABYE.   Anybody else? Are you in love with anybody else?

ELLIE.   Of course not.

MRS HUSHABYE.   Humph! [*The book on the drawing-table catches her eye. She picks it up, and evidently finds the title very unexpected. She looks at Ellie, and asks, quaintly*]. Quite sure youre not in love with an actor?

ELLIE.   No, no. Why? What put such a thing into your head?

MRS HUSHABYE.   This is yours, isnt it? Why else should you be reading Othello?

ELLIE.   My father taught me to love Shakespear.

MRS HUSHABYE   [*flinging the book down on the table*] Really! your father does seem to be about the limit.

ELLIE   [*naïvely*] Do you never read Shakespear, Hesione? That seems to me so extraordinary. I like Othello.

MRS HUSHABYE.   Do you indeed? He was jealous, wasnt he?

ELLIE.   Oh, not that. I think all the part about jealousy is horrible. But dont you think it must have been a wonderful experience for Desdemona, brought up so quietly at home, to meet a man who had been out in the world doing all sorts of brave things and having terrible adventures, and yet finding something in her that made him love to sit and talk with her and tell her about them?

MRS HUSHABYE.   Thats your idea of romance, is it?

ELLIE.   Not romance, exactly. It might really happen.

*Ellie's eyes shew that she is not arguing, but in a daydream. Mrs Hushabye, watching her inquisitively, goes deliberately back to the sofa and resumes her seat beside her.*

MRS HUSHABYE.   Ellie darling: have you noticed that some of those stories that Othello told Desdemona couldnt have happened?

ELLIE.    Oh no. Shakespear thought they could have happened.

MRS HUSHABYE.    Hm! Desdemona thought they could have happened. But they didnt.

ELLIE.    Why do you look so enigmatic about it? You are such a sphinx: I never know what you mean.

MRS HUSHABYE.    Desdemona would have found him out if she had lived, you know. I wonder was that why he strangled her!

ELLIE.    Othello was not telling lies.

MRS HUSHABYE.    How do you know?

ELLIE.    Shakespear would have said if he was. Hesione: there are men who have done wonderful things: men like Othello, only, of course, white, and very handsome, and—

MRS HUSHABYE.    Ah! Now we're coming to it. Tell me all about him. I knew there must be somebody, or youd never have been so miserable about Mangan: youd have thought it quite a lark to marry him.

ELLIE.    [blushing vividly] Hesione: you are dreadful. But I dont want to make a secret of it, though of course I dont tell everybody. Besides, I dont know him.

MRS HUSHABYE.    Dont know him! What does that mean?

ELLIE.    Well, of course I know him to speak to.

MRS HUSHABYE.    But you want to know him ever so much more intimately, eh?

ELLIE.    No no: I know him quite—almost intimately.

MRS HUSHABYE.    You dont know him; and you know him almost intimately. How lucid!

ELLIE.    I mean that he does not call on us. I—I got into conversation with him by chance at a concert.

MRS HUSHABYE.    You seem to have rather a gay time at your concerts, Ellie.

ELLIE.    Not at all: we talk to everyone in the greenroom waiting for our turns. I thought he was one of the artists: he looked so splendid. But he was only one of the committee.

I happened to tell him that I was copying a picture at the National Gallery. I make a little money that way. I cant paint much; but as it's always the same picture I can do it pretty quickly and get two or three pounds for it. It happened that he came to the National Gallery one day.

MRS HUSHABYE. One student's day. Paid sixpence to stumble about through a crowd of easels, when he might have come in next day for nothing and found the floor clear! Quite by accident?

ELLIE [*triumphantly*] No. On purpose. He liked talking to me. He knows lots of the most splendid people. Fashionable women who are all in love with him. But he ran away from them to see me at the National Gallery and persuade me to come with him for a drive round Richmond Park in a taxi.

MRS HUSHABYE. My pettikins, you have been going it. It's wonderful what you good girls can do without anyone saying a word.

ELLIE. I am not in society, Hesione. If I didnt make acquaintances in that way I shouldnt have any at all.

MRS HUSHABYE. Well, no harm if you know how to take care of yourself. May I ask his name?

ELLIE [*slowly and musically*] Marcus Darnley.

MRS HUSHABYE [*echoing the music*] Marcus Darnley! What a splendid name!

ELLIE. Oh, I'm so glad you think so. I think so too; but I was afraid it was only a silly fancy of my own.

MRS HUSHABYE. Hm! Is he one of the Aberdeen Darnleys?

ELLIE. Nobody knows. Just fancy! He was found in an antique chest—

MRS HUSHABYE. A what?

ELLIE. An antique chest, one summer morning in a rose garden, after a night of the most terrible thunderstorm.

MRS HUSHABYE. What on earth was he doing in the

chest? Did he get into it because he was afraid of the lightning?

ELLIE.   Oh no, no: he was a baby. The name Marcus Darnley was embroidered on his babyclothes. And five hundred pounds in gold.

MRS HUSHABYE   [*looking hard at her*] Ellie!

ELLIE.   The garden of the Viscount—

MRS HUSHABYE.   —de Rougemont?

ELLIE   [*innocently*] No: de Larochejaquelin. A French family. A vicomte. His life has been one long romance. A tiger—

MRS HUSHABYE.   Slain by his own hand?

ELLIE.   Oh no: nothing vulgar like that. He saved the life of the tiger from a hunting party: one of King Edward's hunting parties in India. The King was furious: that was why he never had his military services properly recognized. But he doesn't care. He is a Socialist and despises rank, and has been in three revolutions fighting on the barricades.

MRS HUSHABYE.   How can you sit there telling me such lies? You, Ellie, of all people! And I thought you were a perfectly simple, straightforward, good girl.

ELLIE   [*rising, dignified but very angry*] Do you mean to say you dont believe me?

MRS HUSHABYE.   Of course I dont believe you. Youre inventing every word of it. Do you take me for a fool?

*Ellie stares at her. Her candor is so obvious that Mrs Hushabye is puzzled.*

ELLIE.   Goodbye, Hesione. I'm very sorry. I see now that it sounds very improbable as I tell it. But I cant stay if you think that way about me.

MRS HUSHABYE   [*catching her dress*] You shant go. I couldn't be so mistaken: I know too well what liars are like. Somebody has really told you all this.

ELLIE   [*flushing*] Hesione: dont say that you dont believe h i m. I couldnt bear that.

MRS HUSHABYE [*soothing her*] Of course I believe him, dearest. But you should have broken it to me by degrees. [*Drawing her back to her seat*] Now tell me all about him. Are you in love with him?

ELLIE. Oh no. I'm not so foolish. I dont fall in love with people. I'm not so silly as you think.

MRS HUSHABYE. I see. Only something to think about—to give some interest and pleasure to life.

ELLIE. Just so. Thats all, really.

MRS HUSHABYE. It makes the hours go fast, doesnt it? No tedious waiting to go to sleep at nights and wondering whether you will have a bad night. How delightful it makes waking up in the morning! How much better than the happiest dream! All life transfigured! No more wishing one had an interesting book to read, because life is so much happier than any book! No desire but to be alone and not to have to talk to anyone: to be alone and just think about it.

ELLIE [*embracing her*] Hesione: you are a witch. How do you know? Oh, you are the most sympathetic woman in the world.

MRS HUSHABYE [*caressing her*] Pettikins, my pettikins: how I envy you! and how I pity you!

ELLIE. Pity me! Oh, why?

*A very handsome man of fifty, with mousquetaire moustaches, wearing a rather dandified curly brimmed hat, and carrying an elaborate walking-stick, comes into the room from the hall, and stops short at sight of the women on the sofa.*

ELLIE [*seeing him and rising in glad surprise*] Oh! Hesione: this is Mr Marcus Darnley.

MRS HUSHABYE [*rising*] What a lark! He is my husband.

ELLIE. But how—[*She stops suddenly; then turns pale and sways*].

MRS HUSHABYE [*catching her and sitting down with her on the sofa*] Steady, my pettikins.

THE MAN [*with a mixture of confusion and effrontery, de-*

*positing his hat and stick on the teak table*] My real name, Miss Dunn, is Hector Hushabye. I leave you to judge whether that is a name any sensitive man would care to confess to. I never use it when I can possibly help it. I have been away for nearly a month; and I had no idea you knew my wife, or that you were coming here. I am none the less delighted to find you in our little house.

ELLIE   [*in great distress*] I dont know what to do. Please, may I speak to Papa? Do leave me. I cant bear it.

MRS HUSHABYE.   Be off, Hector.

HECTOR.   I—

MRS HUSHABYE.   Quick, quick. Get out.

HECTOR.   If you think it better—[*He goes out, taking his hat with him but leaving the stick on the table*].

MRS HUSHABYE   [*laying Ellie down at the end of the sofa*] Now, pettikins, he is gone. Theres nobody but me. You can let yourself go. Dont try to control yourself. Have a good cry.

ELLIE   [*raising her head*] Damn!

MRS HUSHABYE.   Splendid! Oh, what a relief! I thought you were going to be broken-hearted. Never mind me. Damn him again.

ELLIE.   I am not damning him: I am damning myself for being such a fool. [*Rising*] How could I let myself be taken in so? [*She begins prowling to and fro, her bloom gone, looking curiously older and harder*].

MRS HUSHABYE   [*cheerfully*] Why not, pettikins? Very few young women can resist Hector. I couldnt when I was your age. He is really rather splendid, you know.

ELLIE   [*turning on her*] Splendid! Yes: splendid l o o k-i n g, of course. But how can you love a liar?

MRS HUSHABYE.   I dont know. But you can, fortunately. Otherwise there wouldnt be much love in the world.

ELLIE.   But to lie like that! To be a boaster! a coward!

MRS HUSHABYE   [*rising in alarm*] Pettikins: none of that,

if you please. If you hint the slightest doubt of Hector's courage, he will go straight off and do the most horribly dangerous things to convince himself that he isnt a coward. He has a dreadful trick of getting out of one third-floor window and coming in at another, just to test his nerve. He has a whole drawerful of Albert Medals for saving people's lives.

ELLIE. He never told me that.

MRS HUSHABYE. He never boasts of anything he really did: he cant bear it; and it makes him shy if anyone else does. All his stories are made-up stories.

ELLIE [*coming to her*] Do you mean that he is really brave, and really has adventures, and yet tells lies about things that he never did and that never happened?

MRS HUSHABYE. Yes, pettikins, I do. People dont have their virtues and vices in sets: they have them anyhow: all mixed.

ELLIE [*staring at her thoughtfully*] Theres something odd about this house, Hesione, and even about you. I dont know why I'm talking to you so calmly. I have a horrible fear that my heart is broken, but that heartbreak is not like what I thought it must be.

MRS HUSHABYE [*fondling her*] It's only life educating you, pettikins. How do you feel about Boss Mangan now?

ELLIE [*disengaging herself with an expression of distaste*] Oh, how can you remind me of him, Hesione?

MRS HUSHABYE. Sorry, dear. I think I hear Hector coming back. You dont mind now, do you, dear?

ELLIE. Not in the least. I'm quite cured.

*Mazzini Dunn and Hector come in from the hall.*

HECTOR [*as he opens the door and allows Mazzini to pass in*] One second more, and she would have been a dead woman!

MAZZINI. Dear! dear! what an escape! Ellie, my love: Mr Hushabye has just been telling me the most extraordinary—

ELLIE. Yes: Ive heard it. [*She crosses to the other side of the room*].

HECTOR [*following her*] Not this one: I'll tell it to you after dinner. I think youll like it. The truth is, I made it up for you, and was looking forward to the pleasure of telling it to you. But in a moment of impatience at being turned out of the room, I threw it away on your father.

ELLIE [*turning at bay with her back to the carpenter's bench, scornfully self-possessed*] It was not thrown away. He believed it. I should not have believed it.

MAZZINI [*benevolently*] Ellie is very naughty, Mr Hush-abye. Of course she does not really think that. [*He goes to the bookshelves, and inspects the titles of the volumes*].

*Boss Mangan comes in from the hall, followed by the Captain. Mangan, carefully frock-coated as for church or for a directors' meeting, is about fiftyfive, with a careworn, mistrustful expression, standing a little on an entirely imaginary dignity, with a dull complexion, straight, lustreless hair, and features so entirely commonplace that it is impossible to describe them.*

CAPTAIN SHOTOVER [*to Mrs Hushabye, introducing the newcomer*] Says his name is Mangan. Not ablebodied.

MRS HUSHABYE [*graciously*] How do you do, Mr Mangan?

MANGAN [*shaking hands*] Very pleased.

CAPTAIN SHOTOVER. Dunn's lost his muscle, but recovered his nerve. Men seldom do after three attacks of delirium tremens. [*He goes into the pantry*].

MRS HUSHABYE. I congratulate you, Mr Dunn.

MAZZINI [*dazed*] I am a lifelong teetotaler.

MRS HUSHABYE. You will find it far less trouble to let Papa have his own way than try to explain.

MAZZINI. But three attacks of delirium tremens, really!

MRS HUSHABYE [*to Mangan*] Do you know my husband, Mr. Mangan? [*She indicates Hector*].

MANGAN [*going to Hector, who meets him with out-*

*stretched hand*] Very pleased. [*Turning to Ellie*] I hope, Miss Ellie, you have not found the journey down too fatiguing. [*They shake hands*].

MRS HUSHABYE.   Hector: shew Mr Dunn his room.

HECTOR.   Certainly. Come along, Mr Dunn. [*He takes Mazzini out*].

ELLIE.   You havnt shewn me my room yet, Hesione.

MRS HUSHABYE.   How stupid of me! Come along. Make yourself quite at home, Mr Mangan. Papa will entertain you. [*She calls to the Captain in the pantry*] Papa: come and explain the house to Mr Mangan.

*She goes out with Ellie. The Captain comes from the pantry.*

CAPTAIN SHOTOVER.   Youre going to marry Dunn's daughter. Dont. Youre too old.

MANGAN   [*staggered*] Well! Thats fairly blunt, Captain.

CAPTAIN SHOTOVER.   It's true.

MANGAN.   She doesnt think so.

CAPTAIN SHOTOVER.   She does.

MANGAN.   Older men than I have—

CAPTAIN SHOTOVER   [*finishing the sentence for him*] — made fools of themselves. That, also, is true.

MANGAN   [*asserting himself*] I dont see that this is any business of yours.

CAPTAIN SHOTOVER.   It is everybody's business. The stars in their courses are shaken when such things happen.

MANGAN.   I'm going to marry her all the same.

CAPTAIN SHOTOVER.   How do you know?

MANGAN   [*playing the strong man*] I intend to. I mean to. See? I never made up my mind to do a thing yet that I didnt bring it off. Thats the sort of man I am; and there will be a better understanding between us when you make up your mind to that, Captain.

CAPTAIN SHOTOVER.   You frequent picture palaces.

MANGAN.   Perhaps I do. Who told you?

CAPTAIN SHOTOVER.   Talk like a man, not like a movy. You mean that you make a hundred thousand a year.

MANGAN.   I dont boast. But when I meet a man that makes a hundred thousand a year, I take off my hat to that man, and stretch out my hand to him and call him brother.

CAPTAIN SHOTOVER.   Then you also make a hundred thousand a year, hey?

MANGAN.   No. I cant say that. Fifty thousand, perhaps.

CAPTAIN SHOTOVER.   His half brother only. [*He turns away from Mangan with his usual abruptness, and collects the empty tea-cups on the Chinese tray*].

MANGAN   [*irritated*] See here, Captain Shotover. I dont quite understand my position here. I came here on your daughter's invitation. Am I in her house or in yours?

CAPTAIN SHOTOVER.   You are beneath the dome of heaven, in the house of God. What is true within these walls is true outside them. Go out on the seas; climb the mountains; wander through the valleys. She is still too young.

MANGAN   [*weakening*] But I'm very little over fifty.

CAPTAIN SHOTOVER.   You are still less under sixty. Boss Mangan: you will not marry the pirate's child. [*He carries the tray away into the pantry*].

MANGAN   [*following him to the half door*] What pirate's child. What are you talking about?

CAPTAIN SHOTOVER   [*in the pantry*] Ellie Dunn. You will not marry her.

MANGAN.   Who will stop me?

CAPTAIN SHOTOVER   [*emerging*] My daughter. [*He makes for the door leading to the hall*].

MANGAN   [*following him*] Mrs Hushabye! Do you mean to say she brought me down here to break it off?

CAPTAIN SHOTOVER   [*stopping and turning on him*] I know nothing more than I have seen in her eye. She will break it off. Take my advice: marry a West Indian negress:

they make excellent wives. I was married to one myself for two years.

MANGAN.   Well, I am damned!

CAPTAIN SHOTOVER.   I thought so. I was, too, for many years. The negress redeemed me.

MANGAN   [feebly] This is queer. I ought to walk out of this house.

CAPTAIN SHOTOVER.   Why?

MANGAN.   Well, many men would be offended by your style of talking.

CAPTAIN SHOTOVER.   Nonsense! It's the other sort of talking that makes quarrels. Nobody ever quarrels with me.

*A gentleman, whose firstrate tailoring and frictionless manners proclaim the wellbred West Ender, comes in from the hall. He has an engaging air of being young and unmarried, but on close inspection is found to be at least over forty.*

THE GENTLEMAN.   Excuse my intruding in this fashion; but there is no knocker on the door; and the bell does not seem to ring.

CAPTAIN SHOTOVER.   Why should there be a knocker? Why should the bell ring? The door is open.

THE GENTLEMAN.   Precisely. So I ventured to come in.

CAPTAIN SHOTOVER.   Quite right. I will see about a room for you. [*He makes for the door*].

THE GENTLEMAN   [*stopping him*] But I'm afraid you dont know who I am.

CAPTAIN SHOTOVER.   Do you suppose that at my age I make distinctions between one fellowcreature and another? [*He goes out. Mangan and the newcomer stare at one another*].

MANGAN.   Strange character, Captain Shotover, sir.

THE GENTLEMAN.   Very.

CAPTAIN SHOTOVER   [*shouting outside*] Hesione: another person has arrived and wants a room. Man about town, well dressed, fifty.

THE GENTLEMAN. Fancy Hesione's feelings! May I ask are you a member of the family?

MANGAN. No.

THE GENTLEMAN. I am. At least a connexion.

*Mrs Hushabye comes back.*

MRS HUSHABYE. How do you do? How good of you to come!

THE GENTLEMAN. I am very glad indeed to make your acquaintance, Hesione. [*Instead of taking her hand he kisses her. At the same moment the Captain appears in the doorway*]. You will excuse my kissing your daughter, Captain, when I tell you that—

CAPTAIN SHOTOVER. Stuff! Everyone kisses my daughter. Kiss her as much as you like. [*He makes for the pantry*].

THE GENTLEMAN. Thank you. One moment, Captain. [*The Captain halts and turns. The gentleman goes to him affably*]. Do you happen to remember—but probably you dont, as it occurred many years ago—that your younger daughter married a numskull?

CAPTAIN SHOTOVER. Yes. She said she'd marry anybody to get away from this house. I should not have recognized you: your head is no longer like a walnut. Your aspect is softened. You have been boiled in bread and milk for years and years, like other married men. Poor devil! [*He disappears into the pantry*].

MRS HUSHABYE [*going past Mangan to the gentleman and scrutinizing him*]. I dont believe you are Hastings Utterword.

THE GENTLEMAN. I am not.

MRS HUSHABYE. Then what business had you to kiss me?

THE GENTLEMAN. I thought I would like to. The fact is, I am Randall Utterword, the unworthy younger brother of Hastings. I was abroad diplomatizing when he was married.

LADY UTTERWORD [*dashing in*] Hesione: where is the key of the wardrobe in my room? My diamonds are in my dressing-bag: I must lock it up—[*Recognizing the stranger with a shock*] Randall: how dare you? [*She marches at him past Mrs Hushabye, who retreats and joins Mangan near the sofa*].

RANDALL.   How dare I what? I am not doing anything.

LADY UTTERWORD.   Who told you I was here?

RANDALL.   Hastings. You had just left when I called on you at Claridge's; so I followed you down here. You are looking extremely well.

LADY UTTERWORD.   Dont presume to tell me so.

MRS HUSHABYE.   What is wrong with Mr Randall, Addy?

LADY UTTERWORD [*recollecting herself*] Oh, nothing. But he has no right to come bothering you and Papa without being invited. [*She goes to the window-seat and sits down, turning away from them ill-humoredly and looking into the garden, where Hector and Ellie are now seen strolling together*].

MRS HUSHABYE.   I think you have not met Mr Mangan, Addy.

LADY UTTERWORD [*turning her head and nodding coldly to Mangan*] I beg your pardon. Randall: you have flustered me so: I made a perfect fool of myself.

MRS HUSHABYE. Lady Utterword. My sister. My y o u n g e r sister.

MANGAN [*bowing*] Pleased to meet you, Lady Utterword.

LADY UTTERWORD [*with marked interest*] Who is that gentleman walking in the garden with Miss Dunn?

MRS HUSHABYE.   I dont know. She quarrelled mortally with my husband only ten minutes ago; and I didnt know anyone else had come. It must be a visitor. [*She goes to the window to look*]. Oh, it is Hector. Theyve made it up.

LADY UTTERWORD.   Your husband! That handsome man?

MRS HUSHABYE.   Well, why shouldnt my husband be a handsome man?

RANDALL [*joining them at the window*] One's husband never is, Ariadne. [*He sits by Lady Utterword, on her right*].

MRS HUSHABYE.   One's sister's husband always is, Mr Randall.

LADY UTTERWORD.   Dont be vulgar, Randall. And you, Hesione, are just as bad.

*Ellie and Hector come in from the garden by the starboard door. Randall rises. Ellie retires into the corner near the pantry. Hector comes forward; and Lady Utterword rises looking her very best.*

MRS HUSHABYE.   Hector: this is Addy.

HECTOR [*apparently surprised*] Not this lady.

LADY UTTERWORD [*smiling*] Why not?

HECTOR [*looking at her with a piercing glance of deep but respectful admiration, his moustache bristling*] I thought— [*Pulling himself together*] I beg your pardon, Lady Utterword. I am extremely glad to welcome you at last under our roof. [*He offers his hand with grave courtesy*].

MRS HUSHABYE.   She wants to be kissed, Hector.

LADY UTTERWORD.   Hesione! [*But she still smiles*].

MRS HUSHABYE.   Call her Addy; and kiss her like a good brother-in-law; and have done with it. [*She leaves them to themselves*].

HECTOR.   Behave yourself, Hesione. Lady Utterword is entitled not only to hospitality but to civilization.

LADY UTTERWORD [*gratefully*] Thank you, Hector. [*They shake hands cordially*].

*Mazzini Dunn is seen crossing the garden from starboard to port.*

CAPTAIN SHOTOVER [*coming from the pantry and addressing Ellie*] Your father has washed himself.

ELLIE [*quite self-possessed*] He often does, Captain Shotover.

CAPTAIN SHOTOVER.   A strange conversion! I saw him through the pantry window.

*Mazzini Dunn enters through the port window door, newly washed and brushed, and stops, smiling benevolently, between Mangan and Mrs Hushabye.*

MRS HUSHABYE [*introducing*] Mr Mazzini Dunn, Lady Ut—oh, I forgot: youve met. [*Indicating Ellie*] Miss Dunn.

MAZZINI [*walking across the room to take Ellie's hand, and beaming at his own naughty irony*] I have met Miss Dunn also. She is my daughter. [*He draws her arm through his caressingly*].

MRS HUSHABYE. Of course: how stupid! Mr Utterword, my sister's-er—

RANDALL [*shaking hands agreeably*] Her brother-in-law, Mr Dunn. How do you do?

MRS HUSHABYE. This is my husband.

HECTOR. We have met, dear. Dont introduce us any more. [*He moves away to the big chair, and adds*] Wont you sit down, Lady Utterword? [*She does so very graciously*].

MRS HUSHABYE. Sorry. I hate it: It's like making people shew their tickets.

MAZZINI [*sententiously*] How little it tells us, after all! The great question is, not who we are, but what we are.

CAPTAIN SHOTOVER. Ha! What are you?

MAZZINI [*taken aback*] What am I?

CAPTAIN SHOTOVER. A thief, a pirate, and a murderer.

MAZZINI. I assure you you are mistaken.

CAPTAIN SHOTOVER. An adventurous life; but what does it end in? Respectability. A ladylike daughter. The language and appearance of a city missionary. Let it be a warning to all of you. [*He goes out through the garden*].

DUNN. I hope nobody here believes that I am a thief, a pirate, or a murderer. Mrs Hushabye: will you excuse me a moment? I must really go and explain. [*He follows the Captain*].

MRS HUSHABYE [*as he goes*] It's no use. Youd really better—[*But Dunn has vanished*]. We had better all go out and look for some tea. We never have regular tea; but you can always get some when you want: the servants keep it stewing all day. The kitchen veranda is the best place to ask. May I shew you? [*She goes to the starboard door*].

RANDALL [*going with her*] Thank you, I dont think I'll take any tea this afternoon. But if you will shew me the garden—?

MRS HUSHABYE. Theres nothing to see in the garden except papa's observatory, and a gravel pit with a cave where he keeps dynamite and things of that sort. However, it's pleasanter out of doors; so come along.

RANDALL. Dynamite! Isnt that rather risky?

MRS HUSHABYE. Well, we dont sit in the gravel pit when theres a thunderstorm.

LADY UTTERWORD. Thats something new. What is the dynamite for?

HECTOR. To blow up the human race if it goes too far. He is trying to discover a psychic ray that will explode all the explosives at the will of a Mahatma.

ELLIE. The Captain's tea is delicious, Mr Utterword.

MRS HUSHABYE [*stopping in the doorway*] Do you mean to say that youve had some of my father's tea? that you got round him before you were ten minutes in the house?

ELLIE. I did.

MRS HUSHABYE. You little devil! [*She goes out with Randall*].

MANGAN. Wont you come, Miss Ellie?

ELLIE. I'm too tired. I'll take a book up to my room and rest a little. [*She goes to the bookshelf*].

MANGAN. Right. You cant do better. But I'm disappointed. [*He follows Randall and Mrs Hushabye*].

*Ellie, Hector, and Lady Utterword are left. Hector is close to Lady Utterword. They look at Ellie, waiting for her to go.*

ELLIE [*looking at the title of a book*] Do you like stories of adventure, Lady Utterword?

LADY UTTERWORD  [*patronizingly*] Of course, dear.

ELLIE.  Then I'll leave you to Mr Hushabye. [*She goes out through the hall*].

HECTOR.  That girl is mad about tales of adventure. The lies I have to tell her!

LADY UTTERWORD  [*not interested in Ellie*] When you saw me what did you mean by saying that you thought, and then stopping short? What did you think?

HECTOR  [*folding his arms and looking down at her magnetically*] May I tell you?

LADY UTTERWORD.  Of course.

HECTOR.  It will not sound very civil. I was on the point of saying "I thought you were a plain woman."

LADY UTTERWORD.  Oh for shame, Hector! What right had you to notice whether I am plain or not?

HECTOR.  Listen to me, Ariadne. Until today I have seen only photographs of you; and no photograph can give the strange fascination of the daughters of that supernatural old man. There is some damnable quality in them that destroys men's moral sense, and carries them beyond honor and dishonor. You know that, dont you?

LADY UTTERWORD.  Perhaps I do, Hector. But let me warn you once for all that I am a rigidly conventional woman. You may think because I'm a Shotover that I'm a Bohemian, because we are all so horribly Bohemian. But I'm not. I hate and loathe Bohemianism. No child brought up in a strict Puritan household ever suffered from Puritanism as I suffered from our Bohemianism.

HECTOR.  Our children are like that. They spend their holidays in the houses of their respectable schoolfellows.

LADY UTTERWORD.  I shall invite them for Christmas.

HECTOR.  Their absence leaves us both without our natural chaperons.

LADY UTTERWORD.  Children are certainly very inconvenient sometimes. But intelligent people can always manage, unless they are Bohemians.

HECTOR. You are no Bohemian; but you are no Puritan either: your attraction is alive and powerful. What sort of woman do you count yourself?

LADY UTTERWORD. I am a woman of the world, Hector; and I can assure you that if you will only take the trouble always to do the perfectly correct thing, and to say the perfectly correct thing, you can do just what you like. An ill-conducted, careless woman gets simply no chance. An ill-conducted, careless man is never allowed within arms length of any woman worth knowing.

HECTOR. I see. You are neither a Bohemian woman nor a Puritan woman. You are a dangerous woman.

LADY UTTERWORD. On the contrary, I am a safe woman.

HECTOR. You are a most accursedly attractive woman. Mind: I am not making love to you. I do not like being attracted. But you had better know how I feel if you are going to stay here.

LADY UTTERWORD. You are an exceedingly clever lady-killer, Hector. And terribly handsome. I am quite a good player, myself, at that game. It is quite understood that we are only playing?

HECTOR. Quite. I am deliberately playing the fool, out of sheer worthlessness.

LADY UTTERWORD [*rising brightly*] Well, you are my brother-in-law. Hesione asked you to kiss me. [*He seizes her in his arms, and kisses her strenuously*]. Oh! that was a little more than play, brother-in-law. [*She pushes him suddenly away*]. You shall not do that again.

HECTOR. In effect, you got your claws deeper into me than I intended.

MRS HUSHABYE [*coming in from the garden*] Dont let me disturb you: I only want a cap to put on Daddiest. The sun is setting; and he'll catch cold. [*She makes for the door leading to the hall*].

LADY UTTERWORD. Your husband is quite charming, darling. He has actually condescended to kiss me at last. I shall go into the garden: it's cooler now. [*She goes out by the port door*].

MRS HUSHABYE. Take care, dear child. I dont believe any man can kiss Addy without falling in love with her. [*She goes into the hall*].

HECTOR [*striking himself on the chest*] Fool! Goat!

*Mrs Hushabye comes back with the Captain's cap.*

HECTOR. Your sister is an extremely enterprising old girl. Wheres Miss Dunn!

MRS HUSHABYE. Mangan says she has gone up to her room for a nap. Addy wont let you talk to Ellie: she has marked you for her own.

HECTOR. She has the diabolical family fascination. I began making love to her automatically. What am I to do? I cant fall in love; and I cant hurt a woman's feelings by telling her so when she falls in love with me. And as women are always falling in love with my moustache I get landed in all sorts of tedious and terrifying flirtations in which I'm not a bit in earnest.

MRS HUSHABYE. Oh, neither is Addy. She has never been in love in her life, though she has always been trying to fall in head over ears. She is worse than you, because you had one real go at least, with me.

HECTOR. That was a confounded madness. I cant believe that such an amazing experience is common. It has left its mark on me. I believe that is why I have never been able to repeat it.

MRS HUSHABYE [*laughing and caressing his arm*] We were frightfully in love with one another, Hector. It was such an enchanting dream that I have never been able to grudge it to you or anyone else since. I have invited all sorts of pretty women to the house on the chance of giving you another turn. But it has never come off.

HECTOR. I dont know that I want it to come off. It was damned dangerous. You fascinated me; but I loved you; so it was heaven. This sister of yours fascinates me; but I hate her; so it is hell. I shall kill her if she persists.

MRS HUSHABYE. Nothing will kill Addy: she is as strong as a horse. [*Releasing him*] Now *I* am going off to fascinate somebody.

HECTOR. The Foreign Office toff? Randall?

MRS HUSHABYE. Goodness gracious, no! Why should I fascinate him?

HECTOR. I presume you dont mean the bloated capitalist, Mangan?

MRS HUSHABYE. Hm! I think he had better be fascinated by me than by Ellie. [*She is going into the garden when the Captain comes in from it with some sticks in his hand*]. What have you got there, daddiest?

CAPTAIN SHOTOVER. Dynamite.

MRS HUSHABYE. Youve been to the gravel pit. Dont drop it about the house: theres a dear. [*She goes into the garden, where the evening light is now very red*].

HECTOR. Listen, O sage. How long dare you concentrate on a feeling without risking having it fixed in your consciousness all the rest of your life?

CAPTAIN SHOTOVER. Ninety minutes. An hour and a half. [*He goes into the pantry*].

*Hector, left alone, contracts his brows, and falls into a daydream. He does not move for some time. Then he folds his arms. Then, throwing his hands behind him, and gripping one with the other, he strides tragically once to and fro. Suddenly he snatches his walking-stick from the teak table, and draws it; for it is a sword-stick. He fights a desperate duel with an imaginary antagonist, and after many vicissitudes runs him through the body up to the hilt. He sheathes his sword and throws it on the sofa, falling into another reverie as he does so. He looks straight into the eyes of an imaginary woman; seizes her by the arms; and says in a deep and thrilling tone* "Do you love me!" *The Captain comes out of the pantry at this moment; and Hector, caught with his arms stretched out and his fists clenched, has to account for his attitude by going through a series of gymnastic exercises.*

CAPTAIN SHOTOVER.   That sort of strength is no good. You will never be as strong as a gorilla.

HECTOR.   What is the dynamite for?

CAPTAIN SHOTOVER.   To kill fellows like Mangan.

HECTOR.   No use. They will always be able to buy more dynamite than you.

CAPTAIN SHOTOVER.   I will make a dynamite that he cannot explode.

HECTOR.   And that you can, eh?

CAPTAIN SHOTOVER.   Yes: when I have attained the seventh degree of concentration.

HECTOR.   Whats the use of that? You never do attain it.

CAPTAIN SHOTOVER.   What then is to be done? Are we to be kept for ever in the mud by these hogs to whom the universe is nothing but a machine for greasing their bristles and filling their snouts?

HECTOR.   Are Mangan's bristles worse than Randall's lovelocks?

CAPTAIN SHOTOVER.   We must win powers of life and death over them both. I refuse to die until I have invented the means.

HECTOR.   Who are we that we should judge them?

CAPTAIN SHOTOVER.   What are they that they should judge us? Yet they do, unhesitatingly. There is enmity between our seed and their seed. They know it and act on it, strangling our souls. They believe in themselves. When we believe in ourselves, we shall kill them.

HECTOR.   It is the same seed. You forget that your pirate

has a very nice daughter. Mangan's son may be a Plato: Randall's a Shelley. What was my father?

CAPTAIN SHOTOVER.  The damndest scoundrel I ever met. [*He replaces the drawing-board; sits down at the table; and begins to mix a wash of color*].

HECTOR.  Precisely. Well, dare you kill his innocent grandchildren?

CAPTAIN SHOTOVER.  They are mine also.

HECTOR.  Just so. We are members one of another. [*He throws himself carelessly on the sofa*]. I tell you I have often thought of this killing of human vermin. Many men have thought of it. Decent men are like Daniel in the lion's den: their survival is a miracle; and they do not always survive. We live among the Mangans and Randalls and Billie Dunns as they, poor devils, live among the disease germs and the doctors and the lawyers and the parsons and the restaurant chefs and the tradesmen and the servants and all the rest of the parasites and blackmailers. What are our terrors to theirs? Give me the power to kill them; and I'll spare them in sheer—

CAPTAIN SHOTOVER  [*cutting in sharply*] Fellow feeling?

HECTOR.  No. I should kill myself if I believed that. I must believe that my spark, small as it is, is divine, and that the red light over their door is hell fire. I should spare them in simple magnanimous pity.

CAPTAIN SHOTOVER.  You cant spare them until you have the power to kill them. At present they have the power to kill you. There are millions of blacks over the water for them to train and let loose on us. Theyre going to do it. Theyre doing it already.

HECTOR.  They are too stupid to use their power.

CAPTAIN SHOTOVER  [*throwing down his brush and coming to the end of the sofa*] Do not deceive yourself: they do use it. We kill the better half of ourselves every day to propitiate them. The knowledge that these people are there to render all our aspirations barren prevents us having the aspirations. And when we are tempted to seek their destruction they bring forth demons to delude us, disguised as pretty daughters, and singers and poets and the like, for whose sake we spare them.

HECTOR [*sitting up and leaning towards him*] May not Hesione be such a demon, brought forth by you lest I should slay you?

CAPTAIN SHOTOVER. That is possible. She has used you up, and left you nothing but dreams, as some women do.

HECTOR. Vampire women, demon women.

CAPTAIN SHOTOVER. Men think the world well lost for them, and lose it accordingly. Who are the men that do things? The husbands of the shrew and of the drunkard, the men with the thorn in the flesh. [*Walking distractedly away towards the pantry*] I must think these things out. [*Turning suddenly*] But I go on with the dynamite none the less. I will discover a ray mightier than any X-ray: a mind ray that will explode the ammunition in the belt of my adversary before he can point his gun at me. And I must hurry. I am old: I have no time to waste in talk. [*He is about to go into the pantry, and Hector is making for the hall, when Hesione comes back*].

MRS HUSHABYE. Daddiest: you and Hector must come and help me to entertain all these people. What on earth were you shouting about?

HECTOR [*stopping in the act of turning the door handle*] He is madder than usual.

MRS HUSHABYE. We all are.

HECTOR. I must change. [*He resumes his door opening*].

MRS HUSHABYE. Stop, stop. Come back, both of you. Come back. [*They return, reluctantly*]. Money is running short.

HECTOR. Money! Where are my April dividends?

MRS HUSHABYE. Where is the snow that fell last year?

CAPTAIN SHOTOVER.  Where is all the money you had for that patent lifeboat I invented?

MRS HUSHABYE.  Five hundred pounds; and I have made it last since Easter!

CAPTAIN SHOTOVER.  Since Easter! Barely four months! Monstrous extravagance! I could live for seven years on £500.

MRS HUSHABYE.  Not keeping open house as we do here, Daddiest.

CAPTAIN SHOTOVER.  Only £500 for that lifeboat! I got twelve thousand for the invention before that.

MRS HUSHABYE.  Yes, dear; but that was for the ship with the magnetic keel that sucked up submarines. Living at the rate we do, you cannot afford life-saving inventions. Cant you think of something that will murder half Europe at one bang?

CAPTAIN SHOTOVER.  No. I am ageing fast. My mind does not dwell on slaughter as it did when I was a boy. Why doesn't your husband invent something? He does nothing but tell lies to women.

HECTOR.  Well, that is a form of invention, is it not? However, you are right: I ought to support my wife.

MRS HUSHABYE.  Indeed you shall do nothing of the sort: I should never see you from breakfast to dinner. I want my husband.

HECTOR  [bitterly] I might as well be your lapdog.

MRS HUSHABYE.  Do you want to be my breadwinner, like the other poor husbands?

HECTOR.  No, by thunder! What a damned creature a husband is anyhow!

MRS HUSHABYE  [to the Captain] What about that harpoon cannon?

CAPTAIN SHOTOVER.  No use. It kills whales, not men.

MRS HUSHABYE.  Why not? You fire the harpoon out of a cannon. It sticks in the enemy's general; you wind him in; and there you are.

HECTOR.   You are your father's daughter, Hesione.

CAPTAIN SHOTOVER.   There is something in it. Not to wind in generals: they are not dangerous. But one could fire a grapnel and wind in a machine gun or even a tank. I will think it out.

MRS HUSHABYE [*squeezing the Captain's arm affectionately*] Saved! You are a darling, daddiest. Now we must go back to these dreadful people and entertain them.

CAPTAIN SHOTOVER.   They have had no dinner. Dont forget that.

HECTOR.   Neither have I. And it is dark: it must be all hours.

MRS HUSHABYE.   Oh, Guinness will produce some sort of dinner for them. The servants always take jolly good care that there is food in the house.

CAPTAIN SHOTOVER [*raising a strange wail in the darkness*] What a house! What a daughter!

MRS HUSHABYE [*raving*] What a father!

HECTOR [*following suit*] What a husband!

CAPTAIN SHOTOVER.   Is there no thunder in heaven?

HECTOR.   Is there no beauty, no bravery, on earth?

MRS HUSHABYE.   What do men want? They have their food, their firesides, their clothes mended, and our love at the end of the day. Why are they not satisfied? Why do they envy us the pain with which we bring them into the world, and make strange dangers and torments for themselves to be even with us?

CAPTAIN SHOTOVER [*weirdly chanting*]

I built a house for my daughters, and opened the doors
                              thereof,
That men might come for their choosing, and their betters
                    spring from their love;
            But one of them married a numskull;

HECTOR.　[*taking up the rhythm*]

                The other a liar wed;

MRS HUSHABYE.　[*completing the stanza*]

And now must she lie beside him, even as she made

                her bed.

LADY UTTERWORD.　[*calling from the garden*] Hesione! Hesione! Where are you?

HECTOR.　The cat is on the tiles.

MRS HUSHABYE.　Coming, darling, coming. [*She goes quickly into the garden*].

*The Captain goes back to his place at the table.*

HECTOR.　[*going into the hall*] Shall I turn up the lights for you?

CAPTAIN SHOTOVER.　No. Give me deeper darkness. Money is not made in the light.

### END OF ACT 1

# Act II

*The same room, with the lights turned up and the curtains drawn. Ellie comes in, followed by Mangan. Both are dressed for dinner. She strolls to the drawing-table. He comes between the table and the wicker chair.*

MANGAN.   What a dinner! I dont call it a dinner: I call it a meal.

ELLIE.   I am accustomed to meals, Mr Mangan, and very lucky to get them. Besides, the captain cooked some macaroni for me.

MANGAN   [*shuddering liverishly*] Too rich: I cant eat such things. I suppose it's because I have to work so much with my brain. Thats the worst of being a man of business: you are always thinking, thinking, thinking. By the way, now that we are alone, may I take the opportunity to come to a little understanding with you?

ELLIE   [*settling into the draughtsman's seat*] Certainly. I should like to.

MANGAN   [*taken aback*] Should you? That surprises me; for I thought I noticed this afternoon that you avoided me all you could. Not for the first time either.

ELLIE.   I was very tired and upset. I wasn't used to the ways of this extraordinary house. Please forgive me.

MANGAN.   Oh, thats all right: I dont mind. But Captain

Shotover has been talking to me about you. You and me, you know.

ELLIE  [*interested*] The Captain! What did he say?

MANGAN.  Well, he noticed the difference between our ages.

ELLIE.  He notices everything.

MANGAN.  You dont mind, then?

ELLIE.  Of course I know quite well that our engagement—

MANGAN.  Oh! you call it an engagement.

ELLIE.  Well, isnt it?

MANGAN.  Oh, yes, yes: no doubt it is if you hold to it. This is the first time youve used the word; and I didnt quite know where we stood: thats all. [*He sits down in the wicker chair; and resigns himself to allow her to lead the conversation*]. You were saying—?

ELLIE.  Was I? I forget. Tell me. Do you like this part of the country? I heard you ask Mr Hushabye at dinner whether there are any nice houses to let down here.

MANGAN.  I like the place. The air suits me. I shouldnt be surprised if I settled down here.

ELLIE.  Nothing would please me better. The air suits me too. And I want to be near Hesione.

MANGAN  [*with growing uneasiness*] The air may suit us; but the question is, should we suit one another? Have you thought about that?

ELLIE.  Mr. Mangan: we must be sensible, mustnt we? It's no use pretending that we are Romeo and Juliet. But we can get on very well together if we choose to make the best of it. Your kindness of heart will make it easy for me.

MANGAN  [*leaning forward, with the beginning of something like deliberate unpleasantness in his voice*] Kindness of heart, eh? I ruined your father, didnt I?

ELLIE.  Oh, not intentionally.

MANGAN.  Yes I did. Ruined him on purpose.

ELLIE.   On purpose!

MANGAN.   Not out of ill-nature, you know. And youll admit that I kept a job for him when I had finished with him. But business is business; and I ruined him as a matter of business.

ELLIE.   I dont understand how that can be. Are you trying to make me feel that I need not be grateful to you, so that I may choose freely?

MANGAN   [rising aggressively] No. I mean what I say.

ELLIE.   But how could it possibly do you any good to ruin my father? The money he lost was yours.

MANGAN   [with a sour laugh] W a s mine! It is mine, Miss Ellie, and all the money the other fellows lost too. [He shoves his hands into his pockets and shews his teeth]. I just smoked them out like a hive of bees. What do you say to that? A bit of a shock, eh?

ELLIE.   It would have been, this morning. N o w! you cant think how little it matters. But it's quite interesting. Only, you must explain it to me. I dont understand it. [Propping her elbows on the drawing-board and her chin on her hands, she composes herself to listen with a combination of conscious curiosity with unconscious contempt which provokes him to more and more unpleasantness, and an attempt at patronage of her ignorance].

MANGAN.   Of course you dont understand: what do you know about business? You just listen and learn. Your father's business was a new business; and I dont start new businesses: I let other fellows start them. They put all their money and their friends' money into starting them. They wear out their souls and bodies trying to make a success of them. Theyre what you call enthusiasts. But the first dead lift of the thing is too much for them; and they havnt enough financial experience. In a year or so they have either to let the whole show go bust, or sell out to a new lot of fellows for a few deferred ordinary shares: that is, if theyre lucky enough to get anything at all. As likely as not the very same thing happens to the new lot. They put in more money and a couple of years more work; and then perhaps they have to sell out to a third lot. If it's really a big thing the third lot will have to sell out too, and leave t h e i r work and t h e i r money behind them. And thats where the real business man comes in: where I come in. But I'm cleverer than some: I dont mind dropping a little money to start the process. I took your father's measure. I saw that he had a sound idea, and that he would work himself silly for it if he got the chance. I saw that he was a child in business, and was dead certain to outrun his expenses and be in too great a hurry to wait for his market. I knew that the surest way to ruin a man who doesnt know how to handle money is to give him some. I explained my idea to some friends in the city, and they found the money; for I take no risks in ideas, even when theyre my own. Your father and the friends that ventured their money with him were no more to me than a heap of squeezed lemons. Youve been wasting your gratitude: my kind heart is all rot. I'm sick of it. When I see your father beaming at me with his moist, grateful eyes, regularly wallowing in gratitude, I sometimes feel I must tell him the truth or burst. What stops me is that I know he wouldnt believe me. He'd think it was my modesty, as you did just now. He'd think anything rather than the truth, which is that he's a blamed fool, and I am a man that knows how to take care of himself. [*He throws himself back into the big chair with large self-approval*]. Now what do you think of me, Miss Ellie?

ELLIE [*dropping her hands*]  How strange! that my mother, who knew nothing at all about business, should have been quite right about you! She always said—not before papa, of course, but to us children—that you were just that sort of man.

MANGAN [*sitting up, much hurt*]  Oh! did she? And yet she'd have let you marry me.

ELLIE.   Well, you see, Mr Mangan, my mother married a very good man—for whatever you may think of my father as a man of business, he is the soul of goodness—and she is not at all keen on my doing the same.

MANGAN.   Anyhow, you don't want to marry me now, do you?

ELLIE [*very calmly*]   Oh, I think so. Why not?

MANGAN [*rising aghast*]   Why not?

ELLIE.   I dont see why we shouldnt get on very well together.

MANGAN.   Well, but look here, you know— [*He stops, quite at a loss*].

ELLIE [*patiently*]   Well?

MANGAN.   Well, I thought you were rather particular about people's characters.

ELLIE.   If we women were particular about men's characters, we should never get married at all, Mr Mangan.

MANGAN.   A child like you talking of "we women"! What next! Youre not in earnest?

ELLIE.   Yes I am. Arnt you?

MANGAN.   You mean to hold me to it?

ELLIE.   Do you wish to back out of it?

MANGAN.   Oh no. Not exactly back out of it.

ELLIE.   Well?

*He has nothing to say. With a long whispered whistle, he drops into the wicker chair and stares before him like a beggared gambler. But a cunning look soon comes into his face. He leans over towards her on his right elbow, and speaks in a low steady voice.*

MANGAN.   Suppose I told you I was in love with another woman!

ELLIE [*echoing him*]   Suppose I told you I was in love with another man!

MANGAN [*bouncing angrily out of his chair*]   I'm not joking.

ELLIE.  Who told you *I* was?

MANGAN.  I tell you I'm serious. Youre too young to be serious; but youll have to believe me. I want to be near your friend Mrs Hushabye. I'm in love with her. Now the murder's out.

ELLIE.  I want to be near your friend Mr Hushabye. I'm in love with him. [*She rises and adds with a frank air*] Now we are in one another's confidence, we shall be real friends. Thank you for telling me.

MANGAN [*almost beside himself*]  Do you think I'll be made a convenience of like this?

ELLIE.  Come, Mr Mangan! you made a business convenience of my father. Well, a woman's business is marriage. Why shouldnt I make a domestic convenience of you?

MANGAN.  Because I dont choose, see? Because I'm not a silly gull like your father. Thats why.

ELLIE [*with serene contempt*]  You are not good enough to clean my father's boots, Mr Mangan; and I am paying you a great compliment in condescending to make a convenience of you, as you call it. Of course you are free to throw over our engagement if you like; but, if you do, youll never enter Hesione's house again: I will take care of that.

MANGAN [*gasping*] You little devil, youve done me. [*On the point of collapsing into the big chair again he recovers himself*] Wait a bit, though: youre not so cute as you think. You cant beat Boss Mangan as easy as that. Suppose I go straight to Mrs Hushabye and tell her that youre in love with her husband.

ELLIE.  She knows it.

MANGAN.  You told her!!!

ELLIE.  She told me.

MANGAN [*clutching at his bursting temples*] Oh, this is a crazy house. Or else I'm going clean off my chump. Is she making a swop with you—she to have your husband and you to have hers?

ELLIE.   Well, you dont want us both, do you?

MANGAN   [*throwing himself into the chair distractedly*] My brain wont stand it. My head's going to split. Help! Help me to hold it. Quick: hold it: squeeze it. Save me. [*Ellie comes behind his chair; clasps his head hard for a moment; then begins to draw her hands from his forehead back to his ears*]. Thank you. [*Drowsily*] Thats very refreshing. [*Waking a little*] Don't you hypnotize me, though. Ive seen men made fools of by hypnotism.

ELLIE   [*steadily*] Be quiet. Ive seen men made fools of without hypnotism.

MANGAN   [*humbly*] You dont dislike touching me, I hope. You never touched me before, I noticed.

ELLIE.   Not since you fell in love naturally with a grown-up nice woman, who will never expect you to make love to her. And I will never expect him to make love to me.

MANGAN.   He may, though.

ELLIE   [*making her passes rhythmically*] Hush. Go to sleep. Do you hear? You are to go to sleep, go to sleep, go to sleep; be quiet, deeply deeply quiet; sleep, sleep, sleep, sleep, sleep.

*He falls asleep. Ellie steals away; turns the light out; and goes into the garden.*

*Nurse Guinness opens the door and is seen in the light which comes in from the hall.*

GUINNESS   [*speaking to someone outside*] Mr Mangan's not here, ducky: theres no one here. It's all dark.

MRS HUSHABYE   [*without*] Try the garden. Mr Dunn and I will be in my boudoir. Shew him the way.

GUINNESS.   Yes, ducky. [*She makes for the garden door in the dark; stumbles over the sleeping Mangan; and screams*]. Ahoo! Oh Lord, sir! I beg your pardon, I'm sure: I didnt see you in the dark. Who is it? [*She goes back to the door and turns on the light*]. Oh, Mr Mangan, sir, I hope I havnt hurt you plumping into your lap like that. [*Coming to him*] I was

looking for you, sir. Mrs Hushabye says will you please—
[*Noticing that he remains quite insensible*] Oh, my good Lord,
I hope I havnt killed him. Sir! Mr Mangan! Sir! [*She shakes
him; and he is rolling inertly off the chair on the floor when she
holds him up and props him against the cushion*]. Miss Hessy!
Miss Hessy! Quick, doty darling. Miss Hessy! [*Mrs Hushabye
comes in from the hall, followed by Mazzini Dunn*]. Oh, Miss
Hessy, Ive been and killed him.

*Mazzini runs round the back of the chair to Mangan's right
hand, and sees that the nurse's words are apparently only too
true.*

MAZZINI.   What tempted you to commit such a crime,
woman?

MRS HUSHABYE   [*trying not to laugh*] Do you mean you
did it on purpose?

GUINNESS.   Now is it likely I'd kill any man on purpose?
I fell over him in the dark; and I'm a pretty tidy weight. He
never spoke nor moved until I shook him; and then he
would have dropped dead on the floor. Isnt it tiresome?

MRS HUSHABYE   [*going past the nurse to Mangan's side, and
inspecting him less credulously than Mazzini*] Nonsense! he is
not dead: he is only asleep. I can see him breathing.

GUINNESS.   But why wont he wake?

MAZZINI   [*speaking very politely into Mangan's ear*] Mangan! My dear Mangan! [*He blows into Mangan's ear*].

MRS HUSHABYE.   Thats no good. [*She shakes him vigorously*]. Mr Mangan: wake up. Do you hear? [*He begins to roll
over*]. Oh! Nurse, nurse: he's falling: help me.

*Nurse Guinness rushes to the rescue. With Mazzini's assis-
tance, Mangan is propped safely up again.*

GUINNESS   [*behind the chair; bending over to test the case
with her nose*] Would he be drunk, do you think, pet?

MRS HUSHABYE.   Had he any of Papa's rum?

MAZZINI.   It cant be that: he is most abstemious. I am
afraid he drank too much formerly, and has to drink too

little now. You know, Mrs Hushabye, I really think he has been hypnotized.

GUINNESS. Hip no what, sir?

MAZZINI. One evening at home, after we had seen a hypnotizing performance, the children began playing at it; and Ellie stroked my head. I assure you I went off dead asleep; and they had to send for a professional to wake me up after I had slept eighteen hours. They had to carry me upstairs; and as the poor children were not very strong, they let me slip; and I rolled right down the whole flight and never woke up. [*Mrs Hushabye splutters*]. Oh, you may laugh, Mrs Hushabye; but I might have been killed.

MRS HUSHABYE. I couldnt have helped laughing even if you had been, Mr Dunn. So Ellie has hypnotized him. What fun!

MAZZINI. Oh no, no, no. It was such a terrible lesson to her: nothing would induce her to try such a thing again.

MRS HUSHABYE. Then who did it? *I* didnt.

MAZZINI. I thought perhaps the Captain might have done it unintentionally. He is so fearfully magnetic: I feel vibrations whenever he comes close to me.

GUINNESS. The Captain will get him out of it anyhow, sir: I'll back him for that. I'll go fetch him. [*She makes for the pantry*].

MRS HUSHABYE. Wait a bit. [*To Mazzini*] You say he is all right for eighteen hours?

MAZZINI. Well, *I* was asleep for eighteen hours.

MRS HUSHABYE. Were you any the worse for it?

MAZZINI. I dont quite remember. They had poured brandy down my throat, you see; and—

MRS HUSHABYE. Quite. Anyhow, you survived. Nurse, darling: go and ask Miss Dunn to come to us here. Say I want to speak to her particularly. You will find her with Mr Hushabye probably.

GUINNESS. I think not, ducky: Miss Addy is with him.

But I'll find her and send her to you. [*She goes out into the garden*].

MRS HUSHABYE  [*calling Mazzini's attention to the figure on the chair*] Now, Mr Dunn, look. Just look. Look hard. Do you still intend to sacrifice your daughter to that thing?

MAZZINI  [*troubled*] You have completely upset me, Mrs Hushabye, by all you have said to me. That anyone could imagine that I—*I*, a consecrated soldier of freedom, if I may say so—could sacrifice Ellie to anybody or anyone, or that I should ever have dreamed of forcing her inclinations in any way, is a most painful blow to my—well, I suppose you would say to my good opinion of myself.

MRS HUSHABYE  [*rather stolidly*] Sorry.

MAZZINI  [*looking forlornly at the body*] What is your objection to poor Mangan, Mrs Hushabye? He looks all right to me. But then I am so accustomed to him.

MRS HUSHABYE.  Have you no heart? Have you no sense? Look at the brute! Think of poor weak innocent Ellie in the clutches of this slavedriver, who spends his life making thousands of rough violent workmen bend to his will and sweat for him: a man accustomed to have great masses of iron beaten into shape for him by steam-hammers! to fight with women and girls over a halfpenny an hour ruthlessly! a captain of industry, I think you call him, dont you? Are you going to fling your delicate, sweet, helpless child into such a beast's claws just because he will keep her in an expensive house and make her wear diamonds to shew how rich he is?

MAZZINI  [*staring at her in wide-eyed amazement*] Bless you, dear Mrs Hushabye, what romantic ideas of business you have! Poor dear Mangan isnt a bit like that.

MRS HUSHABYE  [*scornfully*] Poor dear Mangan indeed!

MAZZINI.  But he doesnt know anything about machinery. He never goes near the men: he couldnt manage them: he is afraid of them. I never can get him to take the least interest in the works: he hardly knows more about them than you do. People are cruelly unjust to Mangan: they think he is all rugged strength just because his manners are bad.

MRS HUSHABYE. Do you mean to tell me he isnt strong enough to crush poor little Ellie?

MAZZINI. Of course it's very hard to say how any marriage will turn out; but speaking for myself, I should say that he wont have a dog's chance against Ellie. You know, Ellie has remarkable strength of character. I think it is because I taught her to like Shakespear when she was very young.

MRS HUSHABYE [contemptuously] Shakespear! The next thing you will tell me is that you could have made a great deal more money than Mangan. [She retires to the sofa, and sits down at the port end of it in the worst of humors].

MAZZINI [following her and taking the other end] No: I'm no good at making money. I dont care enough for it, somehow. I'm not ambitious! that must be it. Mangan is wonderful about money: he thinks of nothing else. He is so dreadfully afraid of being poor. I am always thinking of other things: even at the works I think of the things we are doing and not of what they cost. And the worst of it is, poor Mangan doesnt know what to do with his money when he gets it. He is such a baby that he doesnt know even what to eat and drink: he has ruined his liver eating and drinking the wrong things; and now he can hardly eat at all. Ellie will diet him splendidly. You will be surprised when you come to know him better: he is really the most helpless of mortals. You get quite a protective feeling towards him.

MRS HUSHABYE. Then who manages his business, pray?

MAZZINI. I do. And of course other people like me.

MRS HUSHABYE. Footling people, you mean.

MAZZINI. I suppose youd think us so.

MRS HUSHABYE. And pray why dont you do without him if youre all so much cleverer?

MAZZINI. Oh, we couldnt: we should ruin the business

in a year. I've tried; and I know. We should spend too much
on everything. We should improve the quality of the goods
and make them too dear. We should be sentimental about
the hard cases among the workpeople. But Mangan keeps us
in order. He is down on us about every extra half-penny.
We could never do without him. You see, he will sit up all
night thinking of how to save sixpence. Wont Ellie make
him jump, though, when she takes his house in hand!

MRS HUSHABYE.   Then the creature is a fraud even as a
captain of industry!

MAZZINI.   I am afraid all the captains of industry are
what you call frauds, Mrs Hushabye. Of course there are
some manufacturers who really do understand their own
works; but they dont make as high a rate of profit as Mangan
does. I assure you Mangan is quite a good fellow in his way.
He means well.

MRS HUSHABYE.   He doesnt look well. He is not in his
first youth, is he?

MAZZINI.   After all, no husband is in his first youth for
very long, Mrs Hushabye. And men cant afford to marry in
their first youth nowadays.

MRS HUSHABYE.   Now if *I* said that, it would sound witty.
Why cant you say it wittily? What on earth is the matter with
you? Why dont you inspire everybody with confidence? with
respect?

MAZZINI   [*humbly*] I think that what is the matter with
me is that I am poor. You dont know what that means at
home. Mind: I dont say they have ever complained. Theyve
all been wonderful: theyve been proud of my poverty.
Theyve even joked about it quite often. But my wife has had
a very poor time of it. She has been quite resigned—

MRS HUSHABYE   [*shuddering involuntarily*]!!

MAZZINI.   There! You see, Mrs Hushabye. I dont want
Ellie to live on resignation.

MRS HUSHABYE.   Do you want her to have to resign herself to living with a man she doesnt love?

MAZZINI  [*wistfully*] Are you sure that would be worse than living with a man she did love, if he was a footling person?

MRS HUSHABYE  [*relaxing her contemptuous attitude, quite interested in Mazzini now*] You know, I really think you must love Ellie very much; for you become quite clever when you talk about her.

MAZZINI.   I didnt know I was so very stupid on other subjects.

MRS HUSHABYE.   You are, sometimes.

MAZZINI  [*turning his head away; for his eyes are wet*] I have learnt a good deal about myself from you, Mrs Hushabye; and I'm afraid I shall not be the happier for your plain speaking. But if you thought I needed it to make me think of Ellie's happiness you were very much mistaken.

MRS HUSHABYE  [*leaning towards him kindly*] Have I been a beast?

MAZZINI  [*pulling himself together*] It doesnt matter about me, Mrs Hushabye. I think you like Ellie; and that is enough for me.

MRS HUSHABYE.   I'm beginning to like you a little. I perfectly loathed you at first. I thought you the most odious, self-satisfied, boresome elderly prig I ever met.

MAZZINI  [*resigned, and now quite cheerful*] I daresay I am all that. I never have been a favorite with gorgeous women like you. They always frighten me.

MRS HUSHABYE  [*pleased*] Am I a gorgeous woman, Mazzini? I shall fall in love with you presently.

MAZZINI  [*with placid gallantry*] No you wont, Hesione. But you would be quite safe. Would you believe it that quite a lot of women have flirted with me because I am quite safe? But they get tired of me for the same reason.

MRS HUSHABYE [*mischievously*]. Take care. You may not be so safe as you think.

MAZZINI. Oh yes, quite safe. You see, I have been in love really: the sort of love that only happens once. [*Softly*] Thats why Ellie is such a lovely girl.

MRS HUSHABYE. Well, really, you a r e coming out. Are you quite sure you wont let me tempt you into a second grand passion?

MAZZINI. Quite. It wouldnt be natural. The fact is, you dont strike on my box, Mrs Hushabye; and I certainly dont strike on yours.

MRS HUSHABYE. I see. Your marriage was a safety match.

MAZZINI. What a very witty application of the expression I used! I should never have thought of it.

*Ellie comes in from the garden, looking anything but happy.*

MRS HUSHABYE [*rising*] Oh! here is Ellie at last. [*She goes behind the sofa*].

ELLIE [*on the threshold of the starboard door*] Guinness said you wanted me: you and Papa.

MRS HUSHABYE. You have kept us waiting so long that it almost came to—well, never mind. Your father is a very wonderful man [*she ruffles his hair affectionately*]: the only one I ever met who could resist me when I made myself really agreeable. [*She comes to the big chair, on Mangan's left*]. Come here. I have something to shew you. [*Ellie strolls listlessly to the other side of the chair*]. Look.

ELLIE [*contemplating Mangan without interest*] I know. He is only asleep. We had a talk after dinner; and he fell asleep in the middle of it.

MRS HUSHABYE. You did it, Ellie. You put him asleep.

MAZZINI [*rising quickly and coming to the back of the chair*] Oh, I hope not. Did you, Ellie?

ELLIE [*wearily*] He asked me to.

MAZZINI. But it's dangerous. You know what happened to me.

ELLIE [*utterly indifferent*] Oh, I daresay I can wake him. If not, somebody else can.

MRS HUSHABYE. It doesnt matter, anyhow, because I have at last persuaded your father that you dont want to marry him.

ELLIE [*suddenly coming out of her listlessness, much vexed*] But why did you do that, Hesione? I do want to marry him. I fully intend to marry him.

MAZZINI. Are you quite sure, Ellie? Mrs Hushabye has made me feel that I may have been thoughtless and selfish about it.

ELLIE [*very clearly and steadily*] Papa. When Mrs Hushabye takes it on herself to explain to you what I think or dont think, shut your ears tight; and shut your eyes too. Hesione knows nothing about me: she hasnt the least notion of the sort of person I am, and never will. I promise you I wont do anything I dont want to do and mean to do for my own sake.

MAZZINI. You are quite, quite sure?

ELLIE. Quite, quite sure. Now you must go away and leave me to talk to Mrs Hushabye.

MAZZINI. But I should like to hear. Shall I be in the way?

ELLIE [*inexorable*] I had rather talk to her alone.

MAZZINI [*affectionately*] Oh, well, I know what a nuisance parents are, dear. I will be good and go. [*He goes to the garden door*]. By the way, do you remember the address of that professional who woke me up? Dont you think I had better telegraph to him?

MRS HUSHABYE [*moving towards the sofa*] It's too late to telegraph tonight.

MAZZINI. I suppose so. I do hope he'll wake up in the course of the night. [*He goes out into the garden*].

ELLIE [*turning vigorously on Hesione the moment her father is out of the room*] Hesione: what the devil do you mean by making mischief with my father about Mangan?

MRS HUSHABYE [*promptly losing her temper*] Dont you
dare speak to me like that, you little minx. Remember that
you are in my house.

ELLIE.   Stuff! Why dont you mind your own business?
What is it to you whether I choose to marry Mangan or not?

MRS HUSHABYE.   Do you suppose you can bully me, you
miserable little matrimonial adventurer?

ELLIE.   Every woman who hasnt any money is a matrimonial adventurer. It's easy for you to talk: you have never
known what it is to want money; and you can pick
up men as if they were daisies. I am poor and respectable—

MRS HUSHABYE [*interrupting*] Ho! respectable! How did
you pick up Mangan? How did you pick up my husband?
You have the audacity to tell me that I am a—a—a—

ELLIE.   A siren. So you are. You were born to lead men
by the nose: if you werent, Marcus would have waited for
me, perhaps.

MRS HUSHABYE [*suddenly melting and half laughing*] Oh,
my poor Ellie, my pettikins, my unhappy darling! I am so
sorry about Hector. But what can I do? It's not my fault: I'd
give him to you if I could.

ELLIE.   I dont blame you for that.

MRS HUSHABYE.   What a brute I was to quarrel with you
and call you names! Do kiss me and say youre not angry
with me.

ELLIE [*fiercely*] Oh, dont slop and gush and be sentimental. Dont you see that unless I can be hard—as hard as
nails—I shall go mad? I dont care a damn about your calling
me names: do you think a woman in my situation can feel
a few hard words?

MRS HUSHABYE.   Poor little woman! Poor little situation!

ELLIE.   I suppose you think youre being sympathetic.
You are just foolish and stupid and selfish. You see me getting a smasher right in the face that kills a whole part of my
life: the best part that can never come again; and you think

you can help me over it by a little coaxing and kissing. When I want all the strength I can get to lean on: something iron, something stony, I dont care how cruel it is, you go all mushy and want to slobber over me. I'm not angry; I'm not unfriendly; but for God's sake do pull yourself together; and dont think that because youre on velvet and always have been, women who are in hell can take it as easily as you.

MRS HUSHABYE  [*shrugging her shoulders*] Very well. [*She sits down on the sofa in her old place*]. But I warn you that when I am neither coaxing and kissing nor laughing, I am just wondering how much longer I can stand living in this cruel, damnable world. You object to the siren: well, I drop the siren. You want to rest your wounded bosom against a grindstone. Well [*folding her arms*], here is the grindstone.

ELLIE  [*sitting down beside her, appeased*] Thats better: you really have the trick of falling in with everyone's mood; but you dont understand, because you are not the sort of woman for whom there is only one man and only one chance.

MRS HUSHABYE.  I certainly dont understand how your marrying that object [*indicating Mangan*] will console you for not being able to marry Hector.

ELLIE.  Perhaps you dont understand why I was quite a nice girl this morning, and am now neither a girl nor particularly nice.

MRS HUSHABYE.  Oh yes, I do. It's because you have made up your mind to do something despicable and wicked.

ELLIE.  I dont think so, Hesione. I must make the best of my ruined house.

MRS HUSHABYE.  Pooh! Youll get over it. Your house isnt ruined.

ELLIE.  Of course I shall get over it. You dont suppose I'm going to sit down and die of a broken heart, I hope, or be an old maid living on a pittance from the Sick and Indigent Room-keepers' Association. But my heart is broken, all the same. What I mean by that is that I know that what has happened to me with Marcus will not happen to me ever again. In the world for me there is Marcus and a lot of other men of whom one is just the same as another. Well, if I cant have love, thats no reason why I should have poverty. If Mangan has nothing else, he has money.

MRS HUSHABYE.   And are there no y o u n g men with money?

ELLIE.   Not within my reach. Besides, a young man would have the right to expect love from me, and would perhaps leave me when he found I could not give it to him. Rich young men can get rid of their wives, you know, pretty cheaply. But this object, as you call him, can expect nothing more from me than I am prepared to give him.

MRS HUSHABYE.   He will be your owner, remember. If he buys you, he will make the bargain pay him and not you. Ask your father.

ELLIE   [*rising and strolling to the chair to contemplate their subject*] You need not trouble on that score, Hesione. I have more to give Boss Mangan than he has to give me: it is I who am buying him, and at a pretty good price too, I think. Women are better at that sort of bargain than men. I have taken the Boss's measure; and ten Boss Mangans shall not prevent me doing far more as I please as his wife than I have ever been able to do as a poor girl. [*Stooping to the recumbent figure*] Shall they, Boss? I think not. [*She passes on to the drawing-table, and leans against the end of it, facing the windows*]. I shall not have to spend most of my time wondering how long my gloves will last, anyhow.

MRS HUSHABYE   [*rising superbly*] Ellie: you are a wicked sordid little beast. And to think that I actually condescended to fascinate that creature there to save you from him! Well, let me tell you this: if you make this disgusting match, you will never see Hector again if I can help it.

ELLIE   [*unmoved*] I nailed Mangan by telling him that if

he did not marry me he should never see you again. [*She lifts herself on her wrists and seats herself on the end of the table*].

MRS HUSHABYE  [*recoiling*] Oh!

ELLIE.  So you see I am not unprepared for your playing that trump against me. Well, you just try it: thats all. I should have made a man of Marcus, not a household pet.

MRS HUSHABYE  [*flaming*] You dare!

ELLIE  [*looking almost dangerous*] Set him thinking about me if y o u dare.

MRS HUSHABYE.  Well, of all the impudent little fiends I ever met! Hector says there is a certain point at which the only answer you can give to a man who breaks all the rules is to knock him down. What would you say if I were to box your ears?

ELLIE  [*calmly*] I should pull your hair.

MRS HUSHABYE  [*mischievously*] That wouldnt hurt me. Perhaps it comes off at night.

ELLIE  [*so taken aback that she drops off the table and runs to her*] Oh, you dont mean to say, Hesione, that your beautiful black hair is false?

MRS HUSHABYE  [*patting it*] Dont tell Hector. He believes in it.

ELLIE  [*groaning*] Oh! Even the hair that ensnared him false! Everything false!

MRS HUSHABYE.  Pull it and try. Other women can snare men in their hair; but I can swing a baby on mine. Aha! you cant do that, Goldylocks.

ELLIE  [*heartbroken*]. No. You have stolen m y babies.

MRS HUSHABYE.  Pettikins: dont make me cry. You know, what you said about my making a household pet of him is a little true. Perhaps he ought to have waited for you. Would any other woman on earth forgive you?

ELLIE.  Oh, what right had you to take him all for yourself! [*Pulling herself together*] There! You couldnt help it: neither of us could help it. He couldnt help it. No: dont say anything more: I cant bear it. Let us wake the object. [*She begins stroking Mangan's head, reversing the movement with which she put him to sleep*]. Wake up, do you hear? You are to wake up at once. Wake up, wake up, wake—

MANGAN   [*bouncing out of the chair in a fury and turning on them*] Wake up! So you think Ive been asleep, do you? [*He kicks the chair violently back out of his way, and gets between them*]. You throw me into a trance so that I cant move hand or foot—I might have been buried alive! it's a mercy I wasnt—and then you think I was only asleep. If youd let me drop the two times you rolled me about, my nose would have been flattened for life against the floor. But Ive found you all out, anyhow. I know the sort of people I'm among now. Ive heard every word youve said, you and your precious father, and [*to Mrs Hushabye*] you too. So I'm an object, am I? I'm a thing, am I? I'm a fool that hasnt sense enough to feed myself properly, am I? I'm afraid of the men that would starve if it werent for the wages I give them, am I? I'm nothing but a disgusting old skinflint to be made a convenience of by designing women and fool managers of my works, am I? I'm—

MRS HUSHABYE   [*with the most elegant aplomb*] Sh-sh-sh-sh-sh! Mr Mangan: you are bound in honor to obliterate from your mind all you heard while you were pretending to be asleep. It was not meant for you to hear.

MANGAN.   Pretending to be asleep! Do you think if I was only pretending that I'd have sprawled there helpless, and listened to such unfairness, such lies, such injustice and plotting and backbiting and slandering of me, if I could have up and told you what I thought of you! I wonder I didnt burst.

MRS HUSHABYE   [*sweetly*] You dreamt it all, Mr Mangan. We were only saying how beautifully peaceful you looked in your sleep. That was all, wasnt it, Ellie? Believe me, Mr Mangan, all those unpleasant things came into your mind in the last half second before you woke. Ellie rubbed your hair the wrong way; and the disagreeable sensation suggested a disagreeable dream.

MANGAN    [*doggedly*] I believe in dreams.

MRS HUSHABYE.    So do I. But they go by contraries, dont they?

MANGAN    [*depths of emotion suddenly welling up in him*] I shant forget, to my dying day, that when you gave me the glad eye that time in the garden, you were making a fool of me. That was a dirty low mean thing to do. You had no right to let me come near you if I disgusted you. It isnt my fault if I'm old and havnt a moustache like a bronze candlestick as your husband has. There are things no decent woman would do to a man—like a man hitting a woman in the breast.

*Hesione, utterly shamed, sits down on the sofa and covers her face with her hands. Mangan sits down also on his chair and begins to cry like a child. Ellie stares at them. Mrs Hushabye, at the distressing sound he makes, takes down her hands and looks at him. She rises and runs to him.*

MRS HUSHABYE.    Dont cry: I cant bear it. Have I broken your heart? I didnt know you had one. How could I?

MANGAN.    I'm a man aint I?

MRS HUSHABYE    [*half coaxing, half rallying, altogether tenderly*] Oh no: not what I call a man. Only a Boss: just that and nothing else. What business has a Boss with a heart?

MANGAN.    Then youre not a bit sorry for what you did, nor ashamed?

MRS HUSHABYE.    I was ashamed for the first time in my life when you said that about hitting a woman in the breast, and I found out what I'd done. My very bones blushed red. Youve had your revenge, Boss. Arnt you satisfied?

MANGAN.    Serve you right! Do you hear? Serve you right! Youre just cruel. Cruel.

MRS HUSHABYE.    Yes: cruelty would be delicious if one could only find some sort of cruelty that didnt really hurt.

By the way [*sitting down beside him on the arm of the chair*], whats your name? It's not really Boss, is it?

MANGAN    [*shortly*] If you want to know, my name's Alfred.

MRS HUSHABYE    [*springing up*] Alfred! Ellie: he was christened after Tennyson!!!

MANGAN    [*rising*] I was christened after my uncle, and never had a penny from him, damn him! What of it?

MRS HUSHABYE.    It comes to me suddenly that you are a real person: that you had a mother, like anyone else. [*Putting her hands on his shoulders and surveying him*] Little Alf!

MANGAN.    Well, you have a nerve.

MRS HUSHABYE.    And you have a heart, Alfy, a whimpering little heart, but a real one. [*Releasing him suddenly*] Now run and make it up with Ellie. She has had time to think what to say to you, which is more than I had. [*She goes out quickly into the garden by the port door*].

MANGAN.    That woman has a pair of hands that go right through you.

ELLIE.    Still in love with her, in spite of all we said about you?

MANGAN.    Are all women like you two? Do they never think of anything about a man except what they can get out of him? Y o u werent even thinking that about me. You were only thinking whether your gloves would last.

ELLIE.    I shall not have to think about that when we are married.

MANGAN.    And you think I am going to marry you after what I heard there!

ELLIE.    You heard nothing from me that I did not tell you before.

MANGAN.    Perhaps you think I cant do without you.

ELLIE.    I think you would feel lonely without us all now, after coming to know us so well.

MANGAN [*with something like a yell of despair*] Am I never to have the last word?

CAPTAIN SHOTOVER [*appearing at the starboard garden door*] There is a soul in torment here. What is the matter?

MANGAN. This girl doesnt want to spend her life wondering how long her gloves will last.

CAPTAIN SHOTOVER [*passing through*] Dont wear any. I never do. [*He goes into the pantry*].

LADY UTTERWORD [*appearing at the port garden door, in a handsome dinner dress*] Is anything the matter?

ELLIE. This gentleman wants to know is he never to have the last word?

LADY UTTERWORD [*coming forward to the sofa*] I should let him have it, my dear. The important thing is not to have the last word, but to have your own way.

MANGAN. She wants both.

LADY UTTERWORD. She wont get them, Mr Mangan. Providence always has the last word.

MANGAN [*desperately*] Now y o u are going to come religion over me. In this house a man's mind might as well be a football. I'm going. [*He makes for the hall, but is stopped by a hail from the Captain, who has just emerged from his pantry*].

CAPTAIN SHOTOVER. Whither away, Boss Mangan?

MANGAN. To hell out of this house: let that be enough for you and all here.

CAPTAIN SHOTOVER. You were welcome to come: you are free to go. The wide earth, the high seas, the spacious skies are waiting for you outside.

LADY UTTERWORD. But your things, Mr Mangan. Your bags, your comb and brushes, your pyjamas—

HECTOR [*who has just appeared in the port doorway in a handsome Arab costume*] Why should the escaping slave take his chains with him?

MANGAN. Thats right, Hushabye. Keep the pyjamas, my lady; and much good may they do you.

HECTOR   [*advancing to Lady Utterword's left hand*] Let us all go out into the night and leave everything behind us.

MANGAN.   You stay where you are, the lot of you. I want no company, especially female company.

ELLIE.   Let him go. He is unhappy here. He is angry with us.

CAPTAIN SHOTOVER.   Go, Boss Mangan; and when you have found the land where there is happiness and where there are no women, send me its latitude and longitude; and I will join you there.

LADY UTTERWORD.   You will certainly not be comfortable without your luggage, Mr Mangan.

ELLIE   [*impatient*] Go, go: why dont you go? It is a heavenly night: you can sleep on the heath. Take my waterproof to lie on: it is hanging up in the hall.

HECTOR.   Breakfast at nine, unless you prefer to breakfast with the Captain at six.

ELLIE.   Good night, Alfred.

HECTOR.   Alfred! [*He runs back to the door and calls into the garden*] Randall: Mangan's Christian name is Alfred.

RANDALL   [*appearing in the starboard doorway in evening dress*] Then Hesione wins her bet.

*Mrs Hushabye appears in the port doorway. She throws her left arm round Hector's neck; draws him with her to the back of the sofa; and throws her right arm round Lady Utterword's neck.*

MRS HUSHABYE.   They wouldnt believe me, Alf.

*They contemplate him.*

MANGAN.   Is there any more of you coming in to look at me, as if I was the latest thing in a menagerie?

MRS HUSHABYE.   You a r e the latest thing in this menagerie.

*Before Mangan can retort, a fall of furniture is heard from upstairs; then a pistol shot, and a yell of pain. The staring group breaks up in consternation.*

MAZZINI'S VOICE   [*from above*] Help! A burglar! Help!

HECTOR  [*his eyes blazing*] A burglar!!!

MRS HUSHABYE.  No, Hector: youll be shot. [*But it is too late: he has dashed out past Mangan, who hastily moves towards the bookshelves out of his way*].

CAPTAIN SHOTOVER  [*blowing his whistle*] All hands aloft! [*He strides out after Hector*].

LADY UTTERWORD.  My diamonds! [*She follows the Captain*].

RANDALL  [*rushing after her*] No, Ariadne. Let me.

ELLIE.  Oh, is papa shot? [*She runs out*].

MRS HUSHABYE.  Are you frightened, Alf?

MANGAN.  No. It aint my house, thank God.

MRS HUSHABYE.  If they catch a burglar, shall we have to go into court as witnesses, and be asked all sorts of questions about our private lives?

MANGAN.  You wont be believed if you tell the truth.

*Mazzini, terribly upset, with a duelling pistol in his hand, comes from the hall, and makes his way to the drawing-table.*

MAZZINI.  Oh, my dear Mrs Hushabye, I might have killed him. [*He throws the pistol on the table and staggers round to the chair*]. I hope you wont believe I really intended to.

*Hector comes in, marching an old and villainous looking man before him by the collar. He plants him in the middle of the room and releases him.*

*Ellie follows, and immediately runs across to the back of her father's chair and pats his shoulders.*

RANDALL  [*entering with a poker*] Keep your eye on this door, Mangan. I'll look after the other. [*He goes to the starboard door and stands on guard there*].

*Lady Utterword comes in after Randall, and goes between Mrs Hushabye and Mangan.*

*Nurse Guinness brings up the rear, and waits near the door, on Mangan's left.*

MRS HUSHABYE.  What has happened?

MAZZINI.  Your housekeeper told me there was somebody upstairs, and gave me a pistol that Mr Hushabye had been practising with. I thought it would frighten him; but it went off at a touch.

THE BURGLAR.   Yes, and took the skin off my ear. Precious near took the top off my head. Why dont you have a proper revolver instead of a thing like that, that goes off if you as much as blow on it?

HECTOR.   One of my duelling pistols. Sorry.

MAZZINI.   He put his hands up and said it was a fair cop.

THE BURGLAR.   So it was. Send for the police.

HECTOR.   No, by thunder! It was not a fair cop. We were four to one.

MRS HUSHABYE.   What will they do to him?

THE BURGLAR.   Ten years. Beginning with solitary. Ten years off my life. I shant serve it all: I'm too old. It will see me out.

LADY UTTERWORD.   You should have thought of that before you stole my diamonds.

THE BURGLAR.   Well, youve got them back, lady: havnt you? Can you give me back the years of my life you are going to take from me?

MRS HUSHABYE.   Oh, we cant bury a man alive for ten years for a few diamonds.

THE BURGLAR.   Ten little shining diamonds! Ten long black years!

LADY UTTERWORD.   Think of what it is for us to be dragged through the horrors of a criminal court, and have all our family affairs in the papers! If you were a native, and Hastings could order you a good beating and send you away, I shouldnt mind; but here in England there is no real protection for any respectable person.

THE BURGLAR.   I'm too old to be giv a hiding, lady. Send for the police and have done with it. It's only just and right you should.

RANDALL   [who has relaxed his vigilance on seeing the bur-

*glar so pacifically disposed, and comes forward swinging the poker between his fingers like a well-folded umbrella*] It is neither just nor right that we should be put to a lot of inconvenience to gratify your moral enthusiasm, my friend. You had better get out, while you have the chance.

THE BURGLAR [*inexorably*] No. I must work my sin off my conscience. This has come as a sort of call to me. Let me spend the rest of my life repenting in a cell. I shall have my reward above.

MANGAN [*exasperated*] The very burglars cant behave naturally in this house.

HECTOR. My good sir: you must work out your salvation at somebody else's expense. Nobody here is going to charge you.

THE BURGLAR. Oh, you wont charge me, wont you?

HECTOR. No. I'm sorry to be inhospitable; but will you kindly leave the house?

THE BURGLAR. Right. I'll go to the police station and give myself up. [*He turns resolutely to the door; but Hector stops him*].

| | |
|---|---|
| HECTOR | Oh no. You mustnt do that. |
| RANDALL | No, no. Clear out, man, cant you; and dont be a fool. |
| MRS HUSHABYE | Dont be so silly. Cant you repent at home? |

LADY UTTERWORD. You will have to do as you are told.

THE BURGLAR. It's compounding a felony, you know.

MRS HUSHABYE. This is utterly ridiculous. Are we to be forced to prosecute this man when we dont want to?

THE BURGLAR. Am I to be robbed of my salvation to save you the trouble of spending a day at the sessions? Is that justice? Is it right? Is it fair to me?

MAZZINI [*rising and leaning across the table persuasively as if it were a pulpit desk or a shop counter*] Come, come! let me shew you how you can turn your very crimes to account.

Why not set up as a locksmith? You must know more about locks than most honest men?

THE BURGLAR. Thats true, sir. But I couldnt set up as a locksmith under twenty pounds.

RANDALL. Well, you can easily steal twenty pounds. You will find it in the nearest bank.

THE BURGLAR [*horrified*] Oh what a thing for a gentleman to put into the head of a poor criminal scrambling out of the bottomless pit as it were! Oh, shame on you, sir! Oh, God forgive you! [*He throws himself into the big chair and covers his face as if in prayer*].

LADY UTTERWORD. Really, Randall!

HECTOR. It seems to me that we shall have to take up a collection for this inopportunely contrite sinner.

LADY UTTERWORD. But twenty pounds is ridiculous.

THE BURGLAR [*looking up quickly*] I shall have to buy a lot of tools, lady.

LADY UTTERWORD. Nonsense: you have your burgling kit.

THE BURGLAR. Whats a jimmy and a centrebit and an acetylene welding plant and a bunch of skeleton keys? I shall want a forge, and a smithy, and a shop, and fittings. I cant hardly do it for twenty.

HECTOR. My worthy friend, we havnt got twenty pounds.

THE BURGLAR [*now master of the situation*] You can raise it among you, cant you?

MRS HUSHABYE. Give him a sovereign, Hector, and get rid of him.

HECTOR [*giving him a pound*] There! Off with you.

THE BURGLAR [*rising and taking the money very ungratefully*] I wont promise nothing. You have more on you than a quid: all the lot of you, I mean.

LADY UTTERWORD [*vigorously*] Oh, let us prosecute him and have done with it. I have a conscience too, I hope; and

I do not feel at all sure that we have any right to let him go, especially if he is going to be greedy and impertinent.

THE BURGLAR [*quickly*] All right, lady, all right. Ive no wish to be anything but agreeable. Good evening, ladies and gentlemen; and thank you kindly.

*He is hurrying out when he is confronted in the doorway by Captain Shotover.*

CAPTAIN SHOTOVER [*fixing the burglar with a piercing regard*] Whats this? Are there two of you?

THE BURGLAR [*falling on his knees before the Captain in abject terror*] Oh my good Lord, what have I done? Dont tell me its your house Ive broken into, Captain Shotover.

*The Captain seizes him by the collar; drags him to his feet; and leads him to the middle of the group, Hector falling back beside his wife to make way for them.*

CAPTAIN SHOTOVER [*turning him towards Ellie*] Is that your daughter? [*He releases him*].

THE BURGLAR. Well, how do I know, Captain? You know the sort of life you and me has led. Any young lady of that age might be my daughter anywhere in the wide world, as you might say.

CAPTAIN SHOTOVER [*to Mazzini*] You are not Billy Dunn. This is Billy Dunn. Why have you imposed on me?

THE BURGLAR [*indignantly to Mazzini*] Have you been giving yourself out to be me? You, that nigh blew my head off! Shooting yourself, in a manner of speaking!

MAZZINI. My dear Captain Shotover, ever since I came into this house I have done hardly anything else but assure you that I am not Mr William Dunn, but Mazzini Dunn, a very different person.

THE BURGLAR. He dont belong to my branch, Captain. Theres two sets in the family: the thinking Dunns and the drinking Dunns, each going their own ways. I'm a drinking Dunn: he's a thinking Dunn. But that didnt give him any right to shoot me.

CAPTAIN SHOTOVER. So youve turned burglar, have you?

THE BURGLAR. No, Captain: I wouldnt disgrace our old sea calling by such a thing. I am no burglar.

LADY UTTERWORD. What were you doing with my diamonds?

GUINNESS. What did you break into the house for if youre no burglar?

RANDALL. Mistook the house for your own and came in by the wrong window, eh?

THE BURGLAR. Well, it's no use my telling you a lie: I can take in most captains, but not Captain Shotover, because he sold himself to the devil in Zanzibar, and can divine water, spot gold, explode a cartridge in your pocket with a glance of his eye, and see the truth hidden in the heart of man. But I'm no burglar.

CAPTAIN SHOTOVER. Are you an honest man?

THE BURGLAR. I dont set up to be better than my fellow-creatures, and never did, as you well know, Captain. But what I do is innocent and pious. I enquire about for houses where the right sort of people live. I work it on them same as I worked it here. I break into the house; put a few spoons or diamonds in my pocket; make a noise; get caught; and take up a collection. And you wouldnt believe how hard it is to get caught when youre actually trying to. I have knocked over all the chairs in a room without a soul paying any attention to me. In the end I have had to walk out and leave the job.

RANDALL. When that happens, do you put back the spoons and diamonds?

THE BURGLAR. Well, I dont fly in the face of Providence, if thats what you want to know.

CAPTAIN SHOTOVER. Guinness: you remember this man?

GUINNESS. I should think I do, seeing I was married to him, the blackguard!

HESIONE           [*exclaiming*   { Married to him!
LADY UTTERWORD }  *together*]     { Guinness!!

THE BURGLAR. It wasnt legal. Ive been married to no end of women. No use coming that over me.

CAPTAIN SHOTOVER. Take him to the forecastle. [*He flings him to the door with a strength beyond his years*].

GUINNESS. I suppose you mean the kitchen. They wont have him there. Do you expect servants to keep company with thieves and all sorts?

CAPTAIN SHOTOVER. Land-thieves and water-thieves are the same flesh and blood. I'll have no boatswain on my quarter-deck. Off with you both.

THE BURGLAR. Yes, Captain. [*He goes out humbly*].

MAZZINI. Will it be safe to have him in the house like that?

GUINNESS. Why didnt you shoot him, sir? If I'd known who he was, I'd have shot him myself. [*She goes out*].

MRS HUSHABYE. Do sit down, everybody. [*She sits down on the sofa*].

*They all move except Ellie. Mazzini resumes his seat. Randall sits down in the window seat near the starboard door, again making a pendulum of his poker, and studying it as Galileo might have done. Hector sits on his left, in the middle. Mangan, forgotten, sits in the port corner. Lady Utterword takes the big chair. Captain Shotover goes into the pantry in deep abstraction. They all look after him; and Lady Utterword coughs consciously.*

MRS HUSHABYE. So Billy Dunn was poor nurse's little romance. I knew there had been somebody.

RANDALL. They will fight their battles over again and enjoy themselves immensely.

LADY UTTERWORD [*irritably*] You are not married; and you know nothing about it, Randall. Hold your tongue.

RANDALL.   Tyrant!

MRS HUSHABYE.   Well, we have had a very exciting evening. Everything will be an anticlimax after it. We'd better all go to bed.

RANDALL.   Another burglar may turn up.

MAZZINI.   Oh, impossible! I hope not.

RANDALL.   Why not? There is more than one burglar in England.

MRS HUSHABYE.   What do you say, Alf?

MANGAN [*huffily*]   Oh, I dont matter. I'm forgotten. The burglar has put my nose out of joint. Shove me into a corner and have done with me.

MRS HUSHABYE [*jumping up mischievously, and going to him*]   Would you like a walk on the heath, Alfred? With me?

ELLIE.   Go, Mr Mangan. It will do you good. Hesione will soothe you.

MRS HUSHABYE [*slipping her arm under his and pulling him upright*]   Come, Alfred. There is a moon: it's like the night in Tristan and Isolde. [*She caresses his arm and draws him to the port garden door*].

MANGAN [*writhing but yielding*]   How you can have the face—the heart— [*He breaks down and is heard sobbing as she takes him out*].

LADY UTTERWORD.   What an extraordinary way to behave! What is the matter with the man?

ELLIE [*in a strangely calm voice, staring into an imaginary distance*]   His heart is breaking: that is all. [*The Captain appears at the pantry door, listening*]. It is a curious sensation: the sort of pain that goes mercifully beyond our powers of feeling. When your heart is broken, your boats are burned: nothing matters any more. It is the end of happiness and the beginning of peace.

LADY UTTERWORD [*suddenly rising in a rage, to the astonishment of the rest*]   How dare you?

HECTOR.   Good heavens! Whats the matter?

RANDALL [*in a warning whisper*] Tch—tch—tch! Steady.

ELLIE [*surprised and haughty*]   I was not addressing you particularly, Lady Utterword. And I am not accustomed to be asked how dare I.

LADY UTTERWORD.   Of course not. Anyone can see how badly you have been brought up.

MAZZINI.   Oh, I hope not, Lady Utterword. Really!

LADY UTTERWORD.   I know very well what you meant. The impudence!

ELLIE.   What on earth do you mean?

CAPTAIN SHOTOVER [*advancing to the table*] She means that her heart will not break. She has been longing all her life for someone to break it. At last she has become afraid she has none to break.

LADY UTTERWORD [*flinging herself on her knees and throwing her arms round him*] Papa: dont say you think Ive no heart.

CAPTAIN SHOTOVER [*raising her with grim tenderness*] If you had no heart how could you want to have it broken, child?

HECTOR [*rising with a bound*] Lady Utterword: you are not to be trusted. You have made a scene. [*He runs out into the garden through the starboard door*].

LADY UTTERWORD.   Oh! Hector, Hector! [*She runs out after him*].

RANDALL.   Only nerves, I assure you. [*He rises and follows her, waving the poker in his agitation*].
Ariadne! Ariadne! For God's sake be careful. You will—[*He is gone*].

MAZZINI [*rising*] How distressing! Can I do anything, I wonder?

CAPTAIN SHOTOVER [*promptly taking his chair and setting to work at the drawing-board*] No. Go to bed. Goodnight.

MAZZINI [*bewildered*] Oh! Perhaps you are right.

ELLIE. Goodnight, dearest. [*She kisses him*].

MAZZINI. Goodnight, love. [*He makes for the door, but turns aside to the bookshelves*]. I'll just take a book. [*He takes one*]. Goodnight. [*He goes out, leaving Ellie alone with the Captain*].

*The Captain is intent on his drawing. Ellie, standing sentry over his chair, contemplates him for a moment.*

ELLIE. Does nothing ever disturb you, Captain Shotover?

CAPTAIN SHOTOVER. Ive stood on the bridge for eighteen hours in a typhoon. Life here is stormier; but I can stand it.

ELLIE. Do you think I ought to marry Mr Mangan?

CAPTAIN SHOTOVER [*never looking up*] One rock is as good as another to be wrecked on.

ELLIE. I am not in love with him.

CAPTAIN SHOTOVER. Who said you were?

ELLIE. You are not surprised?

CAPTAIN SHOTOVER. Surprised! At m y age!

ELLIE. It seems to me quite fair. He wants me for one thing: I want him for another.

CAPTAIN SHOTOVER. Money?

ELLIE. Yes.

CAPTAIN SHOTOVER. Well, one turns the cheek: the other kisses it. One provides the cash: the other spends it.

ELLIE. Who will have the best of the bargain, I wonder?

CAPTAIN SHOTOVER. You. These fellows live in an office all day. You will have to put up with him from dinner to breakfast; but you will both be asleep most of that time. All day you will be quit of him; and you will be shopping with his money. If that is too much for you, marry a seafaring man: you will be bothered with him only three weeks in the year, perhaps.

ELLIE. That would be best of all, I suppose.

CAPTAIN SHOTOVER. It's a dangerous thing to be married right up to the hilt, like my daughter's husband. The man is at home all day, like a damned soul in hell.

ELLIE. I never thought of that before.

CAPTAIN SHOTOVER. If youre marrying for business, you cant be too businesslike.

ELLIE. Why do women always want other women's husbands?

CAPTAIN SHOTOVER. Why do horse-thieves prefer a horse that is broken-in to one that is wild?

ELLIE [with a short laugh] I suppose so. What a vile world it is!

CAPTAIN SHOTOVER. It doesnt concern me. I'm nearly out of it.

ELLIE. And I'm only just beginning.

CAPTAIN SHOTOVER. Yes; so look ahead.

ELLIE. Well, I think I am being very prudent.

CAPTAIN SHOTOVER. I didnt say prudent. I said look ahead.

ELLIE. Whats the difference?

CAPTAIN SHOTOVER. It's prudent to gain the whole world and lose your own soul. But dont forget that your soul sticks to you if you stick to it; but the world has a way of slipping through your fingers.

ELLIE [wearily, leaving him and beginning to wander restlessly about the room] I'm sorry, Captain Shotover; but it's no use talking like that to me. Old-fashioned people are no use to me. Old-fashioned people think you can have a soul without money. They think the less money you have, the more soul you have. Young people nowadays know better. A soul is a very expensive thing to keep: much more so than a motor car.

CAPTAIN SHOTOVER. Is it? How much does your soul eat?

ELLIE. Oh, a lot. It eats music and pictures and books

and mountains and lakes and beautiful things to wear and nice people to be with. In this country you cant have them without lots of money: that is why our souls are so horribly starved.

CAPTAIN SHOTOVER.    Mangan's soul lives on pigs' food.

ELLIE.    Yes: money is thrown away on him. I suppose his soul was starved when he was young. But it will not be thrown away on me. It is just because I want to save my soul that I am marrying for money. All the women who are not fools do.

CAPTAIN SHOTOVER.    There are other ways of getting money. Why dont you steal it?

ELLIE.    Because I dont want to go to prison.

CAPTAIN SHOTOVER.    Is that the only reason? Are you quite sure honesty has nothing to do with it?

ELLIE.    Oh, you are very old-fashioned, Captain. Does any modern girl believe that the legal and illegal ways of getting money are the honest and dishonest ways? Mangan robbed my father and my father's friends. I should rob all the money back from Mangan if the police would let me. As they wont, I must get it back by marrying him.

CAPTAIN SHOTOVER.    I cant argue: I'm too old: my mind is made up and finished. All I can tell you is that, old-fashioned or new-fashioned, if you sell yourself, you deal your soul a blow that all the books and pictures and concerts and scenery in the world wont heal. [*He gets up suddenly and makes for the pantry*].

ELLIE    [*running after him and seizing him by the sleeve*] Then why did you sell yourself to the devil in Zanzibar?

CAPTAIN SHOTOVER    [*stopping, startled*] What?

ELLIE.    You shall not run away before you answer. I have found out that trick of yours. If you sold yourself, why shouldnt I?

CAPTAIN SHOTOVER.    I had to deal with men so degraded that they wouldnt obey me unless I swore at them and kicked them and beat them with my fists. Foolish people took young thieves off the streets; flung them into a training ship where they were taught to fear the cane instead of fearing God; and thought theyd made men and sailors of them by private subscription. I tricked these thieves into believing I'd sold myself to the devil. It saved my soul from the kicking and swearing that was damning me by inches.

ELLIE [*releasing him*] I shall pretend to sell myself to Boss Mangan to save my soul from the poverty that is damning me by inches.

CAPTAIN SHOTOVER.   Riches will damn you ten times deeper. Riches wont save even your body.

ELLIE.   Old-fashioned again. We know now that the soul is the body, and the body the soul. They tell us they are different because they want to persuade us that we can keep our souls if we let them make slaves of our bodies. I am afraid you are no use to me, Captain.

CAPTAIN SHOTOVER.   What did you expect? A Savior, eh? Are you old-fashioned enough to believe in that?

ELLIE.   No. But I thought you were very wise, and might help me. Now I have found you out. You pretend to be busy, and think of fine things to say, and run in and out to surprise people by saying them, and get away before they can answer you.

CAPTAIN SHOTOVER.   It confuses me to be answered. It discourages me. I cannot bear men and women. I have to run away. I must run away now. [*He tries to*].

ELLIE [*again seizing his arm*] You shall not run away from me. I can hypnotize you. You are the only person in the house I can say what I like to. I know you are fond of me. Sit down. [*She draws him to the sofa*].

CAPTAIN SHOTOVER [*yielding*] Take care: I am in my dotage. Old men are dangerous: it doesnt matter to them what is going to happen to the world.

*They sit side by side on the sofa. She leans affectionately against him with her head on his shoulder and her eyes half closed.*

ELLIE  [*dreamily*]  I should have thought nothing else mattered to old men. They cant be very interested in what is going to happen to themselves.

CAPTAIN SHOTOVER.   A man's interest in the world is only the overflow from his interest in himself. When you are a child your vessel is not yet full; so you care for nothing but your own affairs. When you grow up, your vessel overflows; and you are a politician, a philosopher, or an explorer and adventurer. In old age the vessel dries up: there is no overflow: you are a child again. I can give you the memories of my ancient wisdom: mere scraps and leavings; but I no longer really care for anything but my own little wants and hobbies. I sit here working out my old ideas as a means of destroying my fellow-creatures. I see my daughters and their men living foolish lives of romance and sentiment and snobbery. I see you, the younger generation, turning from their romance and sentiment and snobbery to money and comfort and hard common sense. I was ten times happier on the bridge in the typhoon, or frozen into Arctic ice for months in darkness, than you or they have ever been. You are looking for a rich husband. At your age I looked for hardship, danger, horror, and death, that I might feel the life in me more intensely. I did not let the fear of death govern my life; and my reward was, I had my life. You are going to let the fear of poverty govern your life; and your reward will be that you will eat, but you will not live.

ELLIE  [*sitting up impatiently*]  But what can I do? I am not a sea captain: I cant stand on bridges in typhoons, or go slaughtering seals and whales in Greenland's icy mountains. They wont let women be captains. Do you want me to be a stewardess?

CAPTAIN SHOTOVER.   There are worse lives. The stewardesses could come ashore if they liked; but they sail and sail and sail.

ELLIE.   What could they do ashore but marry for money? I dont want to be a stewardess: I am too bad a sailor. Think of something else for me.

CAPTAIN SHOTOVER.   I cant think so long and continuously. I am too old. I must go in and out. [*He tries to rise*].

ELLIE   [*pulling him back*] You shall not. You are happy here, arnt you?

CAPTAIN SHOTOVER.   I tell you it's dangerous to keep me. I cant keep awake and alert.

ELLIE.   What do you run away for? To sleep?

CAPTAIN SHOTOVER.   No. To get a glass of rum.

ELLIE   [*frightfully disillusioned*] Is t h a t it? How disgusting! Do you like being drunk?

CAPTAIN SHOTOVER.   No: I dread being drunk more than anything in the world. To be drunk means to have dreams; to go soft; to be easily pleased and deceived; to fall into the clutches of women. Drink does that for you when you are young. But when you are old: very very old, like me, the dreams come by themselves. You dont know how terrible that is: you are young: you sleep at night only, and sleep soundly. But later on you will sleep in the afternoon. Later still you will sleep even in the morning; and you will awake tired, tired of life. You will never be free from dozing and dreams: the dreams will steal upon your work every ten minutes unless you can awaken yourself with rum. I drink now to keep sober; but the dreams are conquering: rum is not what it was: I have had ten glasses since you came; and it might be so much water. Go get me another: Guinness knows where it is. You had better see for yourself the horror of an old man drinking.

ELLIE.   You shall not drink. Dream. I like you to dream. You must never be in the real world when we talk together.

CAPTAIN SHOTOVER.   I am too weary to resist or too

weak. I am in my second childhood. I do not see you as you really are. I cant remember what I really am. I feel nothing but the accursed happiness I have dreaded all my life long: the happiness that comes as life goes, the happiness of yielding and dreaming instead of resisting and doing, the sweetness of the fruit that is going rotten.

ELLIE.   You dread it almost as much as I used to dread losing my dreams and having to fight and do things. But that is all over for me: m y dreams are dashed to pieces. I should like to marry a very old, very rich man. I should like to marry you. I had much rather marry you than marry Mangan. Are you very rich?

CAPTAIN SHOTOVER.   No. Living from hand to mouth. And I have a wife somewhere in Jamaica: a black one. My first wife. Unless she's dead.

ELLIE.   What a pity! I feel so happy with you. [*She takes his hand, almost unconsciously, and pats it*]. I thought I should never feel happy again.

CAPTAIN SHOTOVER.   Why?

ELLIE.   Dont you know?

CAPTAIN SHOTOVER.   No.

ELLIE.   Heartbreak. I fell in love with Hector, and didnt know he was married.

CAPTAIN SHOTOVER.   Heartbreak? Are you one of those who are so sufficient to themselves that they are only happy when they are stripped of everything, even of hope?

ELLIE   [*gripping the hand*] It seems so; for I feel now as if there was nothing I could not do, because I want nothing.

CAPTAIN SHOTOVER.   Thats the only real strength. Thats genius. Thats better than rum.

ELLIE   [*throwing away his hand*] Rum! Why did you spoil it?

*Hector and Randall come in from the garden through the starboard door.*

HECTOR. I beg your pardon. We did not know there was anyone here.

ELLIE [*rising*] That means that you want to tell Mr Randall the story about the tiger. Come, Captain: I want to talk to my father; and you had better come with me.

CAPTAIN SHOTOVER [*rising*] Nonsense! the man is in bed.

ELLIE. Aha! Ive caught you. My real father has gone to bed; but the father you gave me is in the kitchen. You knew quite well all along. Come. [*She draws him out into the garden with her through the port door*].

HECTOR. Thats an extraordinary girl. She has the Ancient Mariner on a string like a Pekinese dog.

RANDALL. Now that they have gone, shall we have a friendly chat?

HECTOR. You are in what is supposed to be my house. I am at your disposal.

*Hector sits down in the draughtsman's chair, turning it to face Randall, who remains standing, leaning at his ease against the carpenter's bench.*

RANDALL. I take it that we may be quite frank. I mean about Lady Utterword.

HECTOR. Y o u may. I have nothing to be frank about. I never met her until this afternoon.

RANDALL [*straightening up*] What! But you are her sister's husband.

HECTOR. Well, if you come to that, you are her husband's brother.

RANDALL. But you seem to be on intimate terms with her.

HECTOR. So do you.

RANDALL. Yes; but I a m on intimate terms with her. I have known her for years.

HECTOR. It took her years to get to the same point with you that she got to with me in five minutes, it seems.

RANDALL   [*vexed*] Really, Ariadne is the limit. [*He moves away huffishly towards the windows*].

HECTOR   [*coolly*] She is, as I remarked to Hesione, a very enterprising woman.

RANDALL   [*returning, much troubled*] You see, Hushabye, you are what women consider a good-looking man.

HECTOR.   I cultivated that appearance in the days of my vanity; and Hesione insists on my keeping it up. She makes me wear these ridiculous things [*indicating his Arab costume*] because she thinks me absurd in evening dress.

RANDALL.   Still, you d o keep it up, old chap. Now, I assure you I have not an atom of jealousy in my disposition—

HECTOR.   The question would seem to be rather whether your brother has any touch of that sort.

RANDALL.   What! Hastings! Oh, dont trouble about Hastings. He has the gift of being able to work sixteen hours a day at the dullest detail, and actually likes it. That gets him to the top wherever he goes. As long as Ariadne takes care that he is fed regularly, he is only too thankful to anyone who will keep her in good humor for him.

HECTOR.   And as she has all the Shotover fascination, there is plenty of competition for the job, eh?

RANDALL   [*angrily*] She encourages them. Her conduct is perfectly scandalous. I assure you, my dear fellow, I havnt an atom of jealousy in my composition; but she makes herself the talk of every place she goes to by her thoughtlessness. It's nothing more: she doesnt really care for the men she keeps hanging about her; but how is the world to know that? It's not fair to Hastings. It's not fair to me.

HECTOR.   Her theory is that her conduct is so correct—

RANDALL.   Correct! She does nothing but make scenes from morning till night. You be careful, old chap. She will get you into trouble: that is, she would if she really cared for you.

HECTOR.   Doesnt she?

RANDALL.   Not a scrap. She may want your scalp to add to her collection; but her true affection has been engaged years ago. You had really better be careful.

HECTOR.   Do you suffer much from this jealousy?

RANDALL.   Jealousy! I jealous! My dear fellow, havnt I told you that there is not an atom of—

HECTOR.   Yes. And Lady Utterword told me she never made scenes. Well, dont waste your jealousy on my moustache. Never waste jealousy on a real man: it is the imaginary hero that supplants us all in the long run. Besides, jealousy does not belong to your easy man-of-the-world pose, which you carry so well in other respects.

RANDALL.   Really, Hushabye, I think a man may be allowed to be a gentleman without being accused of posing.

HECTOR.   It is a pose like any other. In this house we know all the poses: our game is to find out the man under the pose. The man under your pose is apparently Ellie's favorite, Othello.

RANDALL.   Some of your games in this house are damned annoying, let me tell you.

HECTOR.   Yes: I have been their victim for many years. I used to writhe under them at first; but I became accustomed to them. At last I learned to play them.

RANDALL.   If it's all the same to you, I had rather you didnt play them on me. You evidently dont quite understand my character, or my notions of good form.

HECTOR.   Is it your notion of good form to give away Lady Utterword?

RANDALL.   [a childishly plaintive note breaking into his huff] I have not said a word against Lady Utterword. This is just the conspiracy over again.

HECTOR.   What conspiracy?

RANDALL.   You know very well, sir. A conspiracy to

make me out to be pettish and jealous and childish and everything I am not. Everyone knows I am just the opposite.

HECTOR   [*rising*] Something in the air of the house has upset you. It often does have that effect. [*He goes to the garden door and calls Lady Utterword with commanding emphasis*] Ariadne!

LADY UTTERWORD   [*at some distance*] Yes.

RANDALL.   What are you calling her for? I want to speak—

LADY UTTERWORD   [*arriving breathless*] Yes. You really are a terribly commanding person. Whats the matter?

HECTOR.   I do not know how to manage your friend Randall. No doubt you do.

LADY UTTERWORD.   Randall: have you been making yourself ridiculous, as usual? I can see it in your face. Really, you are the most pettish creature.

RANDALL.   You know quite well, Ariadne, that I have not an ounce of pettishness in my disposition. I have made myself perfectly pleasant here. I have remained absolutely cool and imperturbable in the face of a burglar. Imperturbability is almost too strong a point of mine. But [*putting his foot down with a stamp, and walking angrily up and down the room*] I insist on being treated with a certain consideration. I will not allow Hushabye to take liberties with me. I will not stand your encouraging people as you do.

HECTOR.   The man has a rooted delusion that he is your husband.

LADY UTTERWORD.   I know. He is jealous. As if he had any right to be! He compromises me everywhere. He makes scenes all over the place. Randall: I will not allow it. I simply will not allow it. You had no right to discuss me with Hector. I will not be discussed by men.

HECTOR.   Be reasonable, Ariadne. Your fatal gift of beauty forces men to discuss you.

LADY UTTERWORD.   Oh indeed! what about your fatal gift of beauty?

HECTOR.   How can I help it?

LADY UTTERWORD.   You could cut off your moustache: I cant cut off my nose. I get my whole life messed up with people falling in love with me. And then Randall says I run after men.

RANDALL.   I—

LADY UTTERWORD.   Yes you do: you said it just now. Why cant you think of something else than women? Napoleon was quite right when he said that women are the occupation of the idle man. Well, if ever there was an idle man on earth, his name is Randall Utterword.

RANDALL.   Ariad—

LADY UTTERWORD [*overwhelming him with a torrent of words*] Oh yes you are: it's no use denying it. What have you ever done? What good are you? You are as much trouble in the house as a child of three. You couldnt live without your valet.

RANDALL.   This is—

LADY UTTERWORD.   Laziness! You are laziness incarnate. You are selfishness itself. You are the most uninteresting man on earth. You cant even gossip about anything but yourself and your grievances and your ailments and the people who have offended you. [*Turning to Hector*] Do you know what they call him, Hector?

HECTOR   ⎱ [*speaking    ⎰ Please dont tell me.
RANDALL  ⎰  together*]   ⎱ I'll not stand it—

LADY UTTERWORD.   Randall the Rotter: that is his name in good society.

RANDALL [*shouting*] I'll not bear it, I tell you. Will you listen to me, you infernal—[*He chokes*].

LADY UTTERWORD.   Well: go on. What were you going to call me? An infernal what? Which unpleasant animal is it to be this time?

RANDALL [*foaming*] There is no animal in the world so hateful as a woman can be. You are a maddening devil. Hushabye: you will not believe me when I tell you that I have loved this demon all my life; but God knows I have paid for it. [*He sits down in the draughtsman's chair, weeping*].

LADY UTTERWORD [*standing over him with triumphant contempt*] Cry-baby!

HECTOR [*gravely, coming to him*] My friend: the Shotover sisters have two strange powers over men. They can make them love; and they can make them cry. Thank your stars that you are not married to one of them.

LADY UTTERWORD [*haughtily*] And pray, Hector—

HECTOR [*suddenly catching her round the shoulders; swinging her right round him and away from Randall; and gripping her throat with the other hand*] Ariadne: if you attempt to start on me, I'll choke you: do you hear? The cat-and-mouse game with the other sex is a good game; but I can play your head off at it. [*He throws her, not at all gently, into the big chair, and proceeds, less fiercely but firmly*]. It is true that Napoleon said that woman is the occupation of the idle man. But he added that she is the relaxation of the warrior. Well, I am the warrior. So take care.

LADY UTTERWORD [*not in the least put out, and rather pleased by his violence*] My dear Hector: I have only done what you asked me to do.

HECTOR. How do you make that out, pray?

LADY UTTERWORD. You called me in to manage Randall, didn't you? You said you couldnt manage him yourself.

HECTOR. Well, what if I did? I did not ask you to drive the man mad.

LADY UTTERWORD. He isnt mad. Thats the way to manage him. If you were a mother, youd understand.

HECTOR. Mother! What are you up to now?

LADY UTTERWORD. It's quite simple. When the children got nerves and were naughty, I smacked them just enough to give them a good cry and a healthy nervous shock. They went to sleep and were quite good afterwards. Well, I cant smack Randall: he is too big; so when he gets nerves and is naughty, I just rag him till he cries. He will be all right now. Look: he is half asleep already. [*Which is quite true*].

RANDALL  [*waking up indignantly*] I'm not. You are most cruel, Ariadne. [*Sentimentally*] But I suppose I must forgive you, as usual. [*He checks himself in the act of yawning*].

LADY UTTERWORD  [*to Hector*] Is the explanation satisfactory, dread warrior?

HECTOR.  Some day I shall kill you, if you go too far. I thought you were a fool.

LADY UTTERWORD  [*laughing*] Everybody does, at first. But I am not such a fool as I look. [*She rises complacently*]. Now, Randall: go to bed. You will be a good boy in the morning.

RANDALL  [*only very faintly rebellious*] I'll go to bed when I like. It isnt ten yet.

LADY UTTERWORD.  It is long past ten. See that he goes to bed at once, Hector. [*She goes into the garden*].

HECTOR.  Is there any slavery on earth viler than this slavery of men to women?

RANDALL  [*rising resolutely*] I'll not speak to her tomorrow. I'll not speak to her for another week. I'll give her s u c h a lesson. I'll go straight to bed without bidding her goodnight. [*He makes for the door leading to the hall*].

HECTOR.  You are under a spell, man. Old Shotover sold himself to the devil in Zanzibar. The devil gave him a black witch for a wife; and these two demon daughters are their mystical progeny. I am tied to Hesione's apron-string; but I'm her husband; and if I did go stark staring mad about her, at least we became man and wife. But why should y o u let yourself be dragged about and beaten by Ariadne as a toy donkey is dragged about and beaten by a child? What do you get by it? Are you her lover?

RANDALL. You must not misunderstand me. In a higher sense—in a Platonic sense—

HECTOR. Psha! Platonic sense! She makes you her servant; and when pay-day comes round, she bilks you: that is what you mean.

RANDALL [*feebly*] Well, if I dont mind, I dont see what business it is of yours. Besides, I tell you I am going to punish her. You shall see: *I* know how to deal with women. I'm really very sleepy. Say goodnight to Mrs Hushabye for me, will you, like a good chap. Goodnight. [*He hurries out*].

HECTOR. Poor wretch! Oh women! women! women! [*He lifts his fists in invocation to heaven*]. Fall. Fall and crush. [*He goes out into the garden*].

# END OF ACT II

# Act III

In the garden, Hector, as he comes out through the glass door of the poop, finds Lady Utterword lying voluptuously in the hammock on the east side of the flagstaff, in the circle of light cast by the electric arc, which is like a moon in its opal globe. Beneath the head of the hammock, a campstool. On the other side of the flagstaff, on the long garden seat, Captain Shotover is asleep, with Ellie beside him, leaning affectionately against him on his right hand. On his left is a deck chair. Behind them in the gloom, Hesione is strolling about with Mangan. It is a fine still night, moonless.

LADY UTTERWORD.   What a lovely night! It seems made for us.

HECTOR.   The night takes no interest in us. What are we to the night? [He sits down moodily in the deck chair].

ELLIE   [dreamily, nestling against the Captain] Its beauty soaks into my nerves. In the night there is peace for the old and hope for the young.

HECTOR.   Is that remark your own?

ELLIE.   No. Only the last thing the Captain said before he went to sleep.

CAPTAIN SHOTOVER.   I'm not asleep.

HECTOR.   Randall is. Also Mr Mazzini Dunn. Mangan too, probably.

MANGAN.   No.

HECTOR.   Oh, you are there. I thought Hesione would
have sent you to bed by this time.

MRS HUSHABYE   [*coming to the back of the garden seat, into
the light, with Mangan*] I think I shall. He keeps telling me he
has a presentiment that he is going to die. I never met a man
so greedy for sympathy.

MANGAN   [*plaintively*] But I have a presentiment. I really
have. And you wouldnt listen.

MRS HUSHABYE.   I was listening for something else.
There was a sort of splendid drumming in the sky. Did none
of you hear it? It came from a distance and then died away.

MANGAN.   I tell you it was a train.

MRS HUSHABYE.   And *I* tell you, Alf, there is no train at
this hour. The last is nine fortyfive.

MANGAN.   But a goods train.

MRS HUSHABYE.   Not on our little line. They tack a truck
on to the passenger train. What can it have been, Hector?

HECTOR.   Heaven's threatening growl of disgust at us
useless futile creatures. [*Fiercely*] I tell you, one of two things
must happen. Either out of that darkness some new creation
will come to supplant us as we have supplanted the animals,
or the heavens will fall in thunder and destroy us.

LADY UTTERWORD   [*in a cool instructive manner, wallowing comfortably in her hammock*] We have not supplanted the
animals, Hector. Why do you ask heaven to destroy this
house, which could be made quite comfortable if Hesione
had any notion of how to live? Dont you know what is wrong
with it?

HECTOR.   We are wrong with it. There is no sense in us.
We are useless, dangerous, and ought to be abolished.

LADY UTTERWORD.   Nonsense! Hastings told me the
very first day he came here, nearly twentyfour years ago,
what is wrong with the house.

CAPTAIN SHOTOVER. What! The numskull said there was something wrong with my house!

LADY UTTERWORD. I said Hastings said it; and he is not in the least a numskull.

CAPTAIN SHOTOVER. Whats wrong with my house?

LADY UTTERWORD. Just what is wrong with a ship, papa. Wasnt it clever of Hastings to see that?

CAPTAIN SHOTOVER. The man's a fool. Theres nothing wrong with a ship.

LADY UTTERWORD. Yes there is.

MRS HUSHABYE. But what is it? Dont be aggravating, Addy.

LADY UTTERWORD. Guess.

HECTOR. Demons. Daughters of the witch of Zanzibar. Demons.

LADY UTTERWORD. Not a bit. I assure you, all this house needs to make it a sensible, healthy, pleasant house, with good appetites and sound sleep in it, is horses.

MRS HUSHABYE. Horses! What rubbish!

LADY UTTERWORD. Yes: horses. Why have we never been able to let this house? Because there are no proper stables. Go anywhere in England where there are natural, wholesome, contented, and really nice English people; and what do you always find? That the stables are the real centre of the household; and that if any visitor wants to play the piano the whole room has to be upset before it can be opened, there are so many things piled on it. I never lived until I learned to ride; and I shall never ride really well because I didnt begin as a child. There are only two classes in good society in England: the equestrian classes and the neurotic classes. It isnt mere convention: everybody can see that the people who hunt are the right people and the people who dont are the wrong ones.

CAPTAIN SHOTOVER. There is some truth in this. My ship made a man of me; and a ship is the horse of the sea.

LADY UTTERWORD. Exactly how Hastings explained your being a gentleman.

CAPTAIN SHOTOVER. Not bad for a numskull. Bring the man here with you next time: I must talk to him.

LADY UTTERWORD. Why is Randall such an obvious rotter? He is well bred; he has been at a public school and a university; he has been in the Foreign Office; he knows the best people and has lived all his life among them. Why is he so unsatisfactory, so contemptible? Why cant he get a valet to stay with him longer than a few months? Just because he is too lazy and pleasure-loving to hunt and shoot. He strums the piano, and sketches, and runs after married women, and reads literary books and poems. He actually plays the flute; but I never let him bring it into my house. If he would only— [*She is interrupted by the melancholy strains of a flute coming from an open window above. She raises herself indignantly in the hammock*]. Randall: you have not gone to bed. Have you been listening? [*The flute replies pertly*]:

How vulgar! Go to bed instantly, Randall: how dare you? [*The window is slammed down. She subsides*]. How can anyone care for such a creature!

MRS HUSHABYE. Addy: do you think Ellie ought to marry poor Alfred merely for his money?

MANGAN [*much alarmed*] Whats that? Mrs. Hushabye: are my affairs to be discussed like this before everybody?

LADY UTTERWORD. I dont think Randall is listening now.

MANGAN. Everybody is listening. It isnt right.

MRS HUSHABYE. But in the dark, what does it matter? Ellie doesnt mind. Do you, Ellie?

ELLIE. Not in the least. What is your opinion, Lady Utterword? You have so much good sense.

MANGAN. But it isnt right. It—[*Mrs Hushabye puts her hand on his mouth*]. Oh, very well.

LADY UTTERWORD. How much money have you, Mr Mangan?

MANGAN. Really—No: I cant stand this.

LADY UTTERWORD. Nonsense, Mr Mangan! It all turns on your income, doesnt it?

MANGAN. Well, if you come to that, how much money has she?

ELLIE. None.

LADY UTTERWORD. You are answered, Mr Mangan. And now, as you have made Miss Dunn throw her cards on the table, you cannot refuse to shew your own.

MRS HUSHABYE. Come, Alf! out with it! How much?

MANGAN [*baited out of all prudence*] Well, if you want to know, I have no money and never had any.

MRS HUSHABYE. Alfred: you mustnt tell naughty stories.

MANGAN. I'm not telling you stories. I'm telling you the raw truth.

LADY UTTERWORD. Then what do you live on, Mr Mangan?

MANGAN. Travelling expenses. And a trifle of commission.

CAPTAIN SHOTOVER. What more have any of us but travelling expenses for our life's journey?

MRS HUSHABYE. But you have factories and capital and things?

MANGAN. People think I have. People think I'm an industrial Napoleon. Thats why Miss Ellie wants to marry me. But I tell you I have nothing.

ELLIE. Do you mean that the factories are like Marcus's tigers? That they dont exist?

MANGAN. They exist all right enough. But theyre not

mine. They belong to syndicates and shareholders and all sorts of lazy good-for-nothing capitalists. I get money from such people to start the factories. I find people like Miss Dunn's father to work them, and keep a tight hand so as to make them pay. Of course I make them keep me going pretty well; but it's a dog's life; and I dont own anything.

MRS HUSHABYE.   Alfred, Alfred: you are making a poor mouth of it to get out of marrying Ellie.

MANGAN.   I'm telling the truth about my money for the first time in my life; and it's the first time my word has ever been doubted.

LADY UTTERWORD.   How sad! Why dont you go in for politics, Mr Mangan?

MANGAN.   Go in for politics! Where have you been living? I a m in politics.

LADY UTTERWORD.   I'm sure I beg your pardon. I never heard of you.

MANGAN.   Let me tell you, Lady Utterword, that the Prime Minister of this country asked me to join the Government without even going through the nonsense of an election, as the dictator of a great public department.

LADY UTTERWORD.   As a Conservative or a Liberal?

MANGAN.   No such nonsense. As a practical business man. [*They all burst out laughing*]. What are you all laughing at?

MRS HUSHABYE.   Oh, Alfred, Alfred!

ELLIE.   You! who have to get my father to do everything for you!

MRS HUSHABYE.   You! who are afraid of your own workmen!

HECTOR.   You! with whom three women have been playing cat and mouse all the evening!

LADY UTTERWORD.   You must have given an immense sum to the party funds, Mr Mangan.

MANGAN.   Not a penny out of my own pocket. The syndicate found the money: they knew how useful I should be to them in the Government.

LADY UTTERWORD. This is most interesting and unexpected, Mr Mangan. And what have your administrative achievements been, so far?

MANGAN. Achievements? Well, I dont know what you call achievements; but Ive jolly well put a stop to the games of the other fellows in the other departments. Every man of them thought he was going to save the country all by himself, and do me out of the credit and out of my chance of a title. I took good care that if they wouldnt let me do it they shouldnt do it themselves either. I may not know anything about my own machinery; but I know how to stick a ramrod into the other fellow's. And now they all look the biggest fools going.

HECTOR. And in heaven's name, what do you look like?

MANGAN. I look like the fellow that was too clever for all the others, dont I? If that isnt a triumph of practical business, what is?

HECTOR. Is this England, or is it a madhouse?

LADY UTTERWORD. Do you expect to save the country, Mr Mangan?

MANGAN. Well, who else will? Will your Mr Randall save it?

LADY UTTERWORD. Randall the Rotter! Certainly not.

MANGAN. Will your brother-in-law save it with his moustache and his fine talk?

HECTOR. Yes, if they will let me.

MANGAN [sneering] Ah! W i l l they let you?

HECTOR. No. They prefer you.

MANGAN. Very well then, as youre in a world where I'm appreciated and youre not, youd best be civil to me, hadnt you? Who else is there but me?

LADY UTTERWORD. There is Hastings. Get rid of your ridiculous sham democracy; and give Hastings the necessary powers, and a good supply of bamboo to bring the British native to his senses: he will save the country with the greatest ease.

CAPTAIN SHOTOVER.   It had better be lost. Any fool can govern with a stick in his hand. *I* could govern that way. It is not God's way. The man is a numskull.

LADY UTTERWORD.   The man is worth all of you rolled into one. What do you say, Miss Dunn?

ELLIE.   I think my father would do very well if people did not put upon him and cheat him and despise him because he is so good.

MANGAN.   [*contemptuously*] I think I see Mazzini Dunn getting into parliament or pushing his way into the Government. Weve not come to that yet, thank God! What do you say, Mrs Hushabye?

MRS HUSHABYE.   Oh, *I* say it matters very little which of you governs the country so long as we govern you.

HECTOR.   We? Who is we, pray?

MRS HUSHABYE.   The devil's granddaughters, dear. The lovely women.

HECTOR   [*raising his hands as before*] Fall, I say; and deliver us from the lures of Satan!

ELLIE.   There seems to be nothing real in the world except my father and Shakespear. Marcus's tigers are false; Mr Mangan's millions are false; there is nothing really strong and true about Hesione but her beautiful black hair; and Lady Utterword's is too pretty to be real. The one thing that was left to me was the Captain's seventh degree of concentration; and that turns out to be—

CAPTAIN SHOTOVER.   Rum.

LADY UTTERWORD   [*placidly*] A good deal of my hair is quite genuine. The Duchess of Dithering offered me fifty guineas for this [*touching her forehead*] under the impression that it was a transformation; but it is all natural except the color.

MANGAN [*wildly*] Look here: I'm going to take off all my clothes. [*He begins tearing off his coat*].

| LADY UTTERWORD | | Mr Mangan! |
| CAPTAIN SHOTOVER | [*in consternation*] | Whats that? |
| HECTOR | | Ha! ha! Do. Do. |
| ELLIE | | Please dont. |

MRS HUSHABYE [*catching his arm and stopping him*] Alfred: for shame! Are you mad?

MANGAN. Shame! What shame is there in this house? Let's all strip stark naked. We may as well do the thing thoroughly when we're about it. Weve stripped ourselves morally naked: well, let us strip ourselves physically naked as well, and see how we like it. I tell you I cant bear this. I was brought up to be respectable. I dont mind the women dyeing their hair and the men drinking: it's human nature. But it's not human nature to tell everybody about it. Every time one of you opens your mouth I go like this [*he cowers as if to avoid a missile*] afraid of what will come next. How are we to have any self-respect if we dont keep it up that we're better than we really are?

LADY UTTERWORD. I quite sympathize with you, Mr Mangan. I have been through it all; and I know by experience that men and women are delicate plants and must be cultivated under glass. Our family habit of throwing stones in all directions and letting the air in is not only unbearably rude, but positively dangerous. Still, there is no use catching physical colds as well as moral ones; so please keep your clothes on.

MANGAN. I'll do as I like: not what you tell me. Am I a child or a grown man? I wont stand this mothering tyranny. I'll go back to the city, where I'm respected and made much of.

MRS HUSHABYE. Goodbye, Alf. Think of us sometimes in the city. Think of Ellie's youth!

ELLIE. Think of Hesione's eyes and hair!

CAPTAIN SHOTOVER.  Think of this garden in which you are not a dog barking to keep the truth out!

HECTOR.  Think of Lady Utterword's beauty! her good sense! her style!

LADY UTTERWORD.  Flatterer. Think, Mr Mangan, whether you can really do any better for yourself elsewhere: that is the essential point, isnt it?

MANGAN  [*surrendering*] All right: all right. I'm done. Have it your own way. Only let me alone. I dont know whether I'm on my head or my heels when you all start on me like this. I'll stay. I'll marry her. I'll do anything for a quiet life. Are you satisfied now?

ELLIE.  No. I never really intended to make you marry me, Mr Mangan. Never in the depths of my soul. I only wanted to feel my strength: to know that you could not escape if I chose to take you.

MANGAN  [*indignantly*] What! Do you mean to say you are going to throw me over after my acting so handsome?

LADY UTTERWORD.  I should not be too hasty, Miss Dunn. You can throw Mr Mangan over at any time up to the last moment. Very few men in his position go bankrupt. You can live very comfortably on his reputation for immense wealth.

ELLIE.  I cannot commit bigamy, Lady Utterword.

| | | |
|---|---|---|
| MRS HUSHABYE | | Bigamy! Whatever on earth are you talking about, Ellie? |
| LADY UTTERWORD | [*exclaiming all together*] | Bigamy! What do you mean, Miss Dunn? |
| MANGAN | | Bigamy! Do you mean to say youre married already? |
| HECTOR | | Bigamy! This is some enigma. |

ELLIE.  Only half an hour ago I became Captain Shotover's white wife.

MRS HUSHABYE.   Ellie! What nonsense! Where?

ELLIE.   In heaven, where all true marriages are made.

LADY UTTERWORD.   Really, Miss Dunn! Really, papa!

MANGAN.   He told me *I* was too old! And him a mummy!

HECTOR   [*quoting Shelley*]

"Their altar the grassy earth outspread,
And their priest the muttering wind."

ELLIE.   Yes: I, Ellie Dunn, give my broken heart and my strong sound soul to its natural captain, my spiritual husband and second father.

*She draws the Captain's arm through hers, and pats his hand. The Captain remains fast asleep.*

MRS HUSHABYE.   Oh, thats very clever of you, pettikins. Very clever. Alfred: you could never have lived up to Ellie. You must be content with a little share of me.

MANGAN   [*sniffing and wiping his eyes*] It isnt kind—[*His emotion chokes him*].

LADY UTTERWORD.   You are well out of it, Mr Mangan. Miss Dunn is the most conceited young woman I have met since I came back to England.

MRS HUSHABYE.   Oh, Ellie isnt conceited. Are you, pettikins?

ELLIE.   I know my strength now, Hesione.

MANGAN.   Brazen, I call you. Brazen.

MRS HUSHABYE.   Tut tut, Alfred: dont be rude. Dont you feel how lovely this marriage night is, made in heaven? Arnt you happy, you and Hector? Open your eyes: Addy and Ellie look beautiful enough to please the most fastidious man: we live and love and have not a care in the world. We women have managed all that for you. Why in the name of common sense do you go on as if you were two miserable wretches?

CAPTAIN SHOTOVER.   I tell you happiness is no good. You can be happy when you are only half alive. I am happier now I am half dead than ever I was in my prime. But there is no blessing on my happiness.

ELLIE   [*her face lighting up*] Life with a blessing! that is what I want. Now I know the real reason why I couldnt marry Mr Mangan: there would be no blessing on our marriage. There is a blessing on my broken heart. There is a blessing on your beauty, Hesione. There is a blessing on your father's spirit. Even on the lies of Marcus there is a blessing; but on Mr Mangan's money there is none.

MANGAN.   I dont understand a word of that.

ELLIE.   Neither do I. But I know it means something.

MANGAN.   Dont say there was any difficulty about the blessing. I was ready to get a bishop to marry us.

MRS HUSHABYE.   Isnt he a fool, pettikins?

HECTOR   [*fiercely*] Do not scorn the man. We are all fools.

*Mazzini, in pyjamas and a richly colored silk dressing-gown, comes from the house, on Lady Utterword's side.*

MRS HUSHABYE.   Oh! here comes the only man who ever resisted me. Whats the matter, Mr Dunn? Is the house on fire?

MAZZINI.   Oh no: nothing's the matter: but really it's impossible to go to sleep with such an interesting conversation going on under one's window, and on such a beautiful night too. I just had to come down and join you all. What has it all been about?

MRS HUSHABYE.   Oh, wonderful things, soldier of freedom.

HECTOR.   For example, Mangan, as a practical business man, has tried to undress himself and has failed ignominiously; whilst you, as an idealist, have succeeded brilliantly.

MAZZINI.   I hope you dont mind my being like this, Mrs Hushabye. [*He sits down on the campstool*].

MRS HUSHABYE.   On the contrary, I could wish you always like that.

LADY UTTERWORD. Your daughter's match is off, Mr Dunn. It seems that Mr Mangan, whom we all supposed to be a man of property, owns absolutely nothing.

MAZZINI. Well of course I knew that, Lady Utterword. But if people believe in him and are always giving him money, whereas they dont believe in me and never give me any, how can I ask poor Ellie to depend on what I can do for her?

MANGAN. Dont you run away with this idea that I have nothing. I—

HECTOR. Oh, dont explain. We understand. You have a couple of thousand pounds in exchequer bills, 50,000 shares worth tenpence a dozen, and half a dozen tabloids of cyanide of potassium to poison yourself with when you are found out. Thats the reality of your millions.

MAZZINI. Oh no, no, no. He is quite honest: the businesses are genuine and perfectly legal.

HECTOR [disgusted] Yah! Not even a great swindler!

MANGAN. So you think. But Ive been too many for some honest men, for all that.

LADY UTTERWORD. There is no pleasing you, Mr Mangan. You are determined to be neither rich nor poor, honest nor dishonest.

MANGAN. There you go again. Ever since I came into this silly house I have been made to look like a fool, though I'm as good a man in this house as in the city.

ELLIE [musically] Yes: this silly house, this strangely happy house, this agonizing house, this house without foundations. I shall call it Heartbreak House.

MRS HUSHABYE. Stop, Ellie; or I shall howl like an animal.

MANGAN [breaks into a low snivelling] !!!

MRS HUSHABYE. There! you have set Alfred off.

ELLIE. I like him best when he is howling.

CAPTAIN SHOTOVER. Silence! [*Mangan subsides into silence*]. I say, let the heart break in silence.

HECTOR. Do you accept that name for your house?

CAPTAIN SHOTOVER. It is not my house: it is only my kennel.

HECTOR. We have been too long here. We do not live in this house: we haunt it.

LADY UTTERWORD [*heart torn*] It is dreadful to think how you have been here all these years while I have gone round the world. I escaped young; but it has drawn me back. It wants to break my heart too. But it shant. I have left you and it behind. It was silly of me to come back. I felt sentimental about Papa and Hesione and the old place. I felt them calling to me.

MAZZINI. But what a very natural and kindly and charming human feeling, Lady Utterword!

LADY UTTERWORD. So I thought, Mr Dunn. But I know now that it was only the last of my influenza. I found that I was not remembered and not wanted.

CAPTAIN SHOTOVER. You left because you did not want us. Was there no heartbreak in that for your father? You tore yourself up by the roots; and the ground healed up and brought forth fresh plants and forgot you. What right had you to come back and probe old wounds?

MRS HUSHABYE. You were a complete stranger to me at first, Addy; but now I feel as if you had never been away.

LADY UTTERWORD. Thank you, Hesione; but the influenza is quite cured. The place may be Heartbreak House to you, Miss Dunn, and to this gentleman from the city who seems to have so little self-control; but to me it is only a very ill-regulated and rather untidy villa without any stables.

HECTOR. Inhabited by—?

ELLIE. A crazy old sea captain and a young singer who adores him.

MRS HUSHABYE. A sluttish female, trying to stave off a

double chin and an elderly spread, vainly wooing a born soldier of freedom.

MAZZINI. Oh, really, Mrs Hushabye—

MANGAN. A member of His Majesty's Government that everybody sets down as a nincompoop: dont forget him, Lady Utterword.

LADY UTTERWORD. And a very fascinating gentleman whose chief occupation is to be married to my sister.

HECTOR. All heartbroken imbeciles.

MAZZINI. Oh no. Surely, if I may say so, rather a favorable specimen of what is best in our English culture. You are very charming people, most advanced, unprejudiced, frank, humane, unconventional, democratic, free-thinking, and everything that is delightful to thoughtful people.

MRS HUSHABYE. You do us proud, Mazzini.

MAZZINI. I am not flattering, really. Where else could I feel perfectly at ease in my pyjamas? I sometimes dream that I am in very distinguished society, and suddenly I have nothing on but my pyjamas! Sometimes I havnt even pyjamas. And I always feel overwhelmed with confusion. But here, I dont mind in the least: it seems quite natural.

LADY UTTERWORD. An infallible sign that you are not now in really distinguished society, Mr Dunn. If you were in my house, you w o u l d feel embarrassed.

MAZZINI. I shall take particular care to keep out of your house, Lady Utterword.

LADY UTTERWORD. You will be quite wrong, Mr Dumn. I should make you very comfortable; and you would not have the trouble and anxiety of wondering whether you should wear your purple and gold or your green and crimson dressing-gown at dinner. You complicate life instead of simplifying it by doing these ridiculous things.

ELLIE. Y o u r house is not Heartbreak House: is it, Lady Utterword?

HECTOR. Yet she breaks hearts, easy as her house is.

That poor devil upstairs with his flute howls when she twists his heart, just as Mangan howls when my wife twists his.

LADY UTTERWORD.    That is because Randall has nothing to do but have his heart broken. It is a change from having his head shampooed. Catch anyone breaking Hastings' heart!

CAPTAIN SHOTOVER.    The numskull wins, after all.

LADY UTTERWORD.    I shall go back to my numskull with the greatest satisfaction when I am tired of you all, clever as you are.

MANGAN    [*huffily*] I never set up to be clever.

LADY UTTERWORD.    I forgot you, Mr Mangan.

MANGAN.    Well, I dont see that quite, either.

LADY UTTERWORD.    You may not be clever, Mr Mangan; but you are successful.

MANGAN.    But I dont want to be regarded merely as a successful man. I have an imagination like anyone else. I have a presentiment—

MRS HUSHABYE.    Oh, you are impossible, Alfred. Here I am devoting myself to you; and you think of nothing but your ridiculous presentiment. You bore me. Come and talk poetry to me under the stars. [*She drags him away into the darkness*].

MANGAN    [*tearfully, as he disappears*] Yes: it's all very well to make fun of me; but if you only knew—

HECTOR    [*impatiently*] How is all this going to end?

MAZZINI.    It wont end, Mr Hushabye. Life doesnt end: it goes on.

ELLIE.    Oh, it cant go on for ever. I'm always expecting something. I dont know what it is; but life must come to a point sometime.

LADY UTTERWORD.    The point for a young woman of your age is a baby.

HECTOR.    Yes, but, damn it, I have the same feeling; and I cant have a baby.

LADY UTTERWORD.    By deputy, Hector.

HECTOR.  But I h a v e children. All that is over and done with for me: and yet I too feel that this cant last. We sit here talking, and leave everything to Mangan and to chance and to the devil. Think of the powers of destruction that Mangan and his mutual admiration gang wield! It's madness: it's like giving a torpedo to a badly brought up child to play at earthquakes with.

MAZZINI.  I know. I used often to think about that when I was young.

HECTOR.  Think! Whats the good of thinking about it? Why didnt you do something?

MAZZINI.  But I did. I joined societies and made speeches and wrote pamphlets. That was all I could do. But, you know, though the people in the societies thought they knew more than Mangan, most of them wouldnt have joined if they had known as much. You see they had never had any money to handle or any men to manage. Every year I expected a revolution, or some frightful smash-up: it seemed impossible that we could blunder and muddle on any longer. But nothing happened, except, of course, the usual poverty and crime and drink that we are used to. Nothing ever does happen. It's amazing how well we get along, all things considered.

LADY UTTERWORD.  Perhaps somebody cleverer than you and Mr Mangan was at work all the time.

MAZZINI.  Perhaps so. Though I was brought up not to believe in anything, I often feel that there is a great deal to be said for the theory of an overruling Providence, after all.

LADY UTTERWORD.  Providence! I meant Hastings.

MAZZINI.  Oh, I beg your pardon, Lady Utterword.

CAPTAIN SHOTOVER.  Every drunken skipper trusts to Providence. But one of the ways of Providence with drunken skippers is to run them on the rocks.

MAZZINI.  Very true, no doubt, at sea. But in politics, I assure you, they only run into jellyfish. Nothing happens.

CAPTAIN SHOTOVER.   At sea nothing happens to the sea. Nothing happens to the sky. The sun comes up from the east and goes down to the west. The moon grows from a sickle to an arc lamp, and comes later and later until she is lost in the light as other things are lost in the darkness. After the typhoon, the flying-fish glitter in the sunshine like birds. It's amazing how t h e y get along, all things considered. Nothing happens, except something not worth mentioning.

ELLIE.   What is that, O Captain, my captain?

CAPTAIN SHOTOVER   [*savagely*] Nothing but the smash of the drunken skipper's ship on the rocks, the splintering of her rotten timbers, the tearing of her rusty plates, the drowning of the crew like rats in a trap.

ELLIE.   Moral: dont take rum.

CAPTAIN SHOTOVER   [*vehemently*] That is a lie, child. Let a man drink ten barrels of rum a day, he is not a drunken skipper until he is a drifting skipper. Whilst he can lay his course and stand on his bridge and steer it, he is no drunkard. It is the man who lies drinking in his bunk and trusts to Providence that I call the drunken skipper, though he drank nothing but the waters of the River Jordan.

ELLIE.   Splendid! And you havnt had a drop for an hour. You see you dont need it: your own spirit is not dead.

CAPTAIN SHOTOVER.   Echoes: nothing but echoes. The last shot was fired years ago.

HECTOR.   And this ship that we are all in? This soul's prison we call England?

CAPTAIN SHOTOVER.   The captain is in his bunk, drinking bottled ditch-water; and the crew is gambling in the forecastle. She will strike and sink and split. Do you think the laws of God will be suspended in favor of England because you were born in it?

HECTOR.   Well, I dont mean to be drowned like a rat in a trap. I still have the will to live. What am I to do?

CAPTAIN SHOTOVER.   Do? Nothing simpler. Learn your business as an Englishman.

HECTOR.   And what may my business as an Englishman be, pray?

CAPTAIN SHOTOVER.   Navigation. Learn it and live; or leave it and be damned.

ELLIE.   Quiet, quiet: youll tire yourself.

MAZZINI.   I thought all that once, Captain; but I assure you nothing will happen.

*A dull distant explosion is heard.*

HECTOR   [*starting up*]. What was that?

CAPTAIN SHOTOVER.   Something happening. [*He blows his whistle*]. Breakers ahead!

*The light goes out.*

HECTOR   [*furiously*] Who put that light out? Who dared put that light out?

NURSE GUINNESS   [*running in from the house to the middle of the esplanade*]. I did, sir. The police have telephoned to say we'll be summoned if we dont put that light out: it can be seen for miles.

HECTOR.   It shall be seen for a hundred miles. [*He dashes into the house*]

NURSE GUINNESS.   The rectory is nothing but a heap of bricks, they say. Unless we can give the rector a bed he has nowhere to lay his head this night.

CAPTAIN SHOTOVER.   The Church is on the rocks, breaking up. I told him it would unless it headed for God's open sea.

NURSE GUINNESS.   And you are all to go down to the cellars.

CAPTAIN SHOTOVER.   Go there yourself, you and all the crew. Batten down the hatches.

NURSE GUINNESS.   And hide beside the coward I married! I'll go on the roof first. [*The lamp lights up again*]There! Mr Hushabye's turned it on again.

THE BURGLAR  [*hurrying in and appealing to Nurse Guinness*] Here: wheres the way to that gravel pit? The boot-boy says theres a cave in the gravel pit. Them cellars is no use. Wheres the gravel pit, Captain?

NURSE GUINNESS.   Go straight on past the flagstaff until you fall into it and break your dirty neck. [*She pushes him contemptuously towards the flagstaff, and herself goes to the foot of the hammock and waits there, as it were by Ariadne's cradle*].

*Another and louder explosion is heard. The burglar stops and stands trembling.*

ELLIE  [*rising*] That was nearer.

CAPTAIN SHOTOVER.   The next one will get us. [*He rises*]. Stand by, all hands, for judgment.

THE BURGLAR.   Oh my Lordy God! [*He rushes away frantically past the flagstaff into the gloom*].

MRS HUSHABYE  [*emerging panting from the darkness*] Who was that running away? [*She comes to Ellie*]. Did you hear the explosions? And the sound in the sky: it's splendid: it's like an orchestra: it's like Beethoven.

ELLIE.   By thunder, Hesione: it i s Beethoven.

*She and Hesione throw themselves into one another's arms in wild excitement. The light increases.*

MAZZINI  [*anxiously*] The light is getting brighter.

NURSE GUINNESS  [*looking up at the house*] It's Mr Hushabye turning on all the lights in the house and tearing down the curtains.

RANDALL  [*rushing in in his pyjamas, distractedly waving a flute*] Ariadne: my soul, my precious, go down to the cellars: I beg and implore you, go down to the cellars!

LADY UTTERWORD  [*quite composed in her hammock*] The governor's wife in the cellars with the servants! Really, Randall!

RANDALL.   But what shall I do if you are killed?

LADY UTTERWORD.   You will probably be killed, too,

Randall. Now play your flute to shew that you are not afraid; and be good. Play us Keep the home fires burning.

NURSE GUINNESS  [*grimly*] T h e y l l keep the home fires burning for us: them up there.

RANDALL  [*having tried to play*] My lips are trembling. I cant get a sound.

MAZZINI.  I hope poor Mangan is safe.

MRS HUSHABYE.  He is hiding in the cave in the gravel pit.

CAPTAIN SHOTOVER.  My dynamite drew him there. It is the hand of God.

HECTOR.  [*returning from the house and striding across to his former place*] There is not half light enough. We should be blazing to the skies.

ELLIE  [*tense with excitement*] Set fire to the house, Marcus.

MRS HUSHABYE.  My house! No.

HECTOR.  I thought of that; but it would not be ready in time.

CAPTAIN SHOTOVER.  The judgment has come. Courage will not save you; but it will shew that your souls are still alive.

MRS HUSHABYE.  Sh-sh! Listen: do you hear it now? It's magnificent.

*They all turn away from the house and look up, listening.*

HECTOR  [*gravely*] Miss Dunn: you can do no good here. We of this house are only moths flying into the candle. You had better go down to the cellar.

ELLIE  [*scornfully*] I d o n t think.

MAZZINI.  Ellie, dear, there is no disgrace in going to the cellar. An officer would order his soldiers to take cover. Mr Hushabye is behaving like an amateur. Mangan and the burglar are acting very sensibly; and it is they who will survive.

ELLIE.   Let them. I shall behave like an amateur. But why should you run any risk?

MAZZINI.   Think of the risk those poor fellows up there are running!

NURSE GUINNESS.   Think of t h e m, indeed, the murdering blackguards! What next?

*A terrific explosion shakes the earth. They reel back into their seats, or clutch the nearest support. They hear the falling of the shattered glass from the windows.*

MAZZINI.   Is anyone hurt?

HECTOR.   Where did it fall?

NURSE GUINNESS   [*in hideous triumph*] Right in the gravel pit: I seen it. Serve un right! I seen it. [*She runs away towards the gravel pit, laughing harshly*].

HECTOR.   One husband gone.

CAPTAIN SHOTOVER.   Thirty pounds of good dynamite wasted.

MAZZINI.   Oh, poor Mangan!

HECTOR.   Are you immortal that you need pity him? Our turn next.

*They wait in silence and intense expectation. Hesione and Ellie hold each other's hand tight.*

*A distant explosion is heard.*

MRS HUSHABYE   [*relaxing her grip*] Oh! they have passed us.

LADY UTTERWORD.   The danger is over, Randall. Go to bed.

CAPTAIN SHOTOVER.   Turn in, all hands. The ship is safe. [*He sits down and goes asleep*].

ELLIE   [*disappointedly*] Safe!

HECTOR   [*disgustedly*] Yes, safe. And how damnably dull the world has become again suddenly! [*He sits down*].

MAZZINI   [*sitting down*] I was quite wrong, after all. It is we who have survived; and Mangan and the burglar—

HECTOR.   —the two burglars—

LADY UTTERWORD. —the two practical men of business—

MAZZINI. —both gone. And the poor clergyman will have to get a new house.

MRS HUSHABYE. But what a glorious experience! I hope theyll come again tomorrow night.

ELLIE [*radiant at the prospect*] Oh, I hope so.

*Randall at last succeeds in keeping the home fires burning on his flute.*

**CURTAIN**

# BANTAM CLASSICS ✪ BANTAM CLASSICS ✪ BANTAM CLASSICS

*Bantam Classics bring you the world's greatest literature—timeless masterpieces of fiction and nonfiction. Beautifully designed and sensibly priced, Bantam Classics are a valuable addition to any home library.*

## The Brontës

| | | |
|---|---|---|
| \_\_\_\_21140-4 | JANE EYRE, Charlotte Brontë | $3.50/$4.50 Canada |
| \_\_\_\_21243-5 | VILLETTE, Charlotte Brontë | $5.95/$6.95 |
| \_\_\_\_21258-3 | WUTHERING HEIGHTS, Emily Brontë | $3.95/$4.95 |

## Charles Dickens

| | | |
|---|---|---|
| \_\_\_\_21223-0 | BLEAK HOUSE | $4.95/$5.95 |
| \_\_\_\_21342-3 | GREAT EXPECTATIONS | $3.95/$4.95 |
| \_\_\_\_21386-5 | OUR MUTUAL FRIEND | $5.95/$6.95 |
| \_\_\_\_21244-3 | A CHRISTMAS CAROL | $2.75/$3.50 |
| \_\_\_\_21189-7 | DAVID COPPERFIELD | $4.95/$5.95 |
| \_\_\_\_21016-5 | HARD TIMES | $3.50/$4.50 |
| \_\_\_\_21265-6 | NICHOLAS NICKLEBY | $5.95/$6.95 |
| \_\_\_\_21102-1 | OLIVER TWIST | $3.95/$4.95 |
| \_\_\_\_21123-4 | THE PICKWICK PAPERS | $4.95/$5.95 |
| \_\_\_\_21176-5 | A TALE OF TWO CITIES | $2.95/$3.50 |

## Henry James

| | | |
|---|---|---|
| \_\_\_\_21127-7 | THE PORTRAIT OF A LADY | $4.50/$5.50 |
| \_\_\_\_21059-9 | THE TURN OF THE SCREW | $3.50/$4.50 |

## Jules Verne

| | | |
|---|---|---|
| \_\_\_\_21356-3 | AROUND THE WORLD IN 80 DAYS | $2.95/$3.50 |
| \_\_\_\_21252-4 | 20,000 LEAGUES UNDER THE SEA | $2.95/$3.50 |
| \_\_\_\_21397-0 | JOURNEY TO THE CENTER OF THE EARTH | $3.95/$4.95 |

**Ask for these books at your local bookstore or use this page to order.**

Please send me the books I have checked above. I am enclosing $\_\_\_\_ (add $2.50 to cover postage and handling). Send check or money order, no cash or C.O.D.'s, please.

Name _____

Address _____

City/State/Zip _____

Send order to: Bantam Books, Dept. CL 3, 2451 S. Wolf Rd., Des Plaines, IL 60018
Allow four to six weeks for delivery.
Prices and availability subject to change without notice. CL 3 4/95